T0357888

Nothin' Comes Easy

Books by Michael Seth Starr

Nothin' Comes Easy: The Life of Rodney Dangerfield

Don Rickles: The Merchant of Venom

Shatner

Ringo: With a Little Help

Black and Blue: The Redd Foxx Story

Hiding in Plain Sight: The Secret Life of Raymond Burr

Bobby Darin: A Life

Mouse in the Rat Pack: The Joey Bishop Story

Art Carney: A Biography

Peter Sellers: A Film History

Nothin' Comes Easy

The Life of
Rodney Dangerfield

Michael Seth Starr

CITADEL PRESS
Kensington Publishing Corp.
kensingtonbooks.com

CITADEL PRESS BOOKS are published by

Kensington Publishing Corp.
900 Third Avenue
New York, NY 10022

10 9 8 7 6 5 4 3 2 1

First Citadel hardcover printing: May 2025

Printed in the United States of America

ISBN: 978-0-8065-4323-9

ISBN: 978-0-8065-4325-3 (e-book)

Library of Congress Control Number: 2024951802

The authorized representative in the EU for product safety and compliance
is eucomply OU, Parnu mnt 139b-14, Apt 123,
Tallinn, Berlin 11317; hello@eucompliancepartner.com

To Gail, my wife and best friend, for her unstinting love, encouragement, and support.

Acknowledgments

THIS BOOK WOULD NOT HAVE BEEN WRITTEN WITHOUT THE EN-thusiasm and encouragement of my editor at Kensington, Gary Gold-stein, who first suggested the idea of a Rodney Dangerfield biography, and who patiently guided me throughout the process.

No book is written in a vacuum, so a big thank-you to the following people who helped me tell Rodney Dangerfield's story: Oliver Stone, David Permut, Dennis Blair, Jay Leno, Bob Nelson, Carol Leifer, Billy Riback, Andrew Buss, Michael O'Keefe, Rita Rudner, Thelma Houston, Harry Basil, Mark Canton, Lily Haydn, Robert Lenz, Ronnie Schell, Mark Drossman, Jeff Abraham, Robert Wuhl, Julie Ancis, Doug Draizin, Adrienne Barbeau, Jeff Altman, Candice Azzara, Patty Bergamaschi, Ilene Graff, Joseph Merhi, Kevin Sasaki, Pauly Shore, Ian Maxtone-Graham, Josh Weinstein, Fabio, Arthur Friedman, Tom Dreesen, Dom Irrera, David Hirshey, Dennis Arfa, Maurice LaMarche.

Nothin' Comes Easy

Prologue

RODDY MCDOWALL'S LETTER ARRIVED LATE IN THE FALL OF 1994, and Rodney Dangerfield was not pleased.

McDowall, the sixty-six-year-old actor, keeper of Hollywood's secrets, and part-time celebrity photographer, was also the chairman of the Actors Branch Executive Committee of the Academy of Motion Picture Arts and Sciences.

On paper, McDowall's position was honorary, yet it carried a certain level of gravitas among the Academy's thousands of members representing many different sides of the film industry.

Rodney Dangerfield had, months earlier, applied to be a card-carrying member of the Academy. And why not? Not only was the seventy-three-year-old comedian hot off his small-but-memorable role as a brutish, incestuous father in Oliver Stone's *Natural Born Killers*—there was talk of a possible Oscar nomination for Best Supporting Actor—but his previous movies, *Caddyshack*, *Easy Money,* and, especially, *Back to School*, had generated a modicum of critical praise and big receipts at the box office. The industry took notice of these big screen bona fides (especially on the money end of things). Dangerfield figured it was best to strike while the iron was hot. At seventy-three years old, he was not getting any younger.

So, it was with a sense of anticipation that Dangerfield opened McDowall's letter, expecting to find that long-elusive acceptance among his show-business peers.

He was crushed to read that the Academy denied his membership on the flimsiest of pretexts.

Dangerfield's movie work, said the letter, signed by McDowall, lacked "enough of the kind of roles that allow a performer to demonstrate the mastery of his craft." In other words: Fuck off. You are a stand-up comedian with no business applying for admittance into this prestigious, elite group representing the best and the brightest of Hollywood. It was that typical West Coast snobbery toward a tried-and-true New Yorker (and a comic, no less).

Rodney Dangerfield's long slog in and up the showbiz ladder had, through the years, hardened his already-no-bullshit attitude. Ten years as a C-level stand-up comic playing C-level clubs. Quitting the business to sell aluminum siding and paint for another decade just to keep the lights on. Slowly working his way back into the clubs under another name lest he publicly flop . . . again. He did not suffer fools gladly, even after a career-changing appearance on *The Ed Sullivan Show* vaulted him into national prominence at the age of forty-five and propelled him on the road to comic immortality.

Rodney Dangerfield was angry at the Academy and at McDowall—and he was not shy in letting everyone know it.

"This is ridiculous, especially since thousands of academy members haven't done any movies to speak of," Dangerfield told the press. "People still quote lines from *Caddyshack*, which I did in 1980. *Back to School*, which I starred in, took in [nearly] $100 million."[1] He was convinced that his take-no-prisoners performance in the ultra-violent *Natural Born Killers* was the reason behind McDowall's letter, that his repulsive character, Ed Wilson, had repelled a sizeable number of Academy members in a role better suited for a "real actor": Nicholson, Pacino, or maybe even (gasp!) Brando.

But Rodney Dangerfield?

"That's not me up there," Dangerfield said. "Even as a stand-up, I'm acting. But like Charlie Chaplin, who was forever 'The Tramp,' I'm locked into an image: the nobody. Maybe the [*Natural Born Killers*] character, which I wrote myself, was so distasteful that it turned the academy off. Certain people—Roddy McDowall included—sometimes let emotion overrule their intelligence."[2]

McDowall did not retort; instead, the Academy's executive director, Bruce Davis, answered the angry comedian by claiming that the organization was now being more selective, that demands for membership were up exponentially ever since the Academy started sending VHS cassettes of movies to members hoping for Oscar consideration. "There's a certain justice in the charge that not every academy member has done work of note," Davis said, peripherally addressing Dangerfield's ire. "Once you accept people, you have them for life. It's a double-edged sword."[3]

The Academy suggested that it might reconsider Dangerfield's application provided he made several more movies and (read between the lines) expanded his repertoire.

Dangerfield was having nothing of it. And anyone who knew Rodney Dangerfield knew that he meant it and knew that what he said for public consumption was only half of the bile he was feeling privately.

"Academy membership isn't something I need," he said. "And now that I've seen the way the academy functions, even the Oscar doesn't mean as much. I know the reality—who are these geniuses who are judging us?"[4]

It was just another in a barrage of the lifelong slings and arrows directed at the bug-eyed, sweaty, herky-jerky, tie-pulling comedian with the doleful countenance. Get in line, he could have said, although now the indelible beaten-down image was played for laughs. Rodney Dangerfield was a millionaire several times over who did not need Hollywood's validation, if that is what you wanted to call it.

He never got a whiff of emotional support from his absentee vaudevillian father or from his loveless, ice-cold mother—and particularly not from the club patrons who, throughout the 1940s, ignored a young Jack Roy—fresh out of Richmond Hill High School in Queens and summers in the Borscht Belt—and watched him board the comedy struggle bus in dumps lurking throughout New York's five boroughs. He was barely able to support himself and, in time, his new bride.

It was not until almost a decade into his second iteration as a comedian, once Jack Roy morphed into Rodney Dangerfield, that he created the catchphrase endearing him to millions of fans, the line that ear-wormed its way into American pop culture and comedy history alongside Jack Benny's thirty-nine-year-old, violin-playing miser ("Your money or your life!" "I'm *thinking*, I'm *thinking*!") or Ralph Kramden's "Hummina hummina hummina," or "Sock it to me" on *Rowan & Martin's Laugh-In,* or Fred Sanford, clutching his chest for the umpteenth feigned heart attack ("I'm coming to join ya, Elizabeth!") on *Sanford and Son*. It was a catchphrase so ubiquitous that, once it gained popularity and entered the American lexicon, it was attached to anything and everything: "Brussel sprouts are the Rodney Dangerfield of vegetables," "Fill-in-the-blank is the Rodney Dangerfield of Fill-in-the blank."). President Ronald Reagan used it in an address to Congress. Jack Benny called it the perfect comedy tagline.

A catchphrase written thousands upon thousands of times in newspapers, magazines, and verbalized in other media to underscore Rodney Dangerfield's immortal five words: "I don't get no respect."

RODNEY DANGERFIELD'S JOURNEY THROUGH LIFE ENCOMPASSED eighty-two years, three public names, very little joy, romances fleeting and permanent, innumerable marijuana joints, other illicit drugs (*snort-snort*), felonious behavior, health crises, a successful New York City comedy club (against all odds), and decades of therapy sessions on his shrinks' couches: "I told my psychiatrist I have suicidal tendencies. He told me from now on I have to pay in advance."

Hell, he was even an Internet pioneer in the Wild West days of the digital age. *Rodney Dangerfield?* Go figure.

In the end, when the "No Respect" comedian passed away, his death made headlines and the tributes poured in, lauding his career and that unforgettable catchphrase, and recounting how the failed comic turned tin man turned comic redux kicked and scraped his way back into show business in his fourth decade on the planet and never looked back.

The legend of Rodney Dangerfield is undeniable. What stood out for me, in authoring this book, was his perseverance in the face of such overwhelming odds. I was impressed at how he launched a second comedy career as a man already in his forties and out of the game for a decade—lost in the weeds of suburban Northern New Jersey selling aluminum siding and paint as Jack Roy, smoking dope, and dealing with an unhappy domestic situation as a husband and father of two children. Through it all, he never abandoned the undeniable urge to get back in the game and to share his seemingly unending reservoir of magical one-liners with a live audience. He never stopped writing jokes—he had a suitcase full of them, in fact; he would say it was a compulsion of his to write, to craft the perfect story-within-a-one-liner that no one would be able to top. Even at the beginning of his comeback, which meant writing jokes on a freelance basis for other comics, including Jackie Mason and Joey Bishop, in the days before the "No Respect" persona was solidified.

Jack Roy was no overnight success story once he re-created himself as Rodney Dangerfield and reentered the world of show business. "You're a bar of soap," he once said. "If you're hot, they'll sell you. If not, you make your own deals."[5] He made his own deals. It took him the good part of five years to finally land that vaunted spot on *The Ed Sullivan Show* and even then another few years before Johnny Carson's *Tonight Show* beckoned. The rest, as they say, is the history of which you will read in this book.

That Rodney Dangerfield accomplished what he did, while battling a lifelong clinical depression that was not medically diagnosed until later in his life, is nearly Shakespearean in scope. He was introduced to marijuana in his early twenties and never looked back, smoking the stuff nearly until his dying day (and even in the hospital while recovering from heart surgery). But he never used marijuana as a crutch; it might have lessened the emotional blows of a monstrously unhappy childhood for a young Jacob Cohen, but it never erased those memories—which the rechristened Rodney Dangerfield tried to deal with through years of psychotherapy and, first and foremost, through his raw, self-effacing comedy, to feel the love and acceptance from an audience that he never felt from his own family.

"I like to do what I'm doing, but we can't change who we are," he once said during his rise to superstardom. "I'm not a happy guy. Comedy is a camouflage for depression. Comics turn to jokes because they don't want to face themselves. Actually, I'm not a happy guy."[6]

Comedians are notoriously competitive, territorial performers vis-à-vis their own material, and Rodney Dangerfield was no different from his colleagues, young and old, in the sneaking suspicion that many of his jokes were purloined by others. The live act was sacred, no matter how many times he performed it—it was his impossibly original calling card that no one could replicate.

"Everybody uses my line and people would think I stole it," he told a reporter. "Here's a joke I made up, about how to look young—hang out with old people. I see that joke, my own joke, on birthday cards. So, I do switches on my own jokes. Like now I'll tell people how to look thin—hang out with fat people."[7]

Later in life, he turned down a lucrative offer to film his stage show in a documentary format—fearing that no one would come to see him live if they had already seen and heard the jokes. Within that context, then, it is remarkable how Rodney Dangerfield nurtured young talent in such a fierce, dog-eat-dog environment as stand-up comedy. The names, by now, are all familiar: Sam Kinison, Louie Anderson, Tim Allen, Jerry Seinfeld, Rita Rudner, Roseanne Barr, Dom Irrera, Harry Basil, Bob Nelson, Carol Leifer, Jim Carrey, Andrew Dice Clay, Bob Saget, Robert Klein (a bit older, but still) . . . the list goes on and on. Rodney was beloved by "the kids" like no other comedian, before or since, and if an up-and-comer had a singular voice or an edge, even better. Rodney's *The 9th Annual Young Comedians Show*, which aired in 1985 on HBO, is, to this day, still considered the biggest launching pad in the history of television for a new generation of comics.

"He was always there for me, always supported me, even when I was experimenting and didn't know what the hell I was doing," Jim Carrey once said. "He sat in the wings with his balls hanging out of his, you know, frigging robe on the side of the stage just howling with laughter, and I'd get off and he'd say, 'Man, they're looking at you like you're from another fucking planet.'"[8]

What readers will learn in the pages of this book is that Rodney Dangerfield lived life by his own rules. He did not care one whit what anyone else thought about his pot-smoking habit or his mode of offstage dress—which, as you will see, was frequently a bathrobe (sometimes open) and slippers, the better in which to feel comfortable, particularly for the rigors of an interview with the press, which he did not particularly enjoy.

He was public but private and did not enjoy talking about his tough, loveless childhood or about his craft, as if trying to explain what fueled his comedy was obvious enough without having to overanalyze everything. In that regard, Rodney Dangerfield was right, since, let's face it, there is nothing more boring than listening to a windy comic break down what makes a joke funny or pontificate on the milieu. Rodney would have none of that in the thousands of interviews he granted after his later-in-life successes, and, in hindsight, it stood him in good stead. If the subject turned serious, he would immediately go into his shtick to throw the interviewer off the scent, and it usually worked. Sure, he dropped a few biographical tidbits into his press clippings over the years, but he also repeated the same lines ad nauseam—that selling paint in the 1950s was a "colorless job," for instance. He saved the majority of his emotional ruminations for his ghostwritten autobiography, published in 2004 shortly before his death. And in that sense, there could never be any annoying or probing follow-up questions.

Rodney had the last laugh.

"You could quote one of his jokes on a tombstone and people would get a kick out of it," Rodney's friend, Jay Leno, told the author. "He was the classic definition of a comedian. He could play an audience in just about any circumstance. You know, some people are very good only in a particular type of crowd. Rodney could play the Sand-and-Gravel Convention. Or he could play Harvard.

"If this was the silent era, he would have been Chaplin."[9]

Chapter One

TUCKED AWAY IN THE CORNER OF RODNEY DANGERFIELD'S OBITU-
aries were a few lines about his father's background in vaudeville.
Nothing more, nothing less. Just a few lines. But the unwritten history of
that part of Rodney Dangerfield's life is that it was a family affair in more
ways than one.

Lost in translation, or, perhaps, not deemed important enough to inves-
tigate, was the fact that his father Phil Roy's vaudeville career ran parallel
with two of comedy's most instantly recognizable names and faces, one of
whom Phil knew personally—names and faces that Rodney Dangerfield
would, in time, equal in the minds of many when listing the pantheon of
unforgettable, instantly recognizable comedians.

JEHAN BEDINI WAS A JUGGLER OF SOME NOTE. HE WAS BORN JEHAN
Pefsner in Lithuania in the Russian Empire in 1880 (or maybe 1875; sources
vary). He arrived in England at the turn of the century with his juggling act
and, with his new partner/sidekick, Arthur—whose full name is lost in the
winds of history—established a vaudeville act called (what else?) Bedini &
Arthur.

Bedini & Arthur traveled the "varieties" circuit throughout Britain,
gaining good press notices along the way. In April 1900, the *Manchester
Courier and Lancashire General Advertiser* raved that "Bedini, the juggler,
who is assisted by Arthur, provides a first-rate turn, and certainly gives the
most delightful performance of the evening."[1]

The act ran its course in England after a while and Bedini headed for
greener pastures. He boarded a steamer bound for New York City and, upon
arriving in the America, anglicized his first name to Jean and looked for

work. A 1904 article in the Washington, D.C., *Evening Star* noted that, in addition to his juggling acumen, Bedini possessed other talents (generating publicity chief among them). A brief time before, he wowed an audience estimated at five thousand onlookers in Chicago by catching an apple thrown from the top of the thirty-three-story Masonic Temple building . . . with a fork clenched between his teeth.[2] Let us see Houdini do *that*. During another promotional stopover Bedini, again clenching a fork in his pearly whites, caught a turnip dropped from the café in the Claus Spreckels building in San Francisco. He eventually dropped the stunt from his repertoire after a one-pound turnip that was dropped from a twelve-story office building in Washington, D.C., hit the fork in his mouth and loosened all of his front teeth.

After bouncing around the theatrical circuit with his juggling act and participating in various burlesque revues, Bedini searched for and found a new stage partner. He relaunched the act as Bedini & Arthur 2.0 to keep his name recognition, such as it was, intact for his newfound American audience.

Bedini's new recruit used the stage name Roy Arthur. He was born Adolf Cohen in 1887 in Philadelphia into a Jewish family that eventually included a brother, Philip, born five years later in 1892. The brothers' parents, Jacob and Sarah (Adelson) Cohen, were Eastern European immigrants who met and married earlier that decade and later settled into a tenement on Manhattan's Lower East Side, an area teeming with various ethnic groups who made the short journey there after landing at Ellis Island in New York Harbor. Somewhere along the way, Adolf (or Adolph, as it was spelled on his tombstone) acquired the family nickname "Bunk," which stuck with him for the rest of his life. He was "Uncle Bunk" to his nephew, Jacob Cohen, who, later in life, morphed into Rodney Dangerfield.

Bedini & Arthur traveled the vaudeville circuit up and down the East Coast and into the Midwest with detours northward into Canada. Roy Arthur, as was common for that time, corked up and worked in blackface—an extension of the nearly defunct "minstrel shows" in which white actors portrayed insultingly buffoonish black characters. He was Bedini's onstage assistant in their act of "ludicrous juggling specialties"; Arthur would comically retrieve the broken plates that Bedini left in his wake. Bedini & Arthur generated positive notices and grabbed attention for their onstage choreography of disaster.

"As a special added attraction to the Dockstader Minstrels this year the Shuberts are featuring Bedini & Arthur, the well-known vaudeville team," noted a 1910 article in the *Buffalo Courier*. "Both artists have become extremely popular through their original and highly entertaining act, which now goes to make up one of the desirable hits in the big minstrel production."[3]

"Bedini & Arthur are the most original and funniest juggling comedians in vaudeville," raved *The Bayonne Herald* in 1903. "They will occupy a strong position on the program at Proctor's Twenty-third Street theatre."[4]

They were still going strong ten years later. "The name of Bedini & Arthur is known wherever the word 'vaudeville' is known, for this team of funsters have appeared all over the world in their laughable feats of juggling, crockery smashing and travesty," proclaimed *The Aberdeen* (Washington) *Herald* in 1913.[5] It is likely that the comedy duo's claim to "have appeared all over the world" was the invention of an overeager press agent (or, perhaps, of Bedini).

Bedini & Arthur were successful enough that, in 1912, Bedini added a third participant to their onstage antics. Young Eddie Cantor was the same age as Adolf "Bunk" Cohen's brother, Philip, and he, too, eventually worked in blackface alongside Roy Arthur in "assisting" Jean Bedini as he shattered plates all over the stage in juggling fun and mayhem. Initially, Cantor, who was trying to find his footing in vaudeville, was relegated to brief appearances with the two established stars. It was an unspectacular entrance for a performer who would, one day, earn the sobriquets "Banjo Eyes" and the "Apostle of Pep" as he blazed a trail through vaudeville, Broadway, movies, radio, and the early days of television as one of the brightest stars in the show business firmament.

Adolf Cohen had discovered Eddie Cantor when he returned for a visit to his old Lower East Side neighborhood. Adolf was enough of a local celebrity as half of Bedini & Arthur that Cantor, who lived a few blocks over on Henry Street, knew his name, and he made it his business to befriend the vaudevillian—and, unsolicited, offered to perform his short act of singing and dancing. Adolf smiled "perfunctorily" and proceeded to ignore the expectant Cantor while he chatted with a small group of friends on a street corner. But he was listening, because he then turned to Eddie Cantor and told him to look him up the following week at the Hammerstein Theater on Broadway, where he was opening with Bedini. When that day arrived, Bedini, the older, more seasoned vaudevillian, took one look at Cantor and hired him on the spot.

For now, Eddie Cantor was just another kid with talent looking for his big break and jumping at the chance to assist a popular vaudeville act. He opened with them later at the Hammerstein Theater: "Bedini & Arthur assisted by Eddie Cantor." It was the first time his name appeared in print; his job was to carry the props on and off the stage while Bedini & Arthur did their thing. The job paid thirty dollars a week; Cantor also ran errands, picked up sandwiches for the headliners, and helped to unpack their trunks and to oversee makeup and costumes.

After a short while, Bedini started to incorporate Cantor into the act, instructing him to work in blackface—"two black-face figures would set him [Bedini] off better, while another white-face might detract from his central position," Cantor wrote. He was *told* to stand in the wings and, when signaled by Bedini, to bring one plate onto the stage, hand it to Arthur, and exit . . . quickly. That did not sit well with the natural born entertainer, and he worked some stage business into his short onstage stint in which he looked "leisurely" at Bedini & Arthur, then cast a "lofty" glance at the audience. It always got a laugh and Bedini, far from being angry, was impressed. He taught Cantor how to roll a plate down his arm and catch it as it dropped off—and that, too, was incorporated into the act.[6]

"That merry twain of jugglers known as Jean Bedini and Roy Arthur come with their usual stunts, including the demolition of more china at one performance than all the restaurants in Edmonton combined in one day," noted *The Edmonton Journal*. "They are assisted this year by Eddie Cantor, a mimic who contrives takeoffs on the act of Rock and Fulton,"[7] the writer alluding to Billy Rock and Maude Fulton, who performed songs and ended their act with a knockabout "Apache" dance routine (so-called for its "savagery"). Cantor also parodied Ruth St. Denis, played Salome, "an artists model," and "danced to Mendelssohn's 'Spring Song' wearing dresses, but always in black-face."

Bedini's two stooges, Cantor and Arthur, worked up their own mini routine, where Arthur chased Cantor around the stage with a hammer and Cantor shouted to the audience, "He means to do me bodily harm!"

"It was the first time any audience heard a negro speak such Oxford English," Cantor noted in the parlance of the day, "and it was the first line I spoke on big-time. From that moment on Arthur and I developed into a sissy-bully team, he the boor and I the cultured, pansy-like negro with spectacles, and anything I could devise to enrage him was effective and brought laughs."[8]

The Bedini-Arthur-Cantor triumvirate hit a wall after two years or so; Cantor was still only earning thirty-five dollars a week (a miniscule raise over his starting salary) and he began to frequently argue with Bedini. He quit the act during an engagement in Cincinnati and contacted vaudeville producer Gus Edwards, whose "Kid Kabaret" revue include George Jessel and who was impressed after watching Cantor with Bedini & Arthur when they shared a bill in Atlantic City. Edwards offered Cantor a whopping raise to seventy-five dollars a week. He was on his way.

Bedini, too, was tiring of the vaudeville grind, the days and nights on the road in different cities for short amounts of time and, on off days, catching all variety of fruits and vegetables with his trusty fork clenched heavenward in his mouth. He wanted to produce revues in the style of Gus Edwards and, sometime in 1914, he dissolved the act and relegated Bedini & Arthur to a footnote in the history of vaudeville. Later, he produced the burlesque review *Madame X* at the New Brighton Theatre in Brooklyn starring... Eddie Cantor.

ROY "BUNK" ARTHUR SAW THE WRITING ON THE WALL AND WAS PREpared for the eventual dissolution of Bedini & Arthur. Unlike his former partner, he was not ready to throw in the towel on his vaudeville career, and he looked no further than his own family to recruit Bedini's replacement: his younger brother, Phil.

Phil Cohen was in his early twenties and had bounced around at a series of jobs. He was a juggler, too, and while not quite on par, yet, with Bedini's skill, he was familiar with the act and replaced Bedini as the catalyst—juggling (and breaking) plates of china, while Roy continued his role in blackface as the comic stooge retrieving the shattered shards and trying to emulate Phil's juggling tricks (with the expected cartoonish results).

So, Phil Cohen changed his stage name to Phil Roy and the new twosome, Roy & Arthur, was born.

They called their act "Fun in a Dining Car" (it was occasionally billed as "China") and hit the road, playing the various vaudeville circuits around the country and in Canada. Roy & Arthur, "High Class Comics," enjoyed a modicum of success and generated positive press notices at nearly every stop along the way.

"Roy and Arthur, with a laughable juggling sketch 'Fun in a Dining Car,' created no little merriment and were given much well merited applause," enthused the *Virginian-Pilot and the Norfolk Landmark* in a review published in June 1916. "The juggling of plates and sticks was both funny and clever, and Roy (sic) was one of the most amusing black-face comedians ever seen on a local stage."[9]

The *Iowa City Press-Citizen:* "Roy & Arthur, the juggling comedians, in 'Fun in a Dining Car'—Pronounced the other of the two best acts of the season. At Clinton recently, at Kansas City before that, and in other large cities, they won praise galore from newspaper critics."[10]

The *Calgary Herald:* "Roy and Arthur in their travesty on juggling entitled 'China' have a specialty which is regarded by unbiased critics as the funniest vaudeville performance in years. Although their manual dexterity is far from being proficient—they possessing (sic) that faculty of being so that they can 'imagine' their efforts yet create a sensation—they depend on their big novelty surprise to win them plaudits, something that has never been missing."[11]

The *Fort Wayne News:* "Phil Roy and Roy Arthur's 'Fun in a Dining Car' is an absurdity with plenty of snap to it. The clumsy attempts of the comedian to emulate the tricks of the straight man in juggling dishes result in fifteen minutes of fun and a general demolishment of everything in sight. The target shooting turn is not entirely new in the idea, but it's the way the old idea is worked out."[12]

Such was the itinerant life of vaudeville that Roy & Arthur encountered many of the up-and-coming and established acts of the day—including Charlie Chaplin. Years later, when he was on *The Tonight Show* in one of his many must-see appearances opposite Johnny Carson, Rodney Dangerfield held up a black-and-white undated photo of his father, a camera slung around his neck, posing with Chaplin.

LIFE ON THE ROAD WAS NOT CONDUCIVE TO LONG-TERM ROMANCE FOR the Cohen brothers, yet somewhere along the way, Phil Cohen met and married a young woman who was from the South and whose name is lost to the vagaries of history. It was a "shotgun wedding," Phil's son would recall, and she died (or left him, no one was quite sure) shortly thereafter. There is no recorded mention of a baby born of the short-lived union.

(Phil's brother, Bunk, took a more traditional route, marrying Mary Kaplan in 1914. They had a son, Jerome.)

In 1917, Phil married Dorothy "Dotty" Teitelbaum, who came from a big Jewish family that included her sisters Rose, Esther, Peggy, and Pearlie and a brother, Joe. The family emigrated to America from Hungary when Dotty was four years old; her father, according to family lore, was a heavy drinker who remained in Hungary and whose name was rarely uttered in the house.

Phil and Dotty's first child, Marion, was born the following year, in 1918, but Phil was on the road virtually every day of the year with his brother, Bunk—an absentee father who rarely returned home to see his wife and baby daughter. It suited him fine; he did what he did when he was off on his own and showed up every now and then to play the role of father and the not-so-devoted husband. When Phil Cohen did arrive back in New York, he did not stay with his wife and daughter but in his own apartment in Manhattan. He would repeat that pattern when another Cohen entered the family fold.

In early 1921, Phil returned home long enough to impregnate Dotty, and, on November 22, 1921, she gave birth to a boy they named Jacob Cohen.

The future Rodney Dangerfield was born in an eighteen-room house on 44 Railroad Avenue in Deer Park, Long Island, owned by Dotty's sister, Rose, and her husband. Later, when Rodney Dangerfield was a household name, there was speculation that the abode in which he entered the world was actually located in Babylon, five miles away. Rodney, though, always considered Deer Park his birthplace.

Phil Cohen turned twenty-nine the very same day that his new son entered the world. Phil and Bunk were working at B. F. Keith's theater on Chestnut Street in Philadelphia when Baby Jacob arrived—baseball star Babe Ruth ("The Sultan of Swat") was on the bill with them—and Phil traveled back to Long Island for the occasion. But, as was his wont, even a new son did not merit much of his attention, and he was quickly on his way back to Philadelphia: after all, the road beckoned. "Dad had no time for kids," his son recalled. "He was always out trying to make new kids."[13]

Chapter Two

It's not easy being me. Nobody was nice. When I was born, the doctor told my mother, "I did all I could but he pulled through anyway." I was an ugly kid, ugly kid. When I was born, I was so ugly the doctor slapped my mother.

DOTTY COHEN HAD LITTLE USE FOR HER NEWBORN SON. SEVERAL weeks after Jacob's birth, she took him back to her crowded apartment in Jamaica, Queens, which was also home to his four-year-old sister Marion, Dotty's three other sisters, and a Swedish carpenter named Mack, who later married Dotty's sister Esther.

"My mother was coldhearted and selfish, and her sisters weren't much better," Rodney Dangerfield recalled. "My mother ran a very cold household. I never got a kiss, a hug, or a compliment. My mother wouldn't even tuck me in and forget about kissing me good night. On my birthdays, I never got a present, a card, nothing."[1]

He remembered Dotty sleeping every day until 11 a.m.—he was on his own for breakfast, which, when he was a bit older, translated to a quick bite at Nedick's cafeteria nearby. Nor did Dotty ever get out of bed to see her son off to school. Rodney recalled how Dotty once stole $100 from him, money that he saved up selling ice cream on the beach. Why? he asked her. Because she needed it. End of story. "That was how she did things."

When I was a kid my parents moved a lot, but I always found them.

* * *

JACOB COHEN'S EARLY YEARS WERE SPENT ON THE ROAD . . . MOVING from one place to another, from Jamaica, Queens, into an apartment in the East Bronx—living with Phil's mother, Sarah, in a one-bedroom apartment in a sixth-floor walkup. Dotty and Marion slept in the living room and Jacob on a cot in the foyer. From there the family schlepped to a place in Far Rockaway for the summer—Jacob sold ice cream on the beach—and then on to Kew Gardens in Queens, so Dotty could be closer to her sister Pearlie. They settled into a one-bedroom flat in an area that was, perhaps, a bit beyond their means with the money Phil Cohen was sending back to his family. "It was too nice," Rodney recalled. "We were much too poor for the neighborhood, and I never fit in there." To help pay the rent, Dotty took in two boarders, "Max—a gangster from Detroit—and his girlfriend, Helene," who slept in the living room, while Jacob, Marion, and Dotty bunked in the bedroom.[2]

Rodney's Aunt Pearlie was not much better than her sister in being cold and selfish. Rodney remembered that Pearlie was going to take Marion to the movies and that he wanted to tag along. Pearlie told him to go wash his face "real good" and then he could accompany them to the theater. "But when I came back out, Pearlie and Marion were gone," he recalled. "I could see them down the block, running away from me. I stood there yelling, 'Pearlie, I washed my hands and face real good . . .'"[3]

When Max and Helene moved out of the apartment, Dotty, Marion, and Jacob moved yet again, this time to a cheaper place in Kew Gardens near the Long Island Railroad.

I asked my old man if I could go ice-skating on the lake. He told me, "Wait till it gets warmer."

JACOB COHEN SAW HIS FATHER TWICE A YEAR—MAYBE THREE TIMES if he was lucky. He would take the train from Kew Gardens into Manhattan, where he and Phil would meet and walk around for an afternoon of little conversation before Phil dropped Jacob off at the subway for his ride back to Queens. There was not much more to their relationship. "I figured out that during my entire childhood," Rodney Dangerfield recalled, "my father saw me for two hours a year." There was the time that Dotty and her sister Esther took Jacob to Atlantic City, not out of the goodness of their hearts, but because Dotty suspected that Phil was shacking up there with one of his women friends. She was right: there he was, on the beach with a lady friend, while Aunt Esther shrieked at him and called his paramour "a whore." Good times.[4]

Life in Queens was not much different from what it had been in the East Bronx, and Jacob Cohen was not a happy child. He remembered listening to fights in the parking lot below his apartment window, and how he always identified with the loser (a lifelong theme). When he was five years old, a creep in the neighborhood offered him a nickel if he would sit on his lap in his office. "He held me and then kissed me on the lips for about five minutes." The man told Jacob not to tell anyone about it, and the boy continued to go there and let the man kiss him. In his autobiography, Rodney Dangerfield said he could not recall how long the abuse continued. "Let's face it," he said. "At five years old, I was a male hooker. Thanks for looking after me, Ma."[5]

Dotty would not even sign Jacob's report card; he was a good student and was bringing home As and Bs. "She said, 'I don't have to look at it. You know what you got.' I never got one hug or kiss in my childhood.

"Where was the love?"[6]

Jacob felt that he never fit in. It did not help his self-esteem when, at the age of ten, he started delivering groceries after school to make a few bucks, depositing packages to the houses and apartments of well-to-do classmates who looked down their noses at the kid from the wrong side of the Kew Gardens tracks. "I'd be going to school with these kids, and after school I'd be delivering orders to their houses, you know what I mean? Also, in those days I experienced quite a bit of anti-Semitism in school, even among the teachers," he said. "And the fact that I came from a split home.

"All in all, I felt on the outside."

Later in his life, when Rodney Dangerfield had conquered show business, he became friendly with Jerry Springer. Rodney was a huge fan of Springer's syndicated daytime television slugfest, *The Jerry Springer Show*. Jerry also grew up in Kew Gardens, near Rodney in fact. He, too, knew the feeling of being looked-down-upon by more affluent neighbors.

"There were really two parts to Kew Gardens," Springer said in recounting the neighborhood in an episode of A&E's *Biography* covering the life of Rodney Dangerfield. "On one side of Lefferts Boulevard you had the private homes. On the side of Lefferts Boulevard where I lived, and he did too, there were a lot of rent-controlled apartments, and it was lower-middle-class."[7]

But Jacob was an enterprising kid, always looking to make a few dollars here and there. As he grew into a teenager, Jacob progressed through school—he was an above-average student—and he held many part-time jobs. He even started his own short-lived newspaper, worked at a newsstand before school, delivered eggs, worked behind the soda fountain at his Aunt Pearlie's drugstore in Astoria, and, when he was fifteen, got a job as a barker for the Academy of Music on 14th Street in Manhattan, trying to corral passersby into the building.

Remember Eddie Cantor and his days with Bedini & Arthur? By this time, he was a huge star. He never forgot how Roy Arthur gave him his start on the stage. He and "Bunk" remained friends and stayed connected through the years. When Bunk's vaudeville career ended, Cantor added his old pal to his staff as a jack-of-all-trades—"a general aide-de-camp, majordomo, valet, and critic"—who not only accompanied "Banjo Eyes" to his various show business engagements but occasionally could be heard cracking wise on Cantor's NBC radio show, *It's Time to Smile*, in the 1940s.

When Jacob was a teenager, Uncle Bunk got his nephew tickets to see Eddie Cantor perform his NBC radio program in Manhattan. Jacob got the best seats in the house—front row, center—but, after one taping, Uncle Bunk pulled him aside. Cantor, he said, was upset because the kid in that seat never laughed and it made him look bad. So, for the next show the following week, Jacob was moved to the last row of seats—and laughed his heart out at anything and everything Cantor said. Uncle Bunk wanted to know why: "I wanna get my seat back in the front row."

Respect.

* * *

WHEN JACOB, WHO NOW WENT BY JACK, TURNED FIFTEEN, HE ENTERED Richmond Hill High School. That same year, he started writing jokes—short one-liners that fell flat with an unsmiling Dotty (when he bothered to repeat one for her). But writing jokes came naturally to Jack; it was one way to escape the loneliness and lovelessness he felt all around him, to get laughs and to be embraced by an imaginary audience, to find approval where none was forthcoming from his parents, who were both too wrapped up in their own lives to give a shit about what their son was feeling. "You wanna escape into unreality," he explained.[8]

At the same time that he was writing jokes, Jack Cohen expanded his mini show-biz empire by starting to perform in amateur shows, performing impressions of W. C. Fields and Al Jolson, neither of which were particularly good. He did not get any encouragement from Dotty or from his father, the vaudevillian. When he turned eighteen, Jack Cohen graduated from Richmond Hill High School (Class of 1939), earned his driver's license—freedom at last!—and bought his first car, an old Ford with a rumble seat. He would occasionally drive the car to the Long Island Railroad station, which had only a few cabs idling outside, and would offer his services as a chauffeur. He made a few bucks that way.

Notably, he also got his first paying job as a comic, but not as Jack Cohen. He used the name Jack Roy, with a tip of the family cap to his father's stage name. He somehow snared his first agent, Jack Miller, who would drive Jack and several other fledgling entertainers to a theater in Newark, New Jersey, which paid them two dollars each to do their thing (which was not much, just a few impressions and some wisecracks). Miller paid his comics in quarters, as if to emphasize their lowest-rung-of-show-business status. Jack Roy remembered the first-ever joke he told onstage opening night: "Would you look at the audience we got here tonight? All these women, they look like a beautiful bed of roses." . . . wait for it . . . "Of course, there's a weed here and there."[9]

Hey, it was a start.

Chapter Three

**I played one club; it was so far out, my act
was reviewed in *Field & Stream*.**

J ACK ROY WAS READY TO HIT THE BIG TIME. HE WAS NINETEEN,
fresh out of high school, had his own car, a new stage name, and a
satchel full of jokes he had been writing for the past four years.

Now came the hard part.

He spent the summer of 1940 in the "Borscht Belt," a veritable training
ground for aspiring comics located ninety miles north of New York City
in the bucolic Catskill Mountains, home to bungalow colonies and hotels
that needed entertainers to keep their patrons happy. Jack spent ten weeks
at a hotel there, earning twelve dollars each week plus room and board. His
act, such as it was, consisted of a few jokes, some songs, and those impersonations of W. C. Fields, Al Jolson, and perhaps a few others.

"I literally got down on my hands and knees and begged for my first job,"
he said later. "After I offered to pay the booking agent his 12 percent in advance, I got ten weeks at a place in Ellenville, N.Y. for $12 a week and room
and board. In those days, you had to do everything . . . comedy, songs, dances,
organize baseball teams . . . the works." That included dancing with the
women whose husbands would be arriving for the weekend from the city.[1]

Jack returned to Queens, and to Dotty, in the fall of 1940, expecting
to find regular work now that he was an experienced entertainer (well, *sort
of*). But all he found were closed doors and agents unwilling to represent a
nineteen-year-old comic with only a summer of Borscht Belt experience un-

der his belt. "All day I walked around in the heat, going from agent to agent, trying to get a job in show business," he recalled. "After three weeks I gave up." He returned to driving a laundry truck and a fish truck.[2]

Jack eventually landed a job as a waiter at the Polish Falcon, a nightclub in Brooklyn, for five dollars a night, and quickly discovered that several of the waiters sang for a few extra bucks . . . so he joined the union (after begging and pleading) and added "singing waiter" to his résumé. On a good weekend, he pocketed twenty to thirty dollars, throwing in some jokes alongside his singing. He worked there for six months and met Sally Marr, who was the club's emcee. She introduced Jack to her son, Lenny Schneider, who was still in the Navy.

Lenny Schneider would find fame (and, ultimately, tragedy) as Lenny Bruce. Lenny "was the nicest kid in the world," Rodney Dangerfield recalled, and a friendship sprung up between the two comics. Rodney remembered hanging out with Lenny Bruce in the 1950s in Bruce's room at the American Hotel in Manhattan—and heading for the bathroom to avoid watching Bruce shoot up to prepare for his act at a club in Greenwich Village.[3]

"I was nineteen working in a place and his mother was mistress of ceremonies," he recalled later. "When I met Lenny he was about seventeen. He was in the Navy and when he got out of the Navy he started going on with me on jobs and we hung out together quite a bit. I knew him well. Lenny was a very giving person, a very nice person [but] he was not understood by all."[4]

One night, Jack Roy showed up to a place in the Bronx called the Neck Inn, expecting to be paid five dollars for emceeing two shows that Saturday night. When he arrived, he was told his services were not needed—one of the waiters was going to emcee the show—but he asked the boss if he could wait on tables, instead, and he ended up making $2.50 for the night. He threw in a few jokes along the way for good measure. He was always pushing, always going. It would eventually pay off.

To make ends meet, and in-between his intermittent gigs, Jack drove a laundry truck on Mondays and Saturdays, and, on Thursdays and Fridays, he drove a fish truck for the Little Fish Market in Kew Gardens, close to home. What spare time he had during the week was spent at Hanson's Drugstore on

51st and Broadway in Manhattan—that mecca for entertainers of all stripes, but particularly for comics both working and unemployed. He could also be found at Kellogg's Cafeteria on 49th Street. His hardscrabble upbringing and his fend-for-himself attitude hardened Jack Roy, even at that young stage of his life, and he was not particularly well liked at Hanson's—and was remembered by his fellow comics as combative . . . and sometimes just downright rude.

"He had a reputation for being angry and they called him 'Angry Jack,'" recalled comedian Bobby Ramsen. "He wasn't very good, but he knew how to tell jokes," said Art Metrano. "We always thought he was like a young Henny Youngman." Jack, it was said, studied Youngman's act at the Paramount Theater in order to create a working template for his machine-gun joke-telling style. It might be apocryphal, but it was not too far a leap to believe that Jack Roy took notes on Youngman's delivery.[5]

"Jack Roy was also known as 'Mad Jack' . . . which comes from his attitude. He was angry on the street all the time," recalled comic Stan Irwin. "He was an angry man but a sweet angry man. At that time you worked joints; you'd change your clothes in the toilet, and if you were lucky you got $5 to $15 a night."[6]

The comics and entertainers at Hanson's also introduced Jack to his life-long love affair with marijuana, which he tried for the first time one night in 1942 when he was hanging around with his pal Joe E. Ross, who was later to star in the classic NBC sitcom *Car 54, Where Are You?*, and a comic named Bobby Byron.

"We were sitting there talking, doing what we were doing, and Bobby and Joe E. decided that they wanted to get high," Jack recalled. "They invited me to join them." Jack refused, at first, but he told them that he would keep them company as they headed back to the Belvedere Hotel on West 48th Street ("I even remember the room, 1411"). When they got upstairs Byron took out a joint and, after he and Ross took a few tokes, they offered it to Jack, who acquiesced. "I felt relaxed, peaceful, everything was okay. That night I found a new friend for the rest of my life."[7]

The small restaurant B&G, located next door to Hanson's, was another hangout for Jack Roy and his fellow show business aspirants. The restaurant's windows were covered with signs advertising their menu items; for kicks, Jack and his friends would sometimes make up their own signs and tape them to the B&G window: "Best Fuckin' Hamburger in Town!" or "Our Soup Will Knock You on Your Ass!" Like that. "That was our experiment for the day," Rodney Dangerfield recalled. "That's what you do when you can't get a job in show business."[8]

SLOWLY BUT SURELY, THROUGH SHEER DETERMINATION AND BULL-headedness, Jack's bookings picked up. He was working slightly classier joints now—the Brass Rail in Brooklyn, the Village Barn in Greenwich Village, Sunrise Village in Bellmore, Long Island—and, on a good weekend, he could pull in between $100 and $150 as an emcee/comic.

He was still living at home, with Dotty, so rent was not an issue, and he expanded beyond the five boroughs and into clubs in South Jersey (Asbury Park), Connecticut (Bridgeport), Boston, New England, Chicago (the Silver Frolics) and farther north in Montreal. It was in that city where an agent named Billy Goldes booked Jack into a place called the Esquire Club, located on Stanley Street. It was a fixture in the city since opening its doors in 1940. Jack figured he had it made—Canada, here I come!—but opening night was a disaster. Nobody laughed at Jack's jokes or his impersonations—not a titter, not a guffaw. Instead, he was met with blank stares. No wonder: what Billy Goldes did not tell Jack was that the Esquire Club catered to a French-speaking audience, who had no idea what the comic emcee was saying. It turned out that Goldes booked Jack into the club in order to get even with its owner over some past slight. Jack Roy did not find that amusing.

> **I'm a bad lover. I once caught a peeping Tom booing me.**

JACK WAS NOT WHAT ANYONE WOULD CALL MOVIE-STAR HANDSOME, but he was not a homely-looking man, either. He had saucer-shaped blue eyes, an aquiline nose that framed his face nicely, and he kept his short, dark, wavy hair slickly parted. He was, in his own way, quite handsome and dapper, despite all the later jokes about his physical appearance. (*I know I'm ugly. I went to a freak show. They let me in for nothing! I was so ugly my mother breastfed me through a straw!*) One-night stands were not uncommon for the young comic in his early twenties as he traversed the country and met willing women in the clubs or during his downtime in whatever city or small-town in which he happened to be working. There was a lot of time to kill between gigs and the road was a lonely existence. Jack claimed that he kept a small blue lightbulb in the glove compartment of his car in case the mood was right. He indulged in sex and marijuana use; the cocaine and rock 'n' roll lifestyle would come years later following his fame and fortune.

"I can't explain it, but there's something about the aura of show business that really helps with the girls," he wrote in his memoir. "If a guy is only fair looking, he becomes good looking when he goes into show business. Not me, but most guys. Girls treat me like I'm their father—they keep asking for money."[9]

Life on the road for a young comic meant no strings attached and no questions asked when it came to one-night stands. Rodney Dangerfield's memoir is sprinkled with tales of sexual derring-do (and a few don'ts) on the nightclub circuit.

He recounted, with particular relish, the time he played a club in Asbury Park, New Jersey, when he was around twenty-one years old. He met a girl after his show that night and they hit it off. There was only one problem: neither of them had a private room and they were hot and heavy in that moment. They took care of that slight blip by driving to a nearby beach and bumping their uglies on the sand until they were stopped by a police officer. But no matter: Jack and his fling then headed back to the room where he was staying, which he shared with his booking agent. They resumed their lovemaking, but Jack did not have a condom. No worries: "Just then, my agent gets out of bed, goes to the closet, takes a rubber out of his coat pocket, hands it to me, and goes right back to bed without a word. Now, that's a booking agent."[10]

Another favorite Dangerfield story unfolded in a New York nightclub he called the House of Scheib's—he was likely referring to Scheib's Place, a former speakeasy at 80 St. Mark's Place. In either event, the place had a mambo

contest each Tuesday night, and Jack Roy got to know one of the female dancers. They began dating until, one night, she told him she was marrying a police
officer from Long Island. Jack knew only one police officer on Long Island,
a childhood acquaintance from Queens who he called "Pete Hartmann" in
his memoirs. As Jack's luck would have it, Pete turned out to be the same guy
his dating companion was set to marry. So, Jack did the right thing: he called
Pete, asked him out for a drink, and told him the woman he was sleeping
with was the same girl Pete was about to make his wife. "When I finished, he
didn't say a word for about five minutes. Then he got up, shook my hand, and
said 'Thanks.' That was it. I didn't hear from him again for years and years."
The old friends eventually reconnected, and Rodney was relieved to hear that
"Pete" never did marry the mambo dancer.[11]

By the mid-1940s, the name Jack Roy started to appear in nightclub and
restaurant newspaper advertisements as these venues advertised their weekly
entertainment slates. The earliest newspaper shout-out to Jack Roy found by
this author appeared in late January 1944 in *The Brooklyn Eagle*, where "Jack
Roy, M.C." was at the Club Warren on Bond Street ("A Paul Lester Attraction"). Jack was joined on the bill by Marguerite, Adele Fox, and the Dick
Ware Orchestra. The following month, "Jack Roy, M.C." was at McGough's,
located at 91st Street and 4th Avenue in Bay Ridge, Brooklyn, with Mary
Mann, Kay Hanson, Peggy Rich, and Ricky Rosborne and his Orchestra. It
was not exactly the Copa, but it was a step up and he had just enough comic
material to squeak by in-between introducing the acts. He returned to Mc-
Gough's four months later in June.

In January 1945, Jack Roy emceed a throwback vaudeville revue at the
RKO Madison Theatre on his home turf in Queens; the following week, he
was at the RKO Bushwick in Brooklyn with Crown Records vocalist and
WMCA radio announcer "Smiling" Jerry Baker and the Crawfords.

"As Jack Roy, his delivery, his subject matter was sort of cult," fellow
comic Stan Irwin said. "He didn't perform the way the majority of other
comics performed. He was just a little angry that he didn't achieve the success
of Jack Roy that he deserved."[12]

He took whatever work was offered, and not only in nightclub venues. In

May 1946, Jack was hired to emcee and tell jokes at a testimonial dinner held at the Williams Lake Hotel in upstate Rosendale, New York, sponsored by the Ulster County Hotel, Restaurant and Liquor Dealers' Association. It was attended by more than two hundred and fifty people. The program included Phil King, he of the noted "hand-balancing act," singer Ginger Harmon, and John Brandon, the "so-called atomic blonde deceptionist"—whatever *that* meant. But, hey, it was a paying gig. And maybe Jack got lucky that night.

"Those were the toughest days," he said. "No one likes to be humiliated. They used to call me 'Angry Jack' because my face was always down when I was young. I have the kind of face that people don't take to even when I'm cheerful. As Jack Roy, I was nothing. I felt like nothing."[13]

The first known press photograph of Jack Roy ran in the January 3, 1947, issue of *The Brooklyn Eagle*. Under the photo of Jack, unsmiling and wearing a tuxedo jacket and bowtie, was this caption: "QUIP-CRACKER—Jack Roy is the comic master of ceremonies at Woodside's Queens Terrace." Over a year later, in April 1948, *The Brooklyn Eagle* ran this first mention of Jack's act: "Jack Roy building up his fan list with his comedy antics at the Park Inn in Valley Stream."[14] It was only one line, but those sixteen words of validation meant the world to him. He was written up again in *The Brooklyn Eagle* the following year (they were big Jack Roy fans): "Jack Roy is a slick comic at Gene's Casa Seville. Held over with songster Donald Novas." That was followed the next day by that same press photo of Jack in his tuxedo and bowtie running opposite "society songbird" Gigi Durston. When all was said and done, Jack was held over six weeks at the Casa Seville, with its "Czechoslovakian crystal, all lucite walls with hidden lighting, stuffed peacocks, and other ornamentation." It was, as they say, a classy joint.

There was a dark side, too.

Years later, Rodney Dangerfield remembered the "animals" he had to deal with in the 1940s club world. There was the night he badmouthed a heckler and, when he left the club after the show, there were three goons waiting for him by the back door. Two guys held him while the third, the heckler, belted him. "I stood there to see how much damage was done. Nothing. As I walked home I thought to myself, 'I'm going to find that guy and beat him up.' The next day I found out someone had killed him after he left me." It was a tough, sometimes dangerous milieu, and it was not always the patrons who were trouble, as Jack Roy learned all too well.[15]

"I worked in all kinds of dumps," he recalled. "I worked 'em all. I worked in a bar once, three shows a night, seven nights a week, and the manager asks me to take a cut in salary! Then, when I didn't, he gets drunk and wants to do some damage to me. You get humble from things like that, you know, you learn humility."[16]

In August 1949, a television audience got its first look at Jack Roy when he made his debut on the New York City TV station WPIX on its *Four-Star Showcase* program. He did not emcee this time—Pete Ivory oversaw those duties—but he joined "the debonair Unger Twins; the dance team of Mara and Maurice"; fellow comedians DeLyon and Ryder; singer Gene Williams; and dancer Rosanna on the sixty-minute program. There is no written or video record of how Jack Roy fared that night, nor are viewership viewers available; chances are it registered an exceedingly small audience in the New York market. Television, which would, decades later, be so important to Rodney Dangerfield's career, was still in its infancy but was growing rapidly, thanks to Milton Berle and his show-stopping *Texaco Star Theater* program on NBC, which premiered in 1948 and put the new medium on the map. Jack Roy, though, would not appear on television again until the 1960s—and then with a new name and a revamped act.

> **My wife was afraid of the dark. Then she saw
> me naked, and now she's afraid of the light.**

BY THE LATE 1940S, JACK ROY WAS DOING A BIT OF SOUL-SEARCHING AS he closed in on his thirtieth birthday, which was still a few years away but close enough. He was still living with Dotty and, despite the marijuana and his prolific sex life on the road, he was thinking of settling into a more traditional lifestyle with which he could merge his comedy career. Giving the business up completely was out of the question, although he knew there was life after show business: he could look no further than his own father, Phil Roy, who segued into a successful career as a New York stockbroker after Roy & Arthur called it quits in the dying days of vaudeville. (Phil eventually moved to Los Angeles to join his brother Adolf, so the old team was reunited, at least in spirit—and no china was broken this time around.)

Jack shared the bill one night with Joyce Indig, and he took a shine to the twenty-two-year-old singer, who was born in April 1927 to Rebecca and Max Indig. She had a younger sister, Carole.

At the time she met Jack Roy, Joyce Indig had compiled an impressive show business résumé. She first surfaced on the scene in 1945, when she was eighteen. In October of that year, she appeared as an actress in an experimental drama called *Seven Mirrors* that opened off-Broadway at the Blackfriars Repertory Theater on West 57th Street. She was listed as one of "the ladies of the epilogue" in a complimentary review in *The Brooklyn Eagle*. Joyce's major talent, though, was as a singer; the *New York Daily News* dubbed her "The warbler with the Casino Russe band."[17] She sang romantic ballads at venues in and around New York City, including the Bayou on West 51st Street and the Ritz Ballroom and across the river in New Jersey at Palisades Amusement Park, where she joined the free daily stage presentation.

Jack Roy was not Joyce's first serious romance. A Brooklyn-born comedian named Van Harris, who worked the Borscht Belt circuit, claimed to have had a "summer romance" with Joyce in the Catskills and made an outlandish claim. "She was a very selfish girl and a very pretty girl," he said. "She had many romances and fell in love with an Italian prizefighter who was married—and he committed suicide over her. She was a rather selfish but lovely girl."

Harris said that his romance with Joyce stuck in Jack Roy's craw in the ensuing years, even after both men were married, Jack wed to Joyce and Harris married to Shirley, who worked as a social director for a Catskills hotel. "Whenever he'd see me, even in the presence of my wife, he would say, 'You ever climb on my wife? You ever climb on my wife?' 'Come on, Rodney, stop the shit.' You know? But that was *Rodney*. That's what he was."[18]

Joyce was an attractive woman with dark hair and high cheekbones; photographs from that time show her wearing her hair in a bob. She signed a deal with Mercury Records and had a minor hit with "Wish Me Luck," which she performed on WNBC radio's *The Skitch Henderson Show* and, in the process, caught the ear of powerful gossip columnist Walter Winchell: "A new name and voice to these ears is Joyce Indig's," Winchell wrote. "We heard her render 'Wish Me Luck' the other morning via Skitch Henderson's offerings and she comes over delightfully."[19] She also merited a mention in Ed Sullivan's syndicated column in the *New York Daily News:* "Joyce Indig at Ruban Blue" (where she was held over).[20]

The music press, too, was taken with Joyce's dulcet tones: "Joyce Indig gets awfully intense singing 'The Best Thing for You' from Berlin's 'Call Me Madame' and a ballad, 'Cross My Heart.'" And this from *The Boston Globe:* "Joyce Indig putting a throb in her voice in 'Cross My Heart' and 'The Best Thing for You.'"[21]

In May 1949, three months before Jack Roy's debut on WPIX, Joyce was a guest on the station's *The Art Ford Show* along with jazz pianist Joe Bushkin and his orchestra, dancer Teddy Hale, and singer Richard Hayes. That fall, she made her singing debut at the Park Avenue, with one gossip columnist clucking that "The Park Ave.'s canary, Joyce Indig, has a new tone. First name Franchot." (She and actor/movie producer Franchot Tone were never an item.)[22] She followed her Park Avenue gig with an opening at the Ritz Café, where she appeared on the *Backstage with Barry Wood* television program on CBS with her "Mood Music in The Modern Manner."

Jack and Joyce were on the way up. Jack, who was identified as "B'way Comedy Star" (really?) snared a spot at Skinny D'Amato's 500 Club in Atlantic City—which had launched Dean Martin and Jerry Lewis into the comic stratosphere and was familiar terrain for Frank Sinatra—and emceed at the Casa Seville on Long Island (Franklin Square), where the "clever comic" was held over. He was working steadily now—the Terrace Garden in Troy, New York, at Iceland Theatre Restaurant closer to home on 53rd Street and Broadway, emceeing a show at Club Charles in Baltimore—and was keeping pace with Joyce, whose photograph ran in the *New York Daily News* during her run at Ruban Bleu.

The couple was doing well, personally *and* professionally. In August 1951, gossip columnist Earl Wilson announced their intentions in one terse line: "Singer Joyce Indig will marry comic Jack Roy."[23]

What Earl Wilson did not mention when announcing the engagement, or perhaps did not know, was that the wedding of Jack Roy and Joyce Indig, which took place that October, signaled the beginning of the end of their performing careers in that phase of their lives. It is unclear if it was Joyce or Jack who pushed for a life of domestic bliss. Perhaps it was a mutually agreed-upon decision, which had to be a tough one. While neither of them had hit the big time—Joyce seemed closer to the top than Jack, at that point—he would later hint that he was not all-in on this plan. Still, he was turning thirty a month after the wedding and while he was working steadily, he had yet to graduate into the big time. How much longer could he tread water?

Rodney Dangerfield would claim later, whenever he recounted his life and career, that he felt it was time to leave "the show" and support his new wife (Joyce stopped working once they were married). He wanted to lead "a so-called normal life," and joked, repeatedly, that he was the only one who knew that he had quit show business.

In one interview, he pinpointed the date of his departure from the dim limelight to an unpleasant experience in the Catskills in 1948, when he played the midnight show and was asked by the angry manager why he was not outside the following morning at 8:30 to lead calisthenics. "That did it," he said, though the story is apocryphal (his last known performance during this phase of his career is 1951).

JACK'S MOTHER, DOTTY, WAS, PREDICTABLY, NOT HAPPY THAT HER SON found a bride, not because she was so attached to him—they could barely stand to be in each other's company—but because she hated any woman who had eyes for her son and would infringe on the money he would throw her way to help keep her going. (Phil Cohen was long out of the picture by this point and gave his ex-wife nothing.)

"We got no wedding present from my mother," Rodney Dangerfield recalled. "When I told my mother I was going to marry Joyce, she looked at me as though I had betrayed her, and then made me promise that I would always support her."

Shortly after the wedding, Jack tried to start a nice routine where he would take Dotty out to dinner every Sunday. "That lasted two Sundays," he recounted. "All through dinner, my mother looked at Joyce with such hatred that from then on, it was just Mom and me having dinner on Sunday nights."[24]

Early in his marriage to Joyce, Jack decided that he wanted to reconnect with his father, whom he had not seen in twenty years, and who was now living in L.A. near his brother, Adolf (Uncle Bunk). Jack and Joyce made the five-day trek to the West Coast by rail, and when they alit in the City of Angels Jack discovered, much to his dismay, that Phil Cohen was working as a shoe salesman in a place called Karl's on Hollywood Boulevard. "Here was this guy who had been a top stockbroker and now he was restocking racks of shoes," he recalled.

Jack figured he would cheer himself up by visiting his Uncle Bunk, who he also had not seen for twenty years, though Phil warned him that Bunk "was not himself." The visit was a short one; Bunk spent their time together yelling at his television set and not paying much attention to his nephew, who made a quick exit and never saw him again.[25]

Family drama aside, Jack Roy might have left the only thing he had known for the past decade, but only physically; he was still a comedian in spirit and he continued to write jokes and add them to his growing joke collection as he segued into his new life at the dawn of the Eisenhower Era.

Who knew? The jokes might come in handy if this working-stiff thing did not pan out.

Chapter Four

I had to tell jokes. I had to write them and tell them. It was like a fix, like I had the habit, you know?

JACK ROY LEFT THE WORLD OF SHOW BUSINESS AND TRANSFORMED himself into a paint and aluminum siding salesman—joining thousands of others nationwide in cashing in on the country's post–World War II preoccupation with encasing their houses in aluminum, and the men willing to do anything and everything (legally and, sometimes, dishonestly) to fulfill their dreams.

The process of aluminum siding was invented in the mid-1940s by the Reynolds Metals Co. in Kentucky, which installed its very first siding job on a cement house, and its adjacent garage, in Louisville in 1945. Aluminum was extremely cost-effective; it was more durable than wood, did not rot or attract termites, and did not need to be painted every few years. The siding business exploded in the ensuing decade along with the booming American economy.[1]

Many men in the aluminum siding business wore a "Ruptured Duck" pin on their lapels to indicate that they had served in the armed forces, giving them another leg up when selling their product. The pin's official name was an "Honorable Service Lapel Button"; veterans referred to it as a "ruptured duck" because the chest on the eagle adorning the pin appeared to burst forward and the bird, at first blush, more closely resembled a duck than an eagle. Another story behind the "Ruptured Duck" pin was that it earned its nickname because the eagle faced right—the direction that armed forces inductees were told to face when coughing as they were being checked for a hernia.

In any event, the pin helped to evoke compassion, admiration, and sympathy from potential aluminum siding and/or paint clients.

(The aluminum siding phenomenon, and the men who toiled in the trenches, is satirized brilliantly in Barry Levinson's 1987 big-screen comedy *Tin Men*, which is set in Baltimore in the early 1960s with stars Richard Dreyfuss and Danny DeVito—and is based on a true story. Dreyfuss and De-Vito play competing aluminum siding salesmen masquerading as *Life* magazine photographers and promising gullible homeowners that, if they replace their homes' wooden exteriors with aluminum, the houses will be featured on the magazine's cover.)

Jack Roy wanted in on the aluminum siding game. As a businessman, he was untested, but as a working comedian and emcee, he knew he could sell himself to perfect strangers. It was, after all, the life he lived for the past decade as a struggling comic, and he had the emotional battle scars to prove it, selling his jokes and impressions to a faceless audience night after night in city after city, town after town. He could sweet-talk with the best of them. And he knew the feeling of being rejected. It would serve him well in the cutthroat business world.

Jack signed on with Pioneer Construction. The company, based in Newark, New Jersey, sold aluminum siding and paint. He was fairly successful at first, scouting out locations in Northern New Jersey, swooping in with the sales pitch and closing the deal—with a joke or two, of course—but when the weather turned cold so did business. Jack and two of his work friends decided to head to the warmer climate of New Orleans, where they stayed for two months before heading back to the New York area. Rodney covered their expenses.

On the way back, they passed through Birmingham, Alabama, where they hooked up with a local siding company run by a guy named Steve Mc-Gill and, before long, they were signing clients left and right. But something seemed a bit off; they took note of the fact that none of the siding work they sold was actually getting done. That was a big problem for Jack and his two guys, since they did not get paid their commissions until the jobs were completed.

Jack figured that McGill owed him and his crew four thousand dollars, and he nagged McGill until the contactor offered to buy them out for seven hundred and fifty dollars. Jack had no other choice and accepted the offer. He drowned his sorrows at a local bar, where, slightly inebriated, he got up, shook out the rust, and did about ten minutes of stand-up to the appreciation of a guy in the bar named Al Fontaine. Fontaine was a local banker who got on the phone, made several calls and, the next day, Jack and his guys got their four thousand dollars from McGill. No questions were asked.[2]

The work, while financially rewarding, was unfulfilling, and Jack felt trapped in a job he hated. "I was extremely unhappy. To me, selling was colorless, uninteresting, boring," he said. "I was like millions of other fellows who are trapped in jobs they hate. A guy feels like he can't take a shot at something else because he's afraid to give up whatever degree of financial security he may have."[3]

It was not much better on the home front, where arguments with Joyce were not uncommon and their marriage teetered on the brink. They were living in an apartment on Yellowstone Boulevard in Forest Hills, Queens, in the mid-1950s; Jack had left Pioneer Construction, and this is the point at which his professional career in the aluminum siding and paint business gets a bit murky. The Tin Man Extraordinaire was now president of three companies, Eastern Home Improvement, Interstate Home Improvement, and Atlantic Home Improvement. They were each connected to Cross Island Home Improvement, which was located in Elmont, on the border between Queens and Long Island, and was run by Benjamin Leimsider. One of Jack's coworkers, Joe Ancis—who would figure heavily into the legends of Lenny Bruce and Rodney Dangerfield—became a close friend and confidant during this time.

Jack was based in Englewood, New Jersey, in Bergen County, just over the river from Manhattan and minutes from the George Washington Bridge. Business was good for a while—Bergen County was, for the most part, middle-class or upper-middle class—and Jack developed strong contacts in the industry together with a loyal clientele. Later, he would describe the job as "colorless"—that was his go-to explanation whenever a reporter asked—but, on the surface, he was doing just fine as a salesman.

His time in the aluminum siding game, however, took a crooked turn. Industry scams were not uncommon, and the FBI was starting to crack down on wonky financial agreements and Tin Men turned Con Men. There was a shady side to the business, and Jack Roy was drawn into its darker corners, which promised quick financial gain by circumventing the law.

Over the course of 1954 and 1955, Jack joined fifteen other men in an aluminum siding fraud that encompassed companies and counties in New York, New Jersey, and Connecticut. The swindle was built around fraudulent loans involving the Federal Housing Authority (FHA). It was brought to the attention of the FBI, which, in conjunction with the U.S. Attorney's Office, was on a crusade against fraudsters bilking the FHA.

Here is how the con game worked: The companies, in total, procured around $600,000 in fake loans for homeowners from the FHA, $60,000 of which was returned to the homeowners in kickbacks. A sales rep would arrange a loan for owners who could not afford home improvements for as much as twice the cost of the job up to $1,500, according to James J. Kelly, the FBI. agent in charge of the case. The homeowner would be identified as a good loan risk (though, in many cases this, too, was a lie) and, when the FHA approved the loan, the salesman took the price of the job and 80 percent of the overpayment, with the other 20 percent kicked back to the homeowners, many of them using the extra cash to pay personal debts, medical bills, auto loans, wedding presents, and taxes.

In this particular case, 74 percent of the FHA loans acquired were fraudulent, according to the FBI; in one instance, the homeowner never received the kickback, while others applied for the loans by promises of commission on contracts obtained from their neighbors.

In some cases, salesman or officers processed the applications for loans of $1,000 to $4,000. When the loans were approved by the FHA, the money would be borrowed from banks or other private institutions. Contracts for minor repairs were negotiated by the salesmen, according to the FBI, and they received 40 to 60 percent commissions on the costs in addition to their commissions as salesmen.[4]

On Saturday morning, October 22, 1955, the FBI arrested Jack Roy (also identified as Jack Cohen), Benjamin Leimsider, Joseph A. Ancis, Murray L. Freeman, Leonard Daffner, and others on racketeering charges. Jack, Leimsider, Daffner, Freeman, and Martin Jacoby's mugshots graced a story in the *New York Daily News* under the headline:

FBI Nabs 15 in Home Improvement Fraud

"Moving quick through the metropolitan area and New Jersey, the FBI yesterday arrested 15 officers and sales representatives of four housing improvement firms on charges of defrauding the government on federally insured loans," the newspaper reported. "To make the racket work, the FBI charged, the suspects promised homeowners kickbacks on the fraudulent loans—but as often as not the kickbacks were not made."[5]

Jack, Joe Ancis, Benjamin Leimsider, and others were hauled before U.S. Commissioner Martin C. Epstein in Brooklyn Federal Court and released on bail. Jack, Ancis, and Leimsider all posted $1,500 bail. Jack called his mother, Dotty, and asked for the bail money; she refused, at first, and then reluctantly relented, but Jack told her to forget about it and "next thing I knew I was in the backseat of a shylock's new Cadillac, where I made a deal."[6]

A week later, Jack and Benjamin Leimsider pleaded guilty in Brooklyn Federal Court before Judge Robert A. Inch and were released on bail. They faced possible twelve-year prison sentences and $30,000 fines.

In February 1956, the two men returned to Brooklyn Federal Court and were fined $6,000 each and given one-year probationary sentences.[7] Jack worked out a deal with his probation officer that he would call him on the phone every week instead of schlepping out to see him in person.

IT WOULD BE EASY TO SAY THAT JACK ROY, AT THE AGE OF THIRTY-FOUR, already washed up as a comedian, took a second hit as a loser in the aluminum siding business.

But he did not—in fact, he thrived.

This time, albeit under heavier scrutiny, Jack got up off the mat, brushed himself off, and launched a new business, National Home Construction

Corp. As before, it was based in Englewood, New Jersey.

Jack placed ads in local newspapers promising $50 for part-time or full-time work at home: "If you have a pleasant speaking voice and can devote 3–4 hours per day, we will train you to become one of our successful telephone solicitors working in your own home. Guarantee. Call Mr. Roy, National Home Construction Corp."

In 1957, National Home Construction Corp. built a waterproof wall of precut stone for a trade show held in the Teaneck Armory in nearby Teaneck, New Jersey. "The new process to be shown publicly for the first time will be the spraying or painting on of a permanent sealer which completely closes all the pores in the material," *The Bergen Record* reported.[8]

Four years later, in 1961, Jack Roy and the National Home Construction Corp. donated the finishing of the four-thousand-square-foot National Hall exhibition area at the Bergen Mall in Paramus, New Jersey. Jack also played host for the reception following the dedication, doing his civic duty with just enough of a forced smile to make it look convincing.

Inside, though, he never left show business, at least not in his heart, and through the years of selling aluminum siding and paint, his arrest by the FBI, and rehabilitating his image, Jack Roy kept writing jokes in his spare time. He sold a few gags to Joey Bishop, among others, and Jack and his friend Joe Ancis would often drive to Hanson's Drugstore in Manhattan, get high, and try to sell Jack's jokes to the other comics.

Comedian Stan Irwin said he "rented" Jack Roy's old stage act. "Jack had a file of jokes in the trunk of his car that he would sell to you for five dollars apiece."[9] Joke-writing was a compulsion for Jack, something he needed to do—"It was like a fix," he said—and his growing joke portfolio would serve him well. "Put it this way," he once said, "Even when I was out of show business I was still writing."[10] But nobody, he thought, could do his material as well as himself.

"It was like a need. I had to work," he said. "I had to tell jokes. I had to write them and tell them. It was like a fix, like I had the habit, you know? Like I had to had to do it, had to do it, had to yell it out, had to get it out, you know?"[11]

The year 1961 marked a milestone birthday for Jack Roy: he turned forty on November 22, and he and Joyce divorced after ten years of a turbulent marriage. But it was not that simple; Joyce had, the previous year, given birth to their first child, a son they named Brian. Jack knew it was time to get back into comedy, the only game he really cared about, but he was also feeling the responsibility of paying child support for Joyce and his one-year-old son, who he loved and to whom he paid as much attention as he possibly could while chasing his comedy dream for a second time.

"I was broke, I owed $20,000," he said. "I couldn't live at home because of the domestic situation. I had to live in a cheap, dirty, low-class hotel in New York. I was so down then that I did the craziest thing in the whole world: I said I'm going back to what I want to do and went back into show business. Everyone said I was nuts. Coming back, you have to take rejection over and over again. But I kept writing jokes. I felt I had something to say: doing a guy where nothing goes right. Everyone could identify with that."[12]

Jack Roy found a "major comic" who he did not name and worked out a deal wherein said comic would pay him 5 percent of his salary for routines. "I supplied him with bits but he didn't pay me so I called it off and went looking for other comedians," Jack said. "Then it dawned on me. There wasn't one guy I was approaching who could deliver my jokes as well as I could . . . and, after over twelve years out of the business, I started from scratch."[13]

"I had my responsibilities, but I felt I also had humor," he said. "I felt I had something to say and I wanted to say it. I quit my job and went out and worked clubs for nothing just to get exposure."[14]

For Jack Roy, Round 2 of the brutal, rough-and-tumble world of comedy meant that failure was not an option.

Chapter Five

**I worked every dungeon there is. Like
this place in Jersey called Aldo's, formerly
Vito's, formerly Nunzio's. I played there for six
months. A rough place. When you entered the
place you went down two steps—physically
and socially.**

JACK ROY DEVOTED HIS ENERGIES INTO GETTING BACK INTO THE
clubs and left the past ten years of his "colorless" career behind him. "I
quit my job and went out and worked nightclubs for nothing just to get the
exposure," he said. "It was quite a gamble. Everybody—including my dog—
said I was nuts. But it paid off."[1]

He was more seasoned now, more attuned to life's vagaries (and failures),
more cynical than he was the first time around. One of the favorite lines he
produced during the aluminum siding years was, "The trouble with me is, I
appeal to everyone who can do me absolutely no good." Words that could fit
just about any situation, words that needed a character around which to form
the image of an everyman schlemiel who, repeatedly, came out on the short
end of the stick.

One of the first people Jack approached, in his long slog on the comeback
trail, was Frank Santore, the manager of the Miami Club on Brighton Street
in Staten Island, who knew Jack from when he played there fifteen years earlier. Santore agreed to give Jack some stage time, and after a decade out of the
game, he shook off the rust and killed that night in November 1961 as the
"Mad Comic Emcee" Jack Roy, sharing the bill with "Decca Recording Star"

Bobby Pace, "Lively Song Stylist" Joy Rogers, and "Lovely Exotic Dancer" Mona Fredericks (Santore obviously liked his adjectives). He was held over another week, and it buoyed his spirits and convinced him it could be different this time around.

"I worked every dungeon there is," he said, tongue not quite planted in cheek. "Like this place in Jersey called Aldo's, formerly Vito's, formerly Nunzio's. I played there for six months. A rough place. When you entered the place you went down two steps—physically and socially."[2]

He approached an agent named Irving "King" Broder, who booked acts into small nightclubs, mostly on Long Island. Jack nagged at Broder, who was not interested in representing a forty-year-old comedian who, for the past decade, was off the stage and lost in suburban New Jersey. Broder did, however, agree to let Jack accompany him on his nightly rounds around the club circuit and, lo and behold—in one of those showbiz stories that seems apocryphal (but was not)—one night Broder's act, a dance team, did not show up for their gig. "I say [to Broder], 'Let me go up. I'll do ten minutes for you, okay?'" Jack recalled. "So finally, I was able to get on a stage for Broder, and I killed that crowd. Even better, I got hired to work that club starting the next weekend.

"And that's how I got back into show business."[3]

Whatever confidence Jack Roy felt about his return to the nightclub stage was tempered by the years of rejection that he experienced in the 1940s in his first time around the comedy circuit. He was cautiously optimistic now but also older and wiser—wary of being let down and embarrassed once again as he reentered an arena dominated by much-younger comics, some of whom, including Joan Rivers and Woody Allen, were a full decade younger and generating lots of positive press with acts tuned to the hipper, Kennedy-era zeitgeist. He was hedging his bets, and rightly so, and what he did next was a stroke of brilliance.

He changed his name—with a little help from a club owner.

In his memoirs, Rodney Dangerfield mentioned only that, early in his comeback bid, he visited a club in which he had worked years before. In reality, it was called the Innwood Lounge and was located on the northern tip of

Manhattan. George McFadden owned the place. McFadden never heard of Jack Roy, but many of his patrons remembered the brusque comic from his appearances there in the '40s—which is exactly what Jack wanted to avoid.

McFadden, as did the other club owners, submitted his performer lineup to the Friday edition of the local papers including the *New York Mirror*, which ran listings of all the acts for the coming weekend. Jack asked Mc-Fadden to change his name—he did not care what it was—so long as people would think they were seeing a new comedian (which, in essence, they were). McFadden chose Rodney Dangerfield, and the legend was born. "He came up with Rodney Dangerfield," he said in a later interview. "I don't know where it came from."[4]

(Rodney's agent at the time, Philip Roy Duke—who also handled comedian/impressionist Will Jordan—laid claim to the name change from Jack Roy to Rodney Dangerfield. When Duke passed away in December 2005 at the age of eighty-four, his obituary in the *Las Vegas Review-Journal* read in part that "He is best known for creating the character Rodney Dangerfield," among other career highlights.)[5]

At first blush, the name Rodney Dangerfield seemed to have been plucked out of thin air. But it was not. At least two episodes of *The Jack Benny Program* on NBC Radio had characters named Rodney Dangerfield. The first time Rodney appeared, he was a cowboy movie star in a 1941 holiday episode of Benny's show called "The Christmas Tree." Jack says his holiday party will include a number of movie stars and, when his wife, Mary Livingstone, asks him to name one, he says, "All right, Rodney Dangerfield."

Jack: "I know he's coming because he already sent me a wire by Western Union."

Mary: "Western Union I heard about, but who is Rodney Dangerfield?"

Jack: "Who is Rodney Dangerfield? Well, I'll be—Mary, did you see *The Fargo Kid Rides the Pony Express on the Santa Fe Trail* at the Hitching Post Theater last week?"

Mary: "No."

Jack: "Well, that was Rodney's greatest performance." (He then proceeds to describe Rodney jumping out of a second-story window with guns blazing as he gallops away.)

The second time Rodney Dangerfield was mentioned in Benny's universe was in the episode "New Year's Date With a French Girl," which aired on NBC on December 30, 1951. Rodney Dangerfield was introduced as "a famous star of stage, screen, radio, and now television." (Jack, of course, wrongly assumed it was *him* to whom they were referring.)

Ricky Nelson, too, used "Rodney Dangerfield" as a pseudonym when he was going on a blind date in a 1962 episode of the ABC television show *The Adventures of Ozzie & Harriet.* The name was mentioned in two scenes. And let us not forget that the protagonist of J. P. Donleavy's 1955 scandalous novel, *The Ginger Man*, was named Sebastian Dangerfield. Hey, you never know.

THE NEWLY RECHRISTENED RODNEY DANGERFIELD DID NOT, AT FIRST, have much more luck than his old nemesis Jack Roy when it came to finding jobs on the nightclub circuit. The gigs were tough to come by and he was getting deeper into debt—$20,000, by his estimate—but he stuck by his guns and soldiered on.

"I remember when I worked once without one person in the audience," he recalled. "It was a club in midtown Manhattan, and the owner told me to go on even though the place was empty. For 20 minutes, I stood up there with jokes. 'Sure is nice to be here tonight, working for nobody,'" I said. A couple of people came in, and I've never been so happy to see anybody."[6]

August 1962 found Rodney Dangerfield playing Bill's Castle in Bridgeport, Connecticut, as one of "The Greatest in Entertainment" acts along with Skippy Cunningham, Barbara Todd, and George Kaye and His Orchestra; in November, he shared a bill with jazz singer June Christy at the Embers in Indianapolis: "The Funtastic Rodney Dangerfield (Who?)"

He returned to Bill's Castle several times in the ensuing year and, in October 1963, moved up a peg on the show business ladder with a mention in Frank Ross's "Sip and Sup" column in the *New York Daily News:* "Brooklyn's [*sic*] Rodney Dangerfield, who wrote for many top comics, debuts his own comedy set tonight at the Town & Country Club in show starring Tony Martin of Hollywood. He's the husband of Cyd Charisse."[7] Later that month, he was back in Queens at the Boulevard Club with Kathy Keegan and the Duquaines.

Rodney met Joan Rivers when they shared a bill with Dick Cavett at Upstairs at the Duplex on Grove Street in Greenwich Village. All three performers worked for free. Cavett remembered the place having "maybe five tables," but it was a mecca for young artists trying to break into the business, among them Hal Holbrook, Woody Allen, JoAnne Worley (later to star on *Rowan & Martin's Laugh-In*), Linda Lavin, and Barbra Streisand. Rivers was not a fan of Rodney's, at least not early on in their relationship. She found him angry, petty, and vindictive.

"His jealousy festered right on the surface as he constantly knocked Dick Cavett, sneering at all 'intellectual comics,'" Rivers recalled. "It was impossible to avoid a run-in with Rodney. I was using a joke based on Irvin Arthur's telephone habits: 'I called my boyfriend at work, and he put me on hold for two years.' Rodney said I could not do that joke. Telephones were his premise. He was very angry. I said, 'Okay, we'll divide up the premises. I'll take marriage, dating, family, children, and pregnancy. You can have telephones, movies, and current events.' He saw no humor in that. He was too angry to have humor about himself."[8]

Rivers remembered that Rodney would talk during other comics' acts, throwing off their timing. "We all have anger," she said, "but Rodney's filled that poor little room."

In September 1964, Rodney appeared on the nationally televised CBS show *On Broadway Tonight* show hosted by Rudy Vallee, in the program's "showcase" portion, with singers Paula Stewart (wife of comedian Jack Carter), Gene Bua, and Adam Wade, dancer Madilyn Clark, and fellow comedian Jerry Shane. The national exposure did not pay immediate dividends; three months later he was still schlepping along with his act in the Encore Room of the Irvington Hotel in Lakewood, New Jersey, as one of the "December Celebrity Stars" along with comedian Morty Gunty, exotic dancer

MI Bonnet, Van Harris (the comic who dated Joyce Indig back in the day), and a handful of other names not heard from again.

He had not really quit the aluminum siding business cold turkey, though, even while he was launching his comedy comeback. Rodney had, though, cut back substantially on that part of his life. Occasionally his two worlds cross-pollinated in weird ways. There was the time, for instance, when he was trying to get agent Dee Anthony to represent him. Dee took Rodney to see Tony Bennett at the Copacabana. After the show, Rodney told Bennett that his siding business was not too far from Bennett's house in Englewood, and Tony invited him over to "bullshit a little." Rodney remembered that he needed to check on a siding job, and Bennett accompanied him to the site— drawing the attention of the neighbors, who wanted to pose for pictures with the famous singer. Bennett graciously signed autographs . . . and Dee Anthony never did represent Rodney.

Rodney and Joyce stayed connected after their divorce. Their past relationship notwithstanding, they shared Brian, of course, and Rodney doted on his son whenever he could. In 1963, Rodney and Joyce reconciled and remarried after two years apart. A year later, Joyce gave birth to their daughter, Melanie, and the family of four moved into a bigger apartment on Manhattan's Upper East Side.

There was a fifth family member who joined the inner circle around this time: Joe Ancis. Rodney and Joe had remained the closest of friends since their days selling (and scamming) aluminum siding clients. Rodney told anyone who would listen that Joe was the funniest guy in the world, though no one really needed convincing, given his influence on the brilliant comedian Lenny Bruce, who was entering the final years of his life and overdosed on morphine in the bathroom of his Hollywood Hills home in 1966 at the age of forty.

"Lenny Bruce idolized Joe, and Lenny's way of working . . . his rhythms, that was all Joe," Rodney recalled in a 1982 television interview. "But Lenny added his own material to that style, ya know? I would say Lenny was great, but Joe was an influence on him and his way of talking: 'Man, let me tell you where it's at,' that whole thing."[9]

The best, most accurate descriptions of Joe Ancis can be found in Albert Goldman's 1971 biography, *Ladies and Gentlemen, Lenny Bruce!!* (from the journalism of Lawrence Schiller). Goldman devotes nearly sixteen pages to Ancis's profound influence on Bruce after they met for the first time at B&G's eatery, located next door to Hanson's Drugstore. Lenny Bruce idolized the beanpole Ancis—"the tall, skinny Ichabod Crane-style cat"[10]—in every aspect of his hep-cat personality: the way he walked, the way he talked, his rapid-fire delivery of one-liners, his Jewishness, his subversiveness, his sexual innuendo, his take-no-prisoners attitude—you name it, Lenny Bruce bought into it. (Bruce's onetime roommate Buddy Hackett did, too—but not to Bruce's extent.)

Rodney knew all of this, of course, from when he first met Joe back in their 1950s siding days, knew of this "young man made of the fragile glass of genius,"[11] and also knew that Joe Ancis was not the competition, that he would never get up onstage and perform. He was not cut from that cloth; he would always remain in the background, a surprisingly shy man with many social phobias (he always carried his own bar of soap in case he needed to use a public restroom, for instance) who could never get up in front of an audience but could keep grown men in stitches, begging for more of his comedic insights and shtick. He was Rodney Dangerfield's father confessor, sounding board, under-the-radar sidekick, life advisor, and mentor rolled into one neurotic package. Their personalities meshed perfectly, two peas in a comedic pod of irreverence and originality, riffing on the vagaries of life, love, and the human condition.

"Joe and I understood each other, and we had the same kind of dark thoughts, so we got along great," Rodney recalled. "But unlike me, Joe never wanted to meet people. He used to say, 'I'm not lookin' to make new friends—I'd like to lose the ones I got' . . . People always wanted to meet Joe, though. He was famous among the hipsters and comedians, who'd heard so much about him, but he didn't want to meet them."[12]

"It was like a love affair. They were in love with each other," Joe's daughter, Julie Ancis, said of her father's relationship with Rodney. "It was a very, very deep friendship. I was too young for Lenny Bruce, but when I've seen him do his thing on videos, his discussions about jazz, that was my father's shit. My dad was heavy into this, and other guys picked it up because it looked like a cool thing, but it was my dad's thing. When I saw Rodney on Johnny Carson, some of the things he said, those were lines my father said. For example, my father used to say all the time, 'What does it all mean?' That was my father. And sometimes I would see Rodney do that on Johnny Carson, but that wasn't his lingo."[13]

THE MID-1960S MARKED A TURNING POINT IN RODNEY DANGERFIELD'S career. He was beginning to make a name for himself as a working comic telling wife jokes with a cynical edge and he was getting noticed. In 1965, he made his first of what would be dozens of appearances on *The Merv Griffin Show*, the former Big Band singer's syndicated television talk show airing in both daytime and late-night timeslots; in some markets, it was up against NBC's powerhouse, *The Tonight Show Starring Johnny Carson*.

Rodney's increased workload translated into more press notices, which were not always glowing. A critic for *Newsday*, for instance, slammed Rodney's appearance at the Living Room, where he shared the bill with Noel Harrison, the singer and son of legendary actor Rex Harrison, and Freddy Cole, the late Nat King Cole's younger brother. Rodney earned $300 a week for that honor. "Comic Rodney Dangerfield seems defeated before he warms up. 'I'm not looking to be a star,' he pleads, 'just good enough to quit my day job.' Don't do it, Rodney."[14]

On the other end of the spectrum, "Rodney Dangerfield, young comic" (*sic*) opened with singer Nancy Wilson at Chicago's famed Mister Kelley's in November 1965 to generous notices (and a $500 weekly paycheck). "There's a new comic by the name of Rodney Dangerfield, who proves to be a bulky individual with a New York city east side [*sic*] accent," noted the critic for the *Chicago Tribune*. "If you're gonna change your name, says Rodney, change it good. A guy like that is funny already, and he gets funnier. I like the part where he says his wife did teach him one thing: Women's clothes go on the wooden hangers."[15]

His schedule was growing busier by the month and Rodney needed someone to manage his career. He approached Jack Rollins, who was managing Woody Allen, Harry Belafonte, and Mike Nichols and Elaine May, but Rollins apparently did not like what he saw (and heard) and took a flyer. Rodney was a straight shooter and had a knack of rubbing people the wrong way. "He wasn't likable in the least," remembered comedian Stanley Dean. "His material, without question, one of the top ten comedians I ever heard . . . but as far as the person goes . . . well, there wasn't much to talk about."[16]

The William Morris Agency sent one of their guys to see Rodney perform fifteen times before finally signing him in 1965 and assigning him to agent Ed Sommerfeld.

"I went into a little club called The Duplex. He got up and said what I considered were some clever and funny things," Sommerfeld recalled. "He explained to me that he would come down to a club just to get the feel of performing again, like a fighter might go to a gymnasium to work out. He still had the bug to perform. I met Joyce, and she was not in favor of this new idea of Rodney going to work telling jokes and writing jokes. He said, 'Joyce, this fellow's with the William Morris Agency, he thinks I'm funny and he thinks he can book me.' And Joyce said, 'Well, you seem like a nice fellow but you're breaking up my marriage.'"[17]

In January 1966, Rodney hit the big time, opening at New York City's legendary Copacabana with singer Sergio Franchi: "Rodney Dangerfield, the comedian, is a find in a subtle way," noted Earl Wilson in his nationally syndicated column. Three days later, Wilson was writing about Rodney at the Copa . . . again. "A platoon of comics turned out to cheer their pal, comedian Rodney Dangerfield, who's featured." And this from "New York Cavalcade" columnist Louis Sobol: "That's quite an entertaining show at the Copa, headed by that dramatic singing man, Sergio Franchi, and highlighted by an unusual comedian, Rodney Dangerfield." Hey, take it any way you can, right? Earl Wilson weighed in again the following week. "Today's Best Laugh: A man knows he's getting old (says Rodney Dangerfield at the Copa) when he can no longer beat women he used to beat to subway seats."[18]

His act was big enough now to graduate to the 1960s-era comedian's rite of passage: a comedy album. Bob Newhart set the standard with his

Grammy-winning 1960 debut album, *The Button-Down Mind of Bob Newhart,* and since then, comics including Joan Rivers, Shelley Berman, Lenny Bruce, Nichols & May, Dick Gregory, Jonathan Winters, and Bill Cosby all had memorialized their acts on wax. In early 1966, Decca Records signed Rodney to a contract for a live album, which he recorded in early March during his run at Upstairs at the Duplex, a cabaret bar on 55 Grove Street in Greenwich Village.

The album, *Rodney Dangerfield: "The Loser,"* dropped in November 1966. Its cover featured a color photograph of a dour-looking Rodney, "The New Comedy Sensation," sitting in the front seat of a 1950s-era car that is being towed while a "Just Married" sign hangs below him on the front door. The ten tracks on the album took a snapshot of Rodney's act: "What's In a Name," "Someone's Gonna Get Hurt," "Lost," "My Neighborhood," "That's Show Biz," and more.

The Loser did not do runaway business in the record stores, nor did it transform Rodney Dangerfield into a major recording star. It did, however, generate positive reviews, and Rodney could notch another small triumph in his comeback belt.

"Rodney Dangerfield is one of the better stand-up comics coming up, and his material on this L.P. is often good for a chuckle or a guffaw," the critic for *The Bergen Record* wrote. "You might also let him expound on the lack of talent on the part of his Jewish friends in such diverse fields as fixing things about the house or engaging in espionage. Not always likely to convulse the listener, but it's a pretty good entry from a performer who shows possibilities of getting better."[19]

Rodney's hot streak continued in April 1966, when he opened for Diana Ross and the Supremes in Miami Beach at the Deauville hotel's Casanova Room. "Rodney Dangerfield, a comedian, opens the show and for the most part his jokes were all right for age or youth," opined a critic for *The Miami News.* "A couple on the borderline brought laughs from the kids so they must know more than we think they do."[20]

He followed that engagement by opening for singer Jimmy Roselli at The Boulevard back home in Queens (Rego Park) and hit the road for Michigan at the Act IV in Detroit—where he followed "The Sparkling Phyllis Mc-Guire." *The Detroit Free Press*: "He's a mature type with a low-keyed style much like that of Jackie Vernon. Billing himself as 'the loser,' he casts himself as the cheerful paranoid, the chap who always misses out on success. He has the New Yorker's habit of inquiring 'You know?' every few lines and takes too much time building to a rather obvious exit line, but he has his funny moments."[21]

Back in New York, he caught a lucky break when Mamie Van Doren, who was set to open at the Latin Quarter, came down with an illness and had to cancel. Rodney replaced her for the night.

Rodney worked with another big name, Peggy Lee, in Boston—he was dubbed "Decca's 'The Loser' for Comedy"—and followed her to Miami Beach when she opened in the Café Cristal in the Diplomat Hotel. "Peggy comes onstage to an audience already warmed up. Rodney Dangerfield is a name you'd associate with a handsome romantic hero. Don't fool yourself. He's a comedian, and a very funny one. This man has a rapid-fire delivery embracing a lot of subjects. They're familiar—wife, children, girls, dates, movies for prospective fathers—but his material is fresh. The Peggy Lee-Dangerfield combination is a fitting one to launch the star-packed nightclub season."[22]

He regrouped with Jimmy Roselli at the Copa (and "The World Famous Copa Girls") in early 1967: "Comic Rodney Dangerfield tells of a relative whose kids are so ugly that in the family album they keep only negatives. He described his crime-ridden neighborhood: 'When I plan a budget I allow for hold-up money.'"[23] One critic who caught Rodney's act at the Copa called him "easily the foremost Angry Young Comedian of our times. A mad, mad, man—but deliciously clever and original."[24]

Angry, maybe. But young? He was forty-five years old.

The positive press certainly helped Rodney's career and his reputation, but he knew he needed that golden spot on a national television show to break through the logjam of comedians who only worked the club circuit.

He could see how the careers of contemporaries such as Don Rickles benefited from national exposure. Rickles was, by now, a semi-regular on *The*

Tonight Show Starring Johnny Carson and was getting hotter by the minute thanks in large part to Carson. Not only could a national television appearance vault a performer into bigger and better venues, but the buzz could also, if it hit the right way, mean a shot in the movies or perhaps starring in a network television series (as it did for both Rickles and Bill Cosby, another frequent Carson guest).

Rodney appeared on *The Mike Douglas Show*—nationally syndicated in daytime and produced in Philadelphia, so that was close by—and on *The Merv Griffin Show,* which, in 1966, was syndicated to stations nationwide that had the option of airing it in the daytime or nighttime hours. Griffin taped his show at the Cort Theatre on West 48th Street in Manhattan, an easy drop-by for Rodney, who could do three minutes of shtick, chat with Merv for a few minutes, and work the clubs that same night.

The Tonight Show was taping its ninety-minute iteration over at Rockefeller Center, but Carson was out of the question, for now. His program was too big for a forty-five-year-old "up-and-comer" like Rodney Dangerfield. There were other reasons why *The Tonight Show* was off-limits. According to Rodney, Carson held a grudge against the comedian after Rodney's manager sent Johnny a nasty letter accusing him of using one of Rodney's jokes on *The Tonight Show* without crediting the source. "This manager takes it on himself to write a letter to *The Tonight Show* saying, 'You won't put Rodney on your show, but you'll steal one of his best jokes,'" recalled comedian Harry Basil, one of Rodney's later collaborators. "Johnny reads the letter on the air and does the joke with no inflection and says, 'If this is his best material, he's in trouble.'

"The joke was, 'How come gas stations leave the cash register open but they'll put the men's room key on a brick?' Rodney's embarrassed and starts writing letters to Johnny trying to apologize. No response."[25]

The Tonight Show would have to wait for now.

Rodney had his eye on a bigger prize: *The Ed Sullivan Show.*

Sullivan's showcase was nearly twenty years old, but it was still CBS's biggest Sunday-night draw with an average audience of thirteen million viewers.

It had not lost too much momentum since February 1964, when the Beatles snared an *Ed Sullivan Show* audience of seventy-three million for their first live appearance in America.

Sullivan taped his show on Broadway and 54th Street—again, like *The Merv Griffin Show*, a convenient landing spot for New York–based comic Rodney Dangerfield. Sullivan provided the icing on the cake by often publicizing his guests in his *New York Daily News* gossip column. A spot on his show was, alongside *The Tonight Show*, the gold standard for performers . . . provided it went well, since a comedian did not get any helpful guffaws from the host, who, unlike Carson, Griffin, Douglas, or Dean Martin, did not join in on the fun by laughing along with his guest.

On *The Ed Sullivan Show*, it was you versus the audience . . . and sometimes you lost . . . and Sullivan never welcomed you back.

Rodney was desperate for a shot on Sullivan's show but could not engender any interest from Sullivan's producers, the host himself, or CBS. So, he came up with a novel way to catch Sullivan's eye.

"I told my agent [Ed Sommerfeld] that I wanted to try for the Sullivan show, and the only way to do it was to audition up there in front of the audience," Rodney said. "You work the dress rehearsal on Sunday before the live telecast. Sullivan's people loved me and booked me for the following week."

Well, not quite. Rodney performed on the dress rehearsal for *The Ed Sullivan Show* in October 1966 . . . then waited . . . and waited . . .

"Then for three weeks I heard nothing, nothing at all—rejected again," he recalled. "Then Bob Precht, the producer, called me up and signed me for a show."

Rodney was booked for Sullivan's live show in March of 1967 and would be paid $1,000 for the privilege. In the interim, when he played the Copa, Ed Sullivan came in to catch his show and loved Rodney's act so much that he rushed up to tell him that he wanted to sign him for his television show. "You already have," Rodney told the flustered host.

He made his debut on *The Ed Sullivan Show* on March 5, 1967, sharing the bill with Sergio Franchi, British comic star Norman Wisdom, Alan King, Dionne Warwick, Gwen Verdon, and actor Robert Horton.

"When that big night came, I remember sitting in my dressing room, waiting for the show to start," Rodney recalled. "I looked out the window. It was raining, but the streets of Manhattan were crowded, and I thought to myself, 'Look at all those people who are gonna miss seeing me tonight on *The Ed Sullivan Show*.'"[26]

He did well, and Sullivan invited him back, bumping his fee up to $1,500. He had made it. "A comedian is only as good as the host lets him be. I love to work for Ed," he said. "It's a live show. That's what I like. I'm the kind of a guy who has hours of material. No set routines."[27]

"My image did it," Rodney said later about his first appearance on *The Ed Sullivan Show*. "The image of a guy in whose life nothing goes right. There are days in everyone's life when he or she is a loser. Maybe you feel like a loser today.

"Nothing went right for you. That's Rodney Dangerfield. And I do everything I can to feed that image. I wear the cheapest suit I can find. The crummiest tie. And I go out there with the worst-looking haircut in the world."[28]

Feared gossip columnist Walter Winchell, who was nearing the end of his career, took notice of Rodney, too, now that he had made the big time. "What's the reason for the glares swapped by comics Rodney Dangerfield and London Lee?" he wondered in a column item printed after Rodney's first *Sullivan Show* appearance.[29] Earlier, Winchell printed an item in his famous slanguage: "Ofergoodnesssakes, don't invite Merv Griffin's producer and comic Rodney Dangerfield to the same subway platform!"[30]

Sullivan himself hinted at Rodney's surly mood in his "Little Old New York" column: "Alan King and comic Rodney Dangerfield feuding over jokes."[31] Later, Rodney and comedian Jackie Vernon "almost came to blows" during a radio talk show in which they "engaged in verbal fisticuffs."

Rodney did not realize it at the time, but his maiden appearance on *The Ed Sullivan Show* established his now-iconic wardrobe template: white shirt, red tie—which he tugged on, nervously—black jacket, and black pants. The red necktie is on display at the National Museum of American History in Washington, D.C.

That one appearance on *The Ed Sullivan Show* boosted Rodney's visibility and gave him, and his career, a cachet that helped to grow the legend. Two months later, in May, he flew to London to make his debut on British television on ITV's *The Eammon Andrews Show*, along with Israeli entertainer Topol—then playing Tevye in *Fiddler on the Roof* on the British stage—as "prime examples of entertainment on both sides of the Atlantic."[32] He returned to *The Ed Sullivan Show* in June, this time sharing the stage with Ed's favorite talking mouse, Topo Gigio, nightclub singer Nancy Ames, rock group The Young Rascals, and fellow comedian Georgie Kaye.

Joey Bishop joined the late-night talk show fray in April 1967 with ABC's *The Joey Bishop Show* (catchy name) and soon Rodney was a welcome guest, not only to perform a few minutes of stand-up but to come over and sit on Joey's couch and chat with the host for whom he once wrote jokes. In August, he joined comedian George Carlin, the Fifth Dimension, and Buddy Greco in *Away We Go*, a summer fill-in for *The Jackie Gleason Show*. (Carlin, still figuring it out and wearing a suit-and-tie, cohosted the hourlong primetime show with Greco.)

And so it went . . . as 1967 turned into 1968, Rodney was all over the tube: multiple guest shots on *The Merv Griffin Show* ("that glib comic Rodney Dangerfield!"), *The Joey Bishop Show, The Mike Douglas Show, The Ed Sullivan Show, The Steve Allen Comedy Hour* (he guested alongside "Miss Peanut Butter"). He made his first guest-starring appearance on a primetime musical comedy series on ABC called *That's Life,* starring Robert Morse and E. J. Peaker as married couple, Bob and Gloria Dickson; Rodney played a delivery guy putting together a Japanese bicycle that Bobby bought for his son. By year's end, he had logged over sixty television appearances regaling audiences with his stories about bad luck, his wife, his neighborhood, and his life as a lovable loser.

He was earning $4,000 a week now and he was being booked into bigger clubs. In January 1968, when Joan Rivers, with whom Rodney played the Living Room, gave birth to her daughter, Melissa, Rodney sent a telegram: "Your jokes may be new—but your delivery is not original."[33]

He played the Latin Quarter in April 1968 as a supporting act for headliner Louis Armstrong, though the appearance nearly hit a snafu: "Comic

Rodney Dangerfield had a billing misunderstanding and almost didn't go on at the Latin Quarter Louis Armstrong Premiere." There was no further word on the "misunderstanding," though perhaps Rodney was unhappy with his billing alongside a pair of jugglers, the Martin Brothers. He was fortunate, later that month, to walk away from a car crash on Park Avenue and 57th Street; his friend, comic Will Jordan, known for his Ed Sullivan impersonation, was not so lucky—he broke five ribs and was out of action for months.

Rodney's star was rising but he still took the smaller jobs—appearing in-person at the opening of the new, spacious camera store Willoughby-Peerless in Herald Square ("The world's unluckiest, unhappiest TV comic star") and honoring club dates, closing out the year at Larry Dixon's Flagship dinner theater on Route 22 in Union, New Jersey.

And . . . still . . . selling aluminum siding every now and then out of the office in Englewood. He remembered closing a job on a Saturday and, the following night, appearing on *The Ed Sullivan Show*. On Monday, when his crew went to install the job, the woman asked one of the guys, "Is Mr. Roy in show business? I think I saw him on *The Ed Sullivan Show*, but they called him Rodney Dangerfield." "Yeah, that's him, his guy answered. "He does some show business on the side."[34]

Chapter Six

With girls, I don't get no respect. I went out with a belly dancer. She told me I turned her stomach.

THE YEAR 1969 WAS RIFE WITH NOTABLE ACHIEVEMENTS: MEN landed on the moon, the "Miracle Mets" won the World Series, Jimi Hendrix electrified Woodstock and . . . Rodney Dangerfield opened a comedy club and made his first appearance in a big-screen movie.

LIFE IN THE ROY HOUSEHOLD WAS NOT A BED OF ROSES, AND DOMESTIC bliss in the couple's apartment on the Upper East Side was a foreign concept to Rodney and Joyce. They fought a lot, which was not great for them or for their children, nine-year-old Brian and four-year-old Melanie.

"It seemed to be like a seesaw. As his success went up, hers deteriorated physically and even mentally," Rodney's agent, Ed Sommerfeld, recalled. "So she had lost that spirit that she formally had, I believe. He said, 'You can't believe it's the same woman, Eddie.' He was in love with the memory he had of her, but he was always aware enough that it was just a memory. He couldn't get that back."[1]

Joyce was plagued by debilitating arthritis and was drinking heavily. When things at home got really bad, Rodney stayed in a nearby hotel. And Rodney being Rodney, even that had its drawbacks. On one of those occasions where he and Joyce were at each other's throats, he was playing a two-week stint at the Living Room in Manhattan. To avoid arguing with Joyce and getting home around 3 or 4 a.m., which would disturb the kids, he got a room on the seventeenth floor of a hotel a few blocks away. He figured the place would be quiet. He was wrong. "So there's a crane working outside my window on a new building and they're . . . making all kinds of noise starting at 7 a.m."

He was always unlucky but, hey, that was his shtick, and it was paying the bills and then some. ("If he ever really stopped worrying," a critic pointed out, "he might lose his gimmick.") There was the day that Rodney was having lunch with a reporter in a Manhattan restaurant when a guy stopped him at the cloakroom. "Are things really that tough?" he asked the supposedly downtrodden comedian. Ed Sullivan once introduced Rodney to his CBS television audience as "The unhappiest person I've ever met in my entire life." And he meant it.

The work was great, of course—the Sullivan show put him on America's map—but Rodney was tiring of life on the road, of the constant traveling across the country to play nightclubs in towns big and small, the trips to L.A. for television appearances on *The Joey Bishop Show* and *The Merv Griffin Show*. (Earlier that year, Merv moved his show from the Cort Theatre on 48th Street to CBS Television City in L.A.'s Fairfax District, losing sidekick Arthur Treacher in the process.) Then it was back to the East Coast to do the *Sullivan Show*, *The Dick Cavett Show* on ABC, and *The Mike Douglas Show*, and to play the nightclub circuit up and down the Eastern Seaboard, from Maine to Miami and then some.

"I don't want to travel anymore," he said around this time. "I want to be in New York where I can do television . . . and watch my children grow up."[2] If he opened his own comedy club, he figured, he could be his own boss and he would be close to his kids and would not have to travel as often, maybe only on weekends. The situation with Joyce was always dicey, anyway; it would behoove him to have a Plan B if it all blew up, which, at this point, was inevitable.

To Rodney Dangerfield, the idea of owning a club was not as far-fetched as it might seem. He knew the ins and outs of the business (at least he thought he did) after toiling in joints big and small lo these many years and dealing with owners both dishonest and on the level, and seeing firsthand how they ran their clubs (and with whom they consorted). The idea had been germinating in his head for a while, and now it was time to pull the trigger.

"See, I had a lot of personal problems," he said. "I thought to myself, I have two kids. I had to bring them up. I had a boy in the hospital for a year and a half. He had a disease of the hips. So what's important to me? To go around the country making money or to stay home and visit him twice a week. So I said, 'I'll open a place.'"[3]

If only it was that easy.

Rodney approached actor/comedian Budd Friedman, who, in 1963, opened the Improv comedy club over on 44th Street and 9th Avenue in the heart of Hell's Kitchen. By the mid-1960s, the Improv established itself as a hip place to see and be seen. Barbra Streisand sang there, Barry Manilow was its on-again/off-again piano player, and future actor Danny Aiello was a bouncer. Rodney was the club's emcee for a time and played there many times, finding a receptive audience.

Robert Klein appeared at the Improv in October 1966 during his run in the Broadway show *The Apple Tree*, whose cast included Alan Alda, Barbara Harris, and Larry Blyden. He described his first experience at the club as "a resounding success" and was surprised, after the show, when "a strange man in a black suit and red tie who was ceaselessly tugging at his collar in nervous discomfort" approached him. "You were brilliant, man," he told him, "and I'm a tough cocksucker, but you have to come here every night for three years to get it right." The stranger then went onstage and "absolutely tore the place apart," Klein recalled. It was Rodney Dangerfield.[4]

"Rodney Dangerfield broke in at the nightclub," Friedman recalled. "He was playing the Living Room at the time and after his show there, he got up on the Improv stage and, a little drunk, alienated everyone in the place. He considered it a challenge, and the next night he came back stone sober and knocked the people out. For two-and-a-half years he was my unofficial emcee and worked out at the club, using the same comedy concept he uses today."[5]

"The Improv was a great place to hang out, a great testing ground for new talent," Rodney said. "At first I wouldn't go on when I was sober. I had personal problems, got drunk and told the audience all about what was happening to me. It was hip, inside stuff, and I began to get a following . . . people came in week after week to see me."

Now, Rodney wanted a piece of the action. He broached the idea to Friedman of buying into the Improv as a partner. It would benefit both of them, he said: Rodney would plug the club during his television appearances and the place would be packed every night, guaranteed. "I'll make a G every week and I'll be able to stay home with my wife and two kids instead of the going-out-of-town hassle," he told Friedman . . . who promptly turned him down.

Rodney was disappointed but did not abandon the idea. "I feel if I can bring business into someone else's club, I can do it for myself," he said.[6]

In 1965, he met a jazz bass player named Anthony Bevacqua at the Living Room and they became good friends who enjoyed each other's company. Rodney and Tony often talked about opening their own club one day if success broke their way. Rodney was now in a position of some strength and, by the middle of 1969, with Budd Friedman in his rearview mirror, he and Tony began to scout locations for the club they hoped to turn into a reality—a place that would carry the name so ubiquitous with Rodney's image. Ed Sullivan broke the news in his "Little Old New York" column in early April: "Hilarious Rodney Dangerfield plans a night club called Dangerfield's."[7]

The prospect of opening a club, and finding financial backing for the venture, was daunting. Notwithstanding the Improv, comedy clubs were scarce in New York City in 1969, and while Rodney Dangerfield had ascended the national stage via his television appearances and busy touring schedule, it was a risky gamble.

Rodney's first course of action was to approach midtown hotels and try to talk the managers into paying the cost of renovating one of their lounges into his new club, which he assured them would be packed every night. No one took the bait.

There was the question of capital, of course, of how Rodney and Tony Bevacqua were going to fund their enterprise. Rodney estimated he had roughly $50,000 in the bank at the time. He was apprised by those in the know that he would realistically need at least $150,000 to open a club when all was said and done. And that was just a guesstimate.

"When Rodney talked to his friends about opening the club, and trying to borrow a few bucks, his friends said, 'You're gonna open a club with a bass player?,'" Bevacqua recalled. "All the clubs were closing; the Copacabana closed, the Persian Room closed and we're opening a club. So, everyone thought we were nuts."

"They say I can't do it, I don't know the restaurant business and all that stuff," Rodney said at the time. "But you want to know something? All these guys that are telling me I can't do it are guys who tried themselves and failed.

"I think I can do it. I know I can. These failure guys look at someone who hits it big and they say, lucky. But you know what my father taught me? He said behind every lucky guy you'll find a brain."[8]

Joyce was not on board with the idea.

"So my wife says to me, 'For the first time in your life you're a success. For the first time in your life you're out of debt. For the first time you could put a little something aside for me and the children. So what do you do? You go into debt again!'"[9]

Rodney spent as much time as he could figuring out the finances and looking for a suitable location for the club when he was in New York. "I figure many people who see me on TV will want to come in and see me in person," he told a reporter. "Even when I'm not performing, I plan to hang around and chat with customers the way [1920s speakeasy owner] Texas Guinan used to do in the old days. You know, in some clubs, performers are hustled on stage and hustled off and they never get a chance to meet anyone. It's going to be different at Dangerfield's."[10]

In August, he took over Jack O'Brian's "Voice of Broadway" column while O'Brian was on vacation, which gave him another platform to talk up his new club. "I'm really looking forward to it," he wrote. "I like people, and it will be like a second home for me, where friends can come in and have a good time. It will be nice to meet, in person, those who have seen me on TV and would like to say hello.

"Anyway, it will be a great challenge. They all laughed at Christopher Columbus. I hope they all keep laughing at me."[11]

He needed a cash infusion for the nightclub and did not take his foot off the gas pedal of his busy nightclub and television career. He returned to *The Ed Sullivan Show*—the door was always open for him—and appeared for a second and third time on ABC's *That's Life* in January and February 1969, guest-starring with Phil Harris and Agnes Moorehead in January and with Tony Randall and Chita Rivera the following month (this time as a milkman musing about his wife's fling at self-improvement).

Next up was an appearance on *NBC Experiment in Television* in an episode called "This Is Sholom Aleichem," starring Jack Gilford as the legendary Yiddish writer. Rodney, Dom DeLuise, and Bel Kaufman, Sholom Aleichem's granddaughter who authored the novel *Up the Down Staircase*, commented on what his writings meant to them.

He was a guest on *That Show with Joan Rivers*, Rivers's first foray into the television talk show arena (via syndication) and joked that he dated a girl who spoke so well "I couldn't take my ears off her." One critic was not impressed with Rodney's act: "Why he's so big is a mystery here. Best way to describe him is if he were a cowboy he'd be the Dick Foran type."[12]

Rodney then headed South for the warmer climes of Miami Beach, where "The Angry Young Comedian" (who was now forty-seven) opened in late January at the Marco Polo Hyatt House on Collins Avenue: "I come from such a tough neighborhood that just the other day they raffled off a police car—with two cops still in it." "Nowadays the kids have a peculiar way of learning arithmetic. The teacher said, 'Johnny, here's fifty cents. Now if you steal another quarter, how much will you have?'"

He returned to the Living Room on 2nd Avenue in late February for a two-week stand—"The other night I had a fight with the dog. My wife said the dog was right"—but was in a foul mood on opening night. "He leads one to believe he wasn't too happy . . . and probably is fulfilling an old contract obligation," noted one critic. "His temper was being taxed, too, by a noisy, inconsiderate, and well-boozed threesome at one table. He got really angry several times with them." Also noted was Rodney's occasional use of profanity: "Dangerfield's lines were funny enough without having to be obscene."[13] In March, he subbed for a vacationing Gene Klavan on Klavan's WNEW radio show in New York.

There was no job too small during this time, regardless of how far it was from the bright lights. Consider Binghamton, New York, where Rodney and singer Lois Walden played the local Jewish Community Center's annual "Broadway to Binghamton" cabaret-style show on a Saturday night. Or a fundraiser for Bergen County Democrats in Paramus, New Jersey, in May 1969. Rodney joined Frank Sinatra, Jr., impressionist David Frye, and singer Aliza Kashi and helped to raise $10,000 for the "Night of Stars." He appeared on locally produced television commercials for Aqueduct Raceway in Queens: "I had eight losers today and when I got home, the kids wanted me to play horsey for them."

Work was work.

RODNEY DANGERFIELD TRACED THE ORIGINS OF HIS IMMORTAL CATCH-phrase "No respect" to the March 1969 publication of Mario Puzo's classic mob novel *The Godfather* and its gloriously epic depiction of Don Vito Corleone's crime family in Staten Island and scions Fredo, Sonny, and Michael Corleone—with its emphasis on "respect" in the ethos of the Mafia. The novel struck a sharp chord and remained on *The New York Times* Best Seller List for sixty-seven weeks, selling over nine million copies in two years and resulting in one of the greatest movies of all time, Francis Ford Coppola's *The Godfather*, which opened in 1972 with stars Marlon Brando, James Caan, Al Pacino, and Robert Duvall, among others, and spawned an equally terrific sequel two years later that snared six Academy Awards (and eleven nominations).

Rodney said he heard wiseguys in the clubs talking about "respect." He did not have a standard catchphrase in his act in those days, not yet, though his go-to line was "nothing goes right"—catchy but lacking the more relatable edge of "no respect." Rodney remembered he was working at Upstairs at the Duplex when he told his first "no respect" joke: "I get no respect. When I was a kid, I played hide-and-seek. They wouldn't even look for me." The response was terrific and that was all he needed. He started peppering his act with "no respect" jokes in the clubs and on television. ("With girls, I don't get no respect. I went out with a belly dancer. She told me I turned her stomach.")

"When you write a joke you have to write an intro to it of some kind, so I wrote 'I don't get no respect' and people seemed to identify with it," he explained. "So I started using it as a handle . . . I guess nobody gets respect in life; whenever something goes wrong you feel that you were mistreated . . ."[14]

The catchphrase caught on like wildfire; journalist Earl Wilson was writing about it as early as March 10, 1969 ("He's right . . . he don't get no respect," he said in a column devoted to an interview with Rodney).

"'I get no respect,' said Rodney Dangerfield. It's his catchphrase, his lament and it's vaulting him into the upper rung of the comics," another columnist noted. "'I just called up my house. My daughter answered and I said, "Lemme talk to mommy." And I hear her say, "Mommy, it's daddy—are you home?" No respect!' That's Rodney, who is from New York and would prefer never to leave the big town although his line of work often takes him out in the hinterlands."[15]

"I found myself starting to pack places," Rodney said. "'No respect' caught on fast."[16]

Whether Rodney told his first "no respect" joke at Upstairs at the Duplex is anyone's guess. Even Rodney himself changed the story every now and then. In 1973, during an appearance on the television show *What's My Line?*, he told host Larry Blyden that he first used the phrase at Georgie Schultz's Brooklyn comedy club, Pips. Schultz, in fact, claimed *he* came up with the line in a routine about a Mafioso who used brute force to counter a lack of respect. Rodney scoffed at the claim. "I should tell you that George Schultz and I are no longer friendly," he said. "I was probably telling it to him. Now he says he gave me a gift. He's nuts. There are people in this world who have to be winners, you know? You tell somebody an idea and suddenly they created it."[17]

To capitalize on his popular catchphrase, Bell Records released Rodney's second album, *I Don't Get No Respect*, a live recording of his stand-up act (venue unknown). Its cover shows Rodney in various stages of distress: overburdened with a shitload of luggage while a porter walks by with an empty handcart; hanging off a diving board with a guy about to stomp on his hand;

and sitting with a lit cigarette looking up at the camera in defeat. "One of my problems, ya know, I don't get no respect. No respect at all," he said, opening the album. "Every time I get in an elevator, the operator says the same thing to me: 'Basement?' The other day I was standing in front of an apartment house. The doorman asked me to get him a cab!" And so on. "He brings out a painful memory in almost everyone who has been victimized by other humans more perverse than he is brave," read one review. "If that's your comedy bag, go for it."[18]

In Rodney's world, "no respect" even extended to his kids. "I am not their favorite on TV," he said. "Melanie prefers 'I Love Lucy.' Brian digs Jackie Gleason—even though I write some of his material. The other day Brian came home and asked me when I was going to be on TV next. I was so happy he'd got some good sense—until he explained, 'My teacher wants to know.'"

Rim shot!

"I bring truisms into the act that everyone can identify with," Rodney explained, and now those "truisms," camouflaged in his "no respect" line, were starting to pay dividends, at least in his professional career. In April 1969, he signed a deal for his first date in Las Vegas, opening that August for Dionne Warwick at the Sands Hotel in its famed Copa Room, the venue that launched Don Rickles into stardom. He did well there and was paid $4,000 for the two-week gig. "Dangerfield works in a familiar tradition of the one-liner comics, but the lines are fresh and amusingly delivered," opined *Los Angeles Times* critic Charles Champlin, reviewing the Warwick/Dangerfield show. "He knew he was moving into a tough neighborhood in Manhattan, he says, when the apartment ad said 'Short run from subway.'"[19]

He was reportedly writing a sitcom (if he was, it never saw the light of day) and Madison Avenue came beckoning, foreshadowing his later success as a pitchman for Miller Lite beer. Rodney was also hired by Buick to film several industrial commercials and he was pitching Bic pens in magazine and newspaper ads.

I guess that's why I broke up with my psychiatrist. No respect from him, either. One day I

**told him I had suicidal tendencies. He told me
from then on, I would have to pay in advance.**

DESPITE, OR MAYBE IN SPITE OF, ALL THE PROFESSIONAL SUCCESS, ROD-
ney was not a happy man. In many of the interviews he granted around this
time, he talked openly of making regular visits to his psychiatrist, no doubt
rehashing his unhappy childhood compounded by his absentee father and
cold, loveless mother. Smoking marijuana helped allay his anxiety, but it did
not cut to the core of what drove his perpetual gloom. "All of our mental atti-
tudes go back to our childhood," he lectured *New York Daily News* columnist
Jack Leahy. "The kids that Hitler taught to hate are still hating today. Down
South, the youngsters who dress up in white sheets to burn crosses with their
fathers are the Ku Kluxers of tomorrow.

"I favor psychiatry for grown-ups," he said. "I'm not saying it has all
the answers, but it does serve a purpose . . . it does give us insights into why
we hurt ourselves in so any ways. The fact that a man goes to a psychiatrist
doesn't necessarily mean he's sick. The sicker ones are those who should go to
psychiatrists but don't.

"I went into show business to get love," he admitted. "I think nine-tenths
of the people in this racket have an identical need . . . People in show business
have this endless desire to be told over and over how wonderful they are. And
that desire drives them to perform before the public."[20]

The situation with Joyce at home was not helping matters, but Rodney
threw himself into his work and was laser-focused on laying the groundwork
for his new comedy club, which was now targeted for a fall 1969 opening. By
June, he closed on a space for Dangerfield's at 1118 1st Avenue between 61st
and 62nd Streets in the shadow of the 59th Street Bridge. Rodney estimated
it would cost him between $75,000 and $100,000 to open the club; he in-
vested a chunk of his own money and borrowed the rest. When all was said
and done, he had sunk $250,000 into the place.

"It's the most exciting venture of my life and I'm going to do it," he declared, somewhat defiantly. "I've been broke before and I'm not afraid to go
for broke again." He figured that getting a crowd into Dangerfield's would

not be a problem—he planned to perform there himself, nightly, and his regular appearances on television would help spread the word (the same guarantee he made to Budd Friedman at the Improv). He envisioned a "small, intimate" nightclub seating about two hundred patrons that could easily be expanded to six hundred or seven hundred if the place took off. (There was an adjoining Chinese laundry that could work if events unfolded in that direction.) Months before Dangerfield's opened its doors, he was already thinking of opening a second club in Miami that he would call Dangerfield's South. Why not think big?

"People tell me I'm nuts," he said. "They say I can't do it, I don't know the restaurant business and all that stuff. But you want to know something? All these guys that are telling me I can't do it are guys who tried themselves and failed . . . I think I can do it. I know I can."[21]

"It was difficult, but we did it because Rodney had credibility," Tony Bevacqua said. "He was on shows already, he was doing TV. So we gathered up enough money to get the place open."

Still, Rodney insisted he did not want to travel anymore and that, at the age of forty-seven, the bloom had wilted off that rose, save for trips to L.A. for network television appearances and for his big out-of-town club dates (including Mr. Kelly's in Chicago and Las Vegas). "I want to be in New York where I can do television and be my own m.c. at my own club . . . and watch my children grow up," he said.

"Everyone said, 'You can't do it, you're crazy.' Well, I just felt I had enough heat going on that I could do it. And it worked out. I got lucky."[22]

"When I started making plans for the club, I figured it could be done for $70,000," he said. "By the time it was finished, it cost a quarter million. A bank vice president gave me the big loan. He told me I was the only man who made him laugh, and when he wished me luck at the opening I knew he was serious."[23]

In early September 1969, in a run-up to the opening of Dangerfield's and to help get the ball rolling, Rodney made his first appearance on *The Tonight Show Starring Johnny Carson*, which taped nearby at the NBC studios in Rockefeller Center. It took a few years, but Carson forgot about the grudge against Rodney's manager, and it was the beginning of a decades-long fruitful relationship that inspired some of the funniest moments in late-night television history.

Comedian Harry Basil recalled how it all unfolded. "Rodney was performing in New York, and he kills in some nightclub and a booker from *The Tonight Show* comes up to him and says, 'Oh my God, you're great! We gotta have you on the show!' Rodney says, 'No, man, Johnny doesn't like me. He's not going to let me on.' The guy says, 'Don't worry about it' and then calls Rodney back and says, 'You're right. He won't let you on.'

"So, Rodney is performing at the Copacabana in the city and he's outside smoking a cigarette and a limo pulls up with Johnny Carson and maybe three or four other people. They go to walk into the nightclub and the bouncer tells them that they're completely sold out. And Rodney overhears this and goes, 'Are you crazy, man? This is Johnny Carson! Johnny, come with me,' and he takes them down the steps through the kitchen, just like the shot in *Goodfellas*, and takes them up to the maître d'. 'Johnny Carson is here, they wouldn't let him in.' 'Oh, Mr. Carson, of course,' and they carry the table over and set him up and Johnny tips the maître d'. Johnny goes to sit down and Rodney gets down close and whispers, 'Johnny, man, I'm sorry. I was wrong. I was wrong.' And a week later Rodney is booked on *The Tonight Show*. Johnny loved him and he wound up being one of his favorite guests."[24]

Rodney followed his first *Tonight Show* spot by driving down to Philadelphia for a spot on *The Mike Douglas Show* (Joan Rivers was Mike's guest host that week), where he was joined by singer Thelma Houston, who was booked as the opening-night act at Dangerfield's. Then he sucked it up and flew to L.A. for *The Merv Griffin Show* (where he plugged the club again).

AND, SOMEHOW, IN ALL THE HUBBUB AND FLYING BACK AND FORTH from New York to the West Coast, Rodney found the time to make his first movie.

It was a low-budget, flight-of-fantasy comedy called *The Projectionist* and filming began in midtown Manhattan in mid-September. Rodney was paid $3,000 for his role. The movie was written and directed by Harry Hurwitz, an artist, college filmmaking instructor, and documentarian of Charlie Chaplin (*The Eternal Tramp*). Comedian Chuck McCann starred as the titular projectionist (his name is never mentioned) at the Midtown Theatre in midtown Manhattan who is terrorized by his boss, Renaldi (Rodney), an obnoxious martinet who berates his employees with nasty, soul-crushing remarks ("Dirt is our enemy and dandruff means dismissal!")

The Projectionist takes refuge in his projection booth, which is off-limits to Renaldi (union rules)—though he barges in there anyway—and which is festooned with movie stills of bygone stars (including Humphrey Bogart, Wallace Beery, John Wayne, and James Stewart).

In order to escape Renaldi's wrath, The Projectionist takes flights of fancy as his imaginary alter ego, the superhero Captain Flash, and inserts himself into various movies in which his coworkers appear as other characters. Renaldi, of course, is Captain Flash's nemesis, The Bat, a nefarious villain surrounded by henchmen who wants to steal an X-ray device invented by a European scientist (played by Jára Kohout, who runs the theatre's candy concession) and whose daughter is played by Ina Balin, aka The Girl, a young woman the Projectionist saw in the theater earlier that day and waxed about eloquently to Harry the usher (Hurwitz in a cameo appearance). The movie premiered at the Rochester Film Festival in October 1970 and did not open widely until the following year.

DANGERFIELD'S OFFICIALLY OPENED ON SEPTEMBER 29, 1969. (RODNEY and crew had a practice run the night before, with around one hundred guests in attendance.) Rodney took out newspaper advertisements for the club with the words "I don't get no respect" alongside a silhouette of his visage akin to Jackie Gleason's face on the moon that is featured in the opening of the syndicated episodes of *The Honeymooners*.

Befitting his "no respect" line, the newspaper ad caused a bit of a ruckus leading into opening night. It included the club's phone number but the phone company had yet to install a phone in Dangerfield's, so reservations were, to say the least, hard to get. Then, someone in the club lost the pages of reservation names, so that some people who showed up—and had reservations—were turned away at the door. On the afternoon of September 29, an employee unlocked the club and put the key in Rodney's dressing room, which caused a mishap because the front door was locked and no one could get in. After someone managed to get inside the club, they broke down the dressing room door to retrieve the key.

Opening night was still a resounding success. "They spilled into the street at Dangerfield's," Earl Wilson reported the next day. "He was warm, winning and likeable." A group of Rodney's celebrity friends—including Joe E. Lewis, Jerry Vale, Milton Berle, Ed McMahon, Fanny Flagg, David Frost (Rodney was a frequent guest on his talk show), Flip Wilson, David Frye, Gene Baylor, and Belle Barth—were on hand to cheer him on. There were fans there, too, including two people from Montreal, who arrived by bus from Worcester, Massachusetts. "Big bus banners spelled out: 'Dangerfield's or bust,'" Ed Sullivan wrote in his column.

Rodney's opening act, Thelma Houston, went over big, too.

"That year was the release of my first album, *Sunshower*, and the album did not get a lot of radio play and it wasn't a commercial success," she recalled. "But it was a critical success in terms of people in the business recognizing me as a new artist and up-and-coming and so forth.

"I was doing this gig in New York at a club with Rodney. He was in-between sets in the little dressing area that they had, and he was telling me, 'I'm going to be opening up my own club and I'm going to call you back and open my club for me.' And I'm thinking, 'Sure.' After this gig I thought no more of it and the next thing . . . sure enough he called me to open up this club. That's when I realized he knew everybody. Everybody came to the opening week of this club. Ed Sullivan was there, all the big names. The show was great, and it was received well and as a result of playing Dangerfield's I got on *The Ed Sullivan Show*. It was huge!"[25]

With Dangerfield's doing a steady business, Rodney was already shooting a television special based on his act that was filmed in the club, with cameos from Ed Sullivan, Joan Rivers, Jerry Vale, Milton Berle, Sergio Franchi, Flip Wilson, David Frost, and several others. He reportedly sunk another $20,000 into the project, tentatively titled *A Night at Dangerfield's*, but the project never came to fruition. Al Jarreau followed Thelma Houston as Rodney's opening act at Dangerfield's and shortly thereafter he snared a recording contract with Columbia Records and a shot on *The David Frost Show*.

Rodney promised a new act every Monday night at Dangerfield's and kept to his word; singers included Laura Lane, Joe Lee Wilson, Barbara Tai Sing, and Jeanine Napoleon opening for the Big Guy. Each table in the club had napkins with a caricature of Rodney and the words "I don't get no respect." Traditions began to take root, with patrons carving their names into the red Dangerfield's lampshades. One night, fifty fans brought a chimp into the club and the animal promptly got sleepy and was put onstage before Rodney. "I'm the owner and I still follow an animal act," he joked. He welcomed it all.

The club was darkly lit; one wag described it as "a mix of cheese and sleaze" and roughly four hundred people could be crammed in and around small black tables. "It was kind of a rectangular room, and the stage was pretty tight because Rodney had a piano and a drum set up there," recalled comedian Bob Nelson. "He had a band that would play; they would smoke a lot of pot and would be in the back dressing room. Then you had to hang out in this little area that was kind of weird. It was a bar in front, a small area, and then you walk to the back of the room."[26]

"It was very dark, because there were tables, little round tables and chairs that were somewhat spread out, you didn't get the boom of laughter that you got in other clubs," comedian Carol Leifer recalled.[27]

Rodney appeared seven nights a week at Dangerfield's in the early days, and by mid-October, two weeks after opening its doors, the endeavor was deemed a bona fide success story. Jack Benny called from California to make a reservation for December (as the story goes, he asked "By the way, what's the minimum?").

Rodney always had a soft spot for Benny, and vice versa.

"He was an ace, he was a doll, and he says to me, 'Rodney, I'm cheap and I'm 39, and that's my image, but your 'no respect,' that's into the soul of everybody, everybody can identify with that," Rodney recalled. "He says to me, 'Every day something happens where people feel they didn't get respect.'"[28]

Rodney kept his promise to mingle with the crowd at Dangerfield's.

After the show, he could be found lounging in his dressing room, with its red-leather couch, usually clad in robe and slippers to welcome friends, glad-handers, and fans with equal aplomb (depending on his mood, which var-ied—remember, this was not a happy man). "I'm glad to be off the road," he told UPI reporter William Verigan. "Living that way is torture, and I love my children and hadn't been with them enough." He did not mention Joyce.[29]

In October, Verigan had visited Rodney at Dangerfield's and described the scene:

> *The dressing room door closes, and the star slumps into a chair. This is when the act ends for most comedians. Locked in seclusion away from the noise of the crowd, a moment to come back to reality. But for Rodney Dangerfield, maybe this is where the act really starts.*

The people who come to his nightclub on New York's East Side know what to expect from over 100 television appearances during the past two years, and there's Rodney in the spotlight just as they know him—a pitiful fellow carrying the weight of the world on his shoulders.

But once he gets away by himself the problems don't stop pressing in on him. "I guess a lot of comedians use the stage to live their fantasies," he said as he leaned back on a red leather couch and chainsmoked cigarettes. "And maybe I do, too, because I find it hard to hold my life up in front of a mirror."[30]

By late November, Rodney was floating the idea of bringing another co-median into Dangerfield's so he could take a break and perform for twenty minutes a night after working nonstop for two and a half months to get the club off the ground. Robert Klein got the call. "In a way, I've made a trap for myself," Rodney said. "No matter how rotten I feel, I've got to go on. If not, the tourists who showed up go away calling my club a fake. Take the other night: I got a fever, bad cold . . . I'm sick as a dog. What do I do? I take a cab down to Dangerfield's, go in, walk out on the floor, and tell the audience I got a bad cold. Then I point out that I'm here, but I can't work, announce no cover or minimum and two drinks on me. Now . . . I can go home and be sick."[31]

A few years earlier, when Robert Klein was working at the Improv, Rodney hooked him up with talent managers Jack Rollins and Charles Joffe and arranged for them to watch Klein perform at the club. Before that night, though, Rodney changed his mind, and as he and Klein were driving down 7th Avenue in Manhattan in Rodney's Impala convertible, he screeched to a halt in front of the Stage Delicatessen, deciding that Klein needed to meet Rollins then and there (since he was bound to be in the eatery, which was a big show-business hangout). Klein described the scene in his book, *The Amorous Busboy of Decatur Avenue,* noting how Rodney introduced him to "a gaunt, lanky man with billowing bags under his eyes: 'Here's that kid I told you about who's the next dimension.'" After meeting Rollins and leaving with Rodney ("I got no beginning, no finish, and I'm weak in the middle"), Klein, the next day, was contacted by five of his previously quiet agents at William Morris.

Klein eventually signed with Rollins and Joffe; Rodney helped him to prepare for his debut on *The Dean Martin Show*: "'Not the intellectual stuff, know what I mean, man?,'" Rodney told him. "Don't make 'em think too much. You use some of those big words, and they don't know what the fuck you're talking about, know what I mean, man?'" (Klein did not make the cut; the show's producer, Greg Garrison, and head writer, Paul Keyes, did not think he was funny enough.)[32]

Rodney closed out the eventful year by flying to Miami to tape an appearance on *The Jackie Gleason Show*. He was back in time to host the New Year's Eve show at Dangerfield's and followed that with another spot on *The Ed Sullivan Show* as the calendar turned to 1970.

Chapter Seven

As soon as I got married, I KNEW I was in trouble. My in-laws sent me a thank-you note.

AS DANGERFIELD'S HUMMED ALONG, RODNEY FELT COMFORTABLE enough to cut back on his seven-nights-a-week, two-shows-a-night schedule. He trimmed his appearances at the club to one show a night, Monday through Thursday, and two shows on Friday and Saturday (the club was closed on Sunday).

Dangerfield's was doing well enough that, within four to five months, Rodney claimed that he was able to pay back all the money he had borrowed from friends and the bank to open the joint—but then his accountant told him about the money he owed in taxes to the IRS. So, it was back to his friends to borrow money . . . again. It would take another two years before the club turned a profit. "This put me in a weird position, because I was now getting really hot in show business, but I couldn't take jobs out of town because I had an obligation to my partner, and to my young kids again," he recalled. "I had to turn down good jobs, much more money than I could make working at the club."[1]

In the meantime, his new schedule at Dangerfield's allowed Rodney to perform elsewhere, even if it was not in the New York area. (He ventured to Mechanicsburg, just outside of Harrisburg, Pennsylvania, for instance, to play a show for the local VFW.) He was always welcome in the Catskills at Kutsher's or the Raleigh Hotel, where he opened over President's Weekend in 1970 and, to publicize his appearance in newspaper ads, they slapped a tricorne Revolutionary War–style hat on the stock image of Rodney with the quote, "If my name was George Washington, I'd get respect." There was a night at Trinchi's in Yonkers and in the 46th St. Theatre in Brooklyn, where "special guest star" Rodney Dangerfield shared the bill with Al Martino in a show sponsored by New York radio station WNEW (emceed by station DJ Ted Brown). Sometimes, Rodney drove out to Pip's, a tiny club in Brooklyn's Sheepshead Bay, to try out new material.

In Rodney's absences from the club, other comics filled in. Scoey Mitchell opened at Dangerfield's and slayed the crowd, as did Milton Berle, who appreciated the club's "blue" comic atmosphere and said he was using words onstage there that he never uttered anywhere else in his lengthy career. "It's fun watching Milton in his natural environment, a nightclub," wrote columnist Jack O'Brian, "but if it's to be this one, don't bring the ladies."[2] Shecky Greene and Phil Harris performed there, too, both with bawdy routines, as did Johnny Carson and Professor Irwin Corey, who subbed his usual absurdism and mangled language for sex talk and profanity. Buddy Hackett, Bob Hope, Ed Sullivan, and Jack Carson were frequent visitors to the club.

One night, a salesman named Jim Dixon (born James La Roe) walked into the club to see the show and astonished everyone with his resemblance to President Richard M. Nixon, who was in his second year in The White House. Rodney dubbed him "Richard M. Dixon" and took him under his wing. Dixon worked corporate events and the like, posing as the president and, later, appearing in a movie called *Richard* as well as in bit parts in other movies and television shows, including *Where the Buffalo Roam*, *Tailgunner Joe*, *The ABC Comedy Hour*, and *The Private Files of J. Edgar Hoover* (all as "Richard Nixon"). "It was weird, the resemblance," Rodney said, and announced plans to include Dixon on an upcoming television show. In 1972, Dixon shared a stage with Shirley MacLaine, Warren Beatty, Eartha Kitt, Ed Ames, and lyricist Alan Jay Lerner at a fundraiser for Democratic senator George McGovern.

Rodney was approached by Ed Sullivan Productions, run by Sullivan's son-in-law, Bob Precht—who had booked Rodney's debut appearance on *The Ed Sullivan Show*, in 1967—to gauge his interest in doing a series (yes, he was interested) and he proceeded to churn out two scripts that included fifteen characters "that would be regularly portrayed in a variety of sketches and walk-ons," he said, mentioning his "Nixon lookalike" (Richard M. Dixon) as one of those characters. The proposed series met the same doomed fate as *An Evening at Dangerfield's*. Rodney also turned down a ten-episode offer from NBC's *The Dean Martin Show* because he did not want to leave the nightclub for another trip to L.A.

His latest album, *I Don't Get No Respect*, was selling well, and Rodney flew down to Miami to do some promotional work for the album, and to fill in for Frank Sinatra at a benefit dinner. "People relate to the 'no respect' theme," he said while flogging the album. "Everyone you talk to has, at one point in their life, felt like they were not treated as they should have been. This feeling is something no later success or money can correct—the feeling that you just don't belong, that you're unloved."[3]

He was always on the move, always open to new opportunities. He became a spokesman, of sorts, for the National Conference of Christians and Jews, which used his name and his signature line, "No Respect," in one of their radio spots. It was an association that would continue for some time thereafter, and included television ads, which Rodney pitched during National Brotherhood Week in spots titled "Brotherhood Begins with Respect." He paid for the taping expenses out of his own pocket as well as the expense of shipping the videos around the country. "I grew up in prejudice; I was the only Jew—and poor—in a wealthy neighborhood," he told a journalist about volunteering for the campaign. "My parents were separated, when other kids had both parents; I had a lowly job of delivery boy, and that made it worse."[4]

He was honored by the National Conference of Christians and Jews the following year, and his devotion to charitable causes cut a wide berth. He was always available for telethons, including Jerry Lewis's Labor Day fundraiser for muscular dystrophy, and he later contributed to the nationally televised *Retarded Children's Telethon* hosted by Steve Allen and Jayne Meadows along with Carol Burnett, Barbara Walters, Buddy Ebsen, Sonny & Cher, and a host of other celebrities—the telecast's cringeworthy title commonplace nomenclature for the times. Two years later, he contributed public service announcements for the Fund for Animals, the organization run by *TV Guide* columnist Cleveland Amory.

The offers were coming in, from the ridiculous to the sublime; he was sporting enough to participate in a preview of Ringling Bros. and Barnum & Bailey's circus show in New York City by riding an elephant in Madison Square Garden (he fell off the beast), while Carnegie Hall beckoned and offered Rodney a solo concert. In April, he was named "Nut of the Year" and gamely posed for photos with emcee Morty Gunty, wearing a giant bolt on his head during a luncheon held at Dangerfield's. It was sponsored by a company with a line of men's grooming products called Nuts & Bolts.

Hey, anything for publicity, ya know.

He went to prison in June 1970, joining singer Eloise Law in performing for the inmates at Rikers Island. The concert was notable enough to be reviewed in *The New York Times*, which, up to this point, rarely, if ever, mentioned Rodney's name despite his booming comedy club on the East Side and his many appearances on *The Ed Sullivan Show*.

"The comedian, Rodney Dangerfield, came on with the line: 'It's a pleasure to be here. I figure this is one audience that's not going to walk out on me' . . . the 48-year-old comic, who has been making it big on television spots the last couple of years, recalls the days of his youth as Jack Roy, when he could never be sure the people would not walk out . . . Mr. Dangerfield is a thick-voiced spieler with a worried look who specializes in the humor of inferiority and self-persecution."[5]

The following month, Rodney and Shelley Berman guest-starred on Robert Klein's CBS summer series, *Comedy Tonight*, which drew comparisons to *Rowan & Martin's Laugh-In* over on NBC but did not move the ratings needle (or the critics).

Life magazine took notice, too, and devoted a page to Rodney in its issue of August 28, 1970, under the headline "A 30-year loser is a winner." Writer Albert Goldman took stock of the Rodney Dangerfield phenomenon, at one point likening him to a spokesman for Richard Nixon's "Silent Majority":

Rodney's nothing new as a comedian—his rabbinical meter, his set 'em up, knock 'em down laff patterns, his stereotypes of sissy Jews and punchy Italians have broken them up in the Catskills for decades. But as a comic symbol, a comic spokesman for every middle-aged, middle-of-the-road Middle American who feels he's out of the money, out of the fun, out in the cold while everybody else is getting his, Rodney Dangerfield is the showbiz counterpart of Spiro T. Agnew.

Rodney's whole act is an extended complaint. He complains about pushy minority groups, exploitative women (even a hooker can make him say "Please!"), snotty kids, unsympathetic wives, crooked business partners, larcenous employees, and cars . . . Sometimes he swerves into surrealism, as in his recollection of a date with a manicurist who held one hand romantically while she dipped the other in his drink.

Whatever his theme, whether he is lamenting his loveless childhood or anticipating his unctuous funeral eulogy, Rodney's refrain, the burden of his lament, is always: "I don't get no respect!" That line is his trademark, his droopy-tailed escutcheon. . . . It's just the sort of line that could go down in the history books as summing up the subliminal attitude of the American people in their greatest spiritual crisis."[6]

In December, Babylon, Long Island, celebrated Rodney Dangerfield Day to commemorate the comedian, who was born at 44 Railroad Avenue in nearby Deer Park. Rodney signed autographs and, when cued, proceeded to press the wrong button to light the town's Christmas tree. He was presented with a plaque citing his contribution to comedy and to the arts —the irony lost on everyone there that day in Babylon (save for Rodney) who likely knew nothing about his miserable childhood. But, hey, the plaque was nice.

The Projectionist finally opened in theaters in January 1971, a year and a half after filming was completed. The reviews were fair to middling, with most critics praising Chuck McCann's performance and giving Rodney a passing grade in his big-screen debut. "Rodney Dangerfield, the comedian who made a career out of complaining 'I get no respect,' makes his screen debut in *The Projectionist*, a fantasy-comedy," noted the *New York Daily News*.

"As the 'heavy,' he may still not get no respect, but his performance is good enough. Chuck McCann, a natural in the title role, sees Dangerfield as the villain in his daydreams, which utilize a good portion of film clips featuring such stars as Humphrey Bogart, Sydney Greenstreet, John Garfield, Errol Flynn, Marilyn Monroe, and Clark Gable . . . But it's all on a sophomoric level."[7]

The New York Times also weighed in, mentioning Rodney only in passing: "Opposed to Captain Flash stands The Bat (Rodney Dangerfield), who in real life manages the theater in which Captain Flash projects and the scientific mastermind sells candy . . . Whatever its 400 failings, there is something to be said for a movie that is occasionally interrupted by previews of coming attractions that include its own world premiere . . ."[8]

"He's still funnier saying, 'I can't get no respect,'" sniped another critic.

The movie opened and closed without much fanfare, and it was relegated to the drive-in circuit shortly thereafter. Rodney rarely mentioned it. "I still don't understand what it was all about," he said years later. "It was a low-budget movie, the kind that you went to location on the subway." Over the years, however, *The Projectionist* achieved something of a cult status and earned a place in the archives of the Museum of Modern Art in New York.[9] In 1980, some theaters resuscitated *The Projectionist* to piggyback on the success of *Caddyshack*, which opened with Rodney in a starring role.

The Projectionist did nothing for Rodney's career, though, and was sometimes forgotten completely. Case in point: Over a year later, Earl Wilson reported that "Rodney Dangerfield'll make his movie debut in the James Caan film 'Barry Segal.'" Caan was hot off his role as Sonny Corleone in *The Godfather*; Rodney was slated to play an aluminum siding salesman and would write his own dialogue. The movie went the way of so many other Hollywood projects and never saw the flickering light of the silver screen.

It would be nearly another decade before Rodney made his next film appearance. One report at the time had him guest starring in the 1972 Smothers Brothers movie *Another Nice Mess* (that did not happen); Philip Roth, the author of *Portnoy's Complaint*, told Rodney that, if it was up to him, he would cast Rodney as Jack Portnoy, the put-upon father of sex-crazed schmuck Alexander Portnoy, in the big-screen version of his book. The movie opened in 1972 with Jack Somack playing Jack Portnoy. Rodney settled for a mock 1971 *Portnoy's Complaint* photo shoot with he and Joan Rivers as Jack and Sophie Portnoy and Dick Cavett as Alexander Portnoy . . . wearing a strait-jacket and boxing gloves.

IN MARCH 1971, CBS CANCELED *The Ed Sullivan Show*, UNCEREMONI-ously ending Sullivan's twenty-three-year Sunday-night run and closing the chapter on a storied television career. "People could count on getting their Petula Clark, Rodney Dangerfield, and dog acts without surprises every Sunday night," wrote one critic. "If CBS wanted a different show, they could have given Sullivan a year or so to experiment with long hair, a Che Guevara mustache or wearing bell bottoms."[10] It marked the end of an era, and, for Rodney, it was a bitter blow for the man who helped propel him to stardom.

There were other transitions.

Phil Cohen died in June 1971 at the age of seventy-eight. He and Rodney did not see much of each other over the years. Phil, the former vaudevillian, found success in the business world in New York and then moved to California to be closer to his brother, Adolf (Roy Arthur from the Roy & Arthur days), who worked closely with Eddie Cantor and who died in 1953.

Phil eventually moved to Florida, where Rodney visited him on occasion, including one day when he took Robert Klein along to meet his father while Rodney was playing the Diplomat Hotel. "Phil Roy was in his early seventies and had throat cancer," Klein recalled. "He had not been around for his son's childhood, and only recently had they had a rapprochement. As we sat on the beach, his father, obviously proud, kept repeating in his fading voice that Rodney should keep hitting the 'no respect' theme. 'Jack, it's a good hook, keep it up.'"[11]

"I asked my old man—he was seventy-six; he died when he was seventy-eight—I said, 'What's the answer to life?,'" Rodney said. "You're an old codger. You lived through vaudeville for twenty-five years. And after that, you were a customs man, in the stock market. You did very well. So, what's the answer to this whole thing?' He looked at me, and he said, 'It's all bullshit.'"[12]

"When my old man was old, I became friendly with him," Rodney told *Rolling Stone* magazine in a 1986 interview. "He was okay, he was a right guy, he was all right. I understood everything. He even cried to me; he said, 'Will you forgive me?' For not seeing me more, you know? I said, 'It's all right, forget it, it's okay."[13]

Rodney flew down to Florida for Phil's funeral, which he called "one of the loneliest moments of my life." He was the only person there; Dotty Cohen had died nine years earlier, in December 1962, at the age of seventy, and Rodney's older sister, Marion Garfinkel, did not attend their father's burial. "I was glad that I'd gotten a little closer to my father," Rodney recalled. "I wouldn't say it made up for all the years he'd basically abandoned me as a kid, but it was something. I guess that underneath it all he wasn't a bad guy. Even though he had walked out on me, still and all I understood him, and there was a part of me that liked him. Knowing my mother, what were his alternatives?"[14]

Back home, the problems between Rodney and Joyce were only amplified and, in 1970, they divorced . . . again . . . only this time it was a permanent conclusion to their two marriages spanning over twenty years. (Joyce never remarried and died in 1975 at the age of fifty.)

Rodney moved out of the apartment and into a new apartment in a building called the Pavilion, located on East 77th Street on the Upper East Side. It overlooked the East River and was a big place, two apartments with the wall knocked down between them. Melanie had her own room, as did Brian and Thelma Gopi, the Jamaican woman who kept house for Rodney. He invited Joe Ancis to move in and Joe, who was separated from his wife but not legally divorced, took him up on his offer.

Joe had his own room, down the hall from Rodney's, and loved to talk to people about his friend in his hep-cat fashion. "He's a very righteous, honorable person," he told a reporter. "He's basically, in the vernacular, a real stand up guy. He's not sycophantic, man. He can't suck, and he refuses to be glibly obsequious, which is part of the politics of show business. He can't make that route, man, and if he did, I think he would be, like, gigantic in a million areas—pictures, television or what have you."[15]

"My parents were separated but not legally divorced," recalled Joe's daughter, Julie Ancis. "My father was living in the apartment with Rodney. My mother did tell me that, when he was home with her, he would be on the phone for hours and hours with Rodney, and Rodney would go over jokes with my dad because he was very careful in crafting his material in terms of timing and where the word hit. And my dad would give a critique around that.

"Growing up, we would all go out to dinner," she said. "It would be me, my brother, oftentimes my mom, Rodney, maybe his girlfriend at the time, Melanie, and Brian. It was a ball and was a lot of fun from the perspective of a teenager.

"Rodney was always kind to me. He had a gluttonous appetite. The appetizers, the drinks, the main course, dessert and then, if I had anything left over on my plate, or my brother [Gordon] did, it was like, 'Hey, Julie, you finished with that?' And then he would grab that and then go home and apparently eat monstrous sandwiches."[16]

"Joe was truly Rodney's best friend, and they had a long history together," recalled Hollywood producer David Permut, who befriended Rodney later in his career. "Joe was eccentric, he was wild. The thing about Joe was that he could talk about anything—ballet, architecture, just about anything. He really had an awareness beyond the scope of entertainment. He had such an amazing sophistication.

"Rodney always respected and admired Joe. He was kind of legendary in the world of comedy [but] most people outside of that sphere don't really know who he was. He was unbelievably smart, sophisticated, worldly, there was nothing he couldn't talk about."[17]

"It was Joe and Rodney," recalled Rodney's booking agent, Dennis Arfa. "And they were sick-funny. They were sickos. I mean, Joe would try to put his pants on and not have his skin touch the pants. You know, it was like, neurotic shit. But they were very hipster. There was a real hipster persona to Joe. You look at Joe and you go, eh, a regular guy. But a real hip guy. And a lot of the language between Rodney and Joe, it was 'square fucks' and 'Cuban hookers,' all of that was between Joe and Rodney. They had a good language together."[18]

Arfa recalled the time Rodney and Joe invited a young woman up to their apartment—not for any funny business, but because she could yodel. "It was probably one o'clock in the morning and they wanted to see this girl. They were just so hysterical listening to this woman yodel and were just having a good time.

"Rodney was a good party boy," he said. "He would chase women. He would be on a plane, and he would start off with a question like, 'Are you married? Are you available? Are you happily married?' He would cut to all the chases. He had big balls that way."[19]

It was not surprising for his new neighbors to see Rodney walking his beloved silver poodle, Keno, and wearing his customary bathrobe and slippers. (Rodney loved his dog dearly and once spent $800 on a mink coat for Keno, who also was occasionally photographed in his master's arms for newspaper interviews.) Rodney often greeted visitors, including journalists, to his big apartment or in his dressing room at Dangerfield's wearing the bathrobe (hopefully closed, though some men have noted this was not always the case). Modesty was not one of Rodney Dangerfield's bigger virtues.

When Joe was not in the apartment, he could often be found holding court at Dangerfield's. His daughter Julie said he did not like to hang out with too many people.

"He was not quiet. He was brilliant in a lot of ways. He got me into the arts. He knew every painting, all the museums. We would go to Europe to see the art. He was very cultured and loved opera and ballet. He would take me every week to see the New York City Ballet, and he was heavy into Miles Davis. My dad was a very deep thinker . . . funny thinking, you know? He would make observations about people or about life. Like we would be in the car and would see a homeless person or a bum or a drug addict and he would say, 'Can you imagine that person was a cute little baby once?'"[20]

BY LATE 1971, RODNEY WAS, ONCE AGAIN, WORKING ON A PROPOSED half-hour syndicated color television series, this time to be produced by Viacom and planned for a 1973 primetime launch. "I'm going to do a pilot film for a series about a comedian named Rodney Dangerfield who owns a club called Dangerfield's," he said. "We'll do it in New York, re-create the club on a TV set, and if it works out I'll have a continuing plug for the club as well as a national TV show."

Rodney insisted on footing the bill for the pilot, figuring that his share of the profits would be much bigger if it were picked up by a network. "It's a question of believing in yourself," he said. "And I believe I can do it. After all, Lucille Ball did it, and Jackie Gleason did it, and they didn't do too bad. People got respect for them."

In addition to a cast including a bartender, a chef, two waiters, a hat check girl, and his (fictional) wife, he planned to use a number of struggling young comedians he had seen at the Improv and on television talk shows.

The project generated positive press but never materialized—a fortuitous stroke of luck in Rodney's burgeoning career. In May, word broke that Rodney, Nipsey Russell, and Dom DeLuise would be joining *The Dean Martin Show* as regulars for the 1972–73 television season to help offset the loss of *Martin Show* regular Paul Lynde, who left to film his own sitcom, *The Paul Lynde Show*, which lasted one season on ABC.

Rodney was no stranger to Martin's popular NBC variety series and dropped in every once in a while for a guest-starring spot. Producer Greg Garrison offered him the chance to play a barber the preceding season, but he turned it down (the role went to Lonnie Shorr). "Greg also asked me to do *The Marty Feldman Show,* but I turned that one down, too," he said. "I'm looking for the least tension. There is no tension in Dean's show."[21]

He would appear in all twenty-eight shows of the new season along with Russell and DeLuise (in a barber shop) and holdovers Kay Medford and Lou Jacobi (in diner sketches). He was guaranteed to appear in reruns, bringing his *Dean Martin Show* episode count to forty. It meant the dreaded flight to L.A. and time away from the club, but it was an offer he could not afford to pass up and it represented a golden publicity opportunity for Dangerfield's.

(*The Dean Martin Show* was entering its eighth season; Martin, who famously hated to rehearse—it interrupted his golf game—only showed up in his tuxedo on shooting days and reportedly had never visited his own office at NBC.)

The setup for *The Dean Martin Show* had Rodney chatting with Martin in a specially built nightclub set called the Club Ding-a-ling. (Rodney said he tried to get Garrison to name it Club Dangerfield's, but no dice.) The sketches were taped on Friday nights and sometimes on Sundays; Rodney flew out to L.A. the day of the tapings, went to his hotel, had a swim, and then reported to the studio in Burbank for work.

"The set for our bits was always the same—me, Dean, a table, and two chairs," Rodney recalled. "For our first show together, it took Dean and me just three or four minutes to film our routine and we were done. 'Okay, great, see ya next week,' right? Wrong. That was the last time I saw Dean. For the next seven Sundays, I flew from New York to California, went into an empty studio, sat down at that table by myself, and did four skits [for two shows] while talking to an empty chair. Later, the crew filled in shots of the audience laughing, and they filled in Dean Martin, too."[22]

Somehow, between jetting back and forth between L.A. and New York, Rodney found time to cobble together a cookbook.

I Couldn't Stand My Wife's Cooking, So I Opened a Restaurant was published in the fall of 1972 with the subtitle *Respectable Recipes Spiced with Humor.* The cover featured the requisite black-and-white photo of Rodney's face, onto which was added a white chef's hat and a white chef's smock—and two meaty arms crossed in front of him. "I dedicate this book to many people . . . to all my friends, relatives, and neighbors who have eaten over at my house . . . I'm sorry." The 244-page book was seasoned with recipes and gags. (Sample: "As soon as I got married, I KNEW I was in trouble. My in-laws sent me a thank-you note.") There were recipes for, among other savory dishes, "Orange-Cranberry Salad," "Tutti-Frutti Noodle Pudding," "Memphis Kishka Balls," and "Women's Lib Pot Roast."[23] The book sold a few copies and Rodney promoted it with a cooking segment on *The Dinah Shore Show.*

In short order, another publisher, Price/Stern/Sloan, released a flimsy paperback called *I Don't Get No Respect: Rodney Dangerfield,* which vanished quickly. "It's out only two weeks," Rodney said, "and already it's selling in the dozens." It was more akin to a pamphlet of Rodney's G-rated jokes, each one illustrated with drawings on the opposite page depicting the punch line.

Example: "And the day I got married was really embarrassing. The judge said: 'If anyone is against this marriage, speak now or forever hold your peace.' I looked around. Her family had formed a double line."[24]

DANGERFIELD'S WAS GOING GREAT GUNS IN ITS FOURTH YEAR. JACK Benny saw Rodney one night on *The Tonight Show Starring Johnny Carson* and called Rodney, at the club, to tell him how much he loved one of his jokes about his wife putting down a steak: "How do you forget the plate?" Benny later came into the club to watch Rodney's act and invited him out to dinner. Rodney declined, using the excuse of needing to finish writing a project. "The truth was that I didn't go because I knew I couldn't be myself with Jack Benny," he recalled. "I mean, I'd have to play a part and be a gentleman. Can you picture me saying to Jack Benny, 'Man, I'm so depressed. It's all too fucking much'?"[25]

(Nearly a decade later, Rodney was awarded the prestigious Jack Benny Award from the students of UCLA, joining Johnny Carson, Steve Martin, Chevy Chase, and John Belushi as alumni. He was cited for his "outstanding contributions to his craft and his immense popularity among young adults.")

Comedian Dennis Blair, a regular performer at Dangerfield's, remembers "The characters in that club. I swear to God, some of my best memories. I mean, there was Bobby Kimball, who was the maître d'. Big burly Scottish guy or British, I forget. But he would take no prisoners. And the greatest thing that he did . . . he would have to phone in American Express credit card numbers, but he forgot to turn the mic off because he would announce Rodney offstage. He would leave the mic on, so while Rodney or whoever was on, you would hear Bobby: 'American Express, 2-5-6.'

"Then there was Bernie the bartender and Teddy, they were characters, too. I mean, Bernie was like the king of dad jokes. All the waiters and the staff, they were great. I don't think they ever spent any money on updating anything. It was dark in there, with dark red curtains. The tables were tiny."[26]

On April 3, 1973, two men, one armed with a shotgun, the other with a pistol, robbed the place at around 1:40 in the morning and escaped with $3,000 from the bar's cash register. The papers went to town with Rodney "getting no respect," of course, but it was no laughing matter. Rodney was sitting at a table with Joe Ancis after the last show that night when the men broke in. "The club is dimly lit and all of a sudden I heard somebody say, 'Down on the floor! This is for real!,'" Rodney recounted. "My God, I thought I was on the set of a B-movie. I didn't hesitate, though. I dove on the floor like everybody else. I looked up and saw this Mutt and Jeff team. One guy, 5-feet-6, was wearing a shotgun; the other guy, about 6-feet-2, had a pistol. They both had Spanish accents and were wearing wide-brim hats, like sombreros." The two men fled the club and hailed a cab, which dropped them off in the Bronx. The crime went unsolved.

Still, the club hummed along, and Rodney was happy to publicize his prized possession, giving interviews in his office at Dangerfield's and buzzing journalists into the inner sanctum.

The club drew a mix of tourists—honeymooners, businessmen, "grand-motherly types in sensible shoes and velvet hats" from Middle America. Following the opening act, Rodney's voice proclaimed over the PA system "I don't get no respect . . . no respect" and then he appeared onstage, sometimes bumming a cigarette from a patron, and schmoozing with the crowd before launching into his act: "Ah, life is just a bowl of pits. For me, nothing comes easy. Last night a hooker made me say please."[27]

The club was a New York City landmark by now; Dustin Hoffman hung around Dangerfield's to prepare for his Oscar-nominated role as Lenny Bruce in Bob Fosse's 1974 biopic *Lenny*, and a smattering of commercials (beer, cologne, "golden oldies" records) were filmed there. The story, told by several people, including Rodney, was that Hoffman was coming to Dangerfield's a few days a week and he asked Joe Ancis, "So, do you think I'm doing a good job?" Joe's response: "No."

"Joe Ancis would walk through," recalled Dennis Blair. "Rodney and I would be at the table writing something and Rodney had a dog named Keno, who would just sit and stare at him all day. Joe was walking through, and Rodney goes, 'Hey, Joe, what's with Keno? He keeps staring at me.' And Joe keeps walking without breaking his stride and goes, 'Man, you're a star.' He

Rodney's father, Phil Roy, and "Uncle Bunk" (in blackface) in 1915 as the vaudeville team Roy & Arthur. Their specialty act of comically clumsy juggling was called "Fun in a Dining Car." *Author collection.*

At the New Orpheum

Phil Roy and Roy Arthur, presenting "Fun in a Dining Car," at the rpheum first half this week.

Jack Roy morphed into Rodney Dangerfield in the early 1960s as he mounted his comedy comeback. *Michael Ochs Archive. Getty Images.*

Rodney Dangerfield poses for a portrait circa 1960 in New York City. *Michael Ochs Archive. Getty Images.*

Rodney got his big break
on *The Ed Sullivan Show*
in March 1967.
He was forty-five years old.
CBS Photo Archive. Getty Images.

Rodney appeared semi-regularly
on *The Ed Sullivan Show* until
its cancellation by CBS in 1971.
CBS Photo Archive. Getty Images.

Rodney in his requisite robe
with his beloved poodle, Keno.
*Photograph by Tim Boxer/
Archive Photos. Getty Images.*

Rodney in his office
at Dangerfield's.
His legendary comedy club
on Manhattan's Upper East Side
opened its doors
in September 1969.
*Photograph by Tim Boxer/
Archive Photos. Getty Images.*

Rodney was a huge fan of
The Jerry Springer Show.
Here he is with his wife Joan
and host Jerry Springer.
Courtesy Linda Shafran.

Movie stardom: Rodney as Al Czervik
in *Caddyshack* (1980).
Photograph by Steve Schapiro/
Corbis Premium Historical.
Getty Images.

Rodney played
loutish photographer
Monty Capuletti
in *Easy Money* (1983).
*Silver Screen Collection/
Moviepix. Getty Images.*

Rodney and his friend
Sam Kinison
in the comedy
Back to School (1986),
Rodney's most successful
big-screen venture.
*Archive Photos/Moviepix.
Getty Images.*

The younger comics, including Andrew Dice Clay, shown here with Rodney in 1989, loved him for his encouragement and support. *Photograph by Jeff Kravitz/ FilmMagic, Inc. Getty Images.*

He's not pigeon-proof: Mr. "No Respect" in a publicity photo. *Photograph by Arthur Schatz/ The Chronicle Collection. Getty Images.*

Rock 'n' roll comic: Rodney and Ozzy Osbourne at the Hollywood premiere of *Little Nicky* in Los Angeles. *Photograph by S. Granitz/WireImage. Getty Images.*

Rodney and his wife, Joan, attend a gala.
Photograph by Frederick M. Brown.
Getty Images.

Rodney celebrated his eightieth birthday
on *The Tonight Show with Jay Leno* in 2001.
He suffered a mild heart attack that same night.
Photograph by Kevin Winter. Getty Images.

Rodney received a star on the
Hollywood Walk of Fame in 2002
at the age of eighty-one.
Photograph by Vince Bucci. Getty Images.

Rodney at the world premiere
of pal Jim Carrey's movie
Bruce Almighty in 2003,
about a month after undergoing
brain surgery.
Photograph by S.Granitz/WireImage.
Getty Images.

Rodney's tombstone says it all.
Photograph by Bill Tompkins/
Michael Ochs Archives. Getty Images.

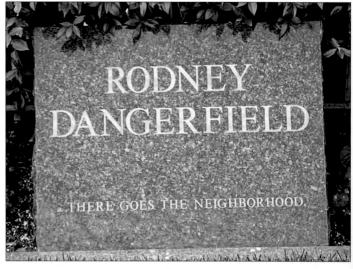

was smart and funny. No desire of wanting to perform for Joe, he just wanted to hang out and do what he did. He was really great."[28]

Dangerfield's was a big draw during prom season, too, with high school kids from the suburbs schlepping into the city for a show. "I do quite well in my own club, or I'd go to Vegas," Rodney said. He reportedly turned down offers of $30,000 to appear in Sin City. "People have a good time at my place, and I like to see people walk out happy. There aren't many places left where you see people laugh. My place is probably the only one left that has a comedian working steady . . . my nightclub routine involves making one hundred fifty to two hundred jokes in forty-five minutes. A laugh a minute isn't enough; you need three or four." He was even talking about opening up another comedy club in Las Vegas.

Dangerfield's also drew a crowd of policemen and local wiseguys who mixed freely in the club's darkened atmosphere. So beloved was Rodney by the New York Police Department that he was surprised with a badge, and a police uniform, from the local Patrolmen's Benevolent Association making him an honorary police officer. That drew the ire of New York Police Commissioner Michael Codd, who was not a fan of celebrities—including Rodney, Frank Sinatra, and attorney F. Lee Bailey—being given honorary badges due to an uptick in police impersonators. The PBA chief pointed out to Codd that Rodney's badge was slightly smaller than the regulation badge worn by members of the NYPD. The "controversy," such as it was, blew over quickly. Rodney kept the badge (and the uniform).

Chapter Eight

I know I'm ugly. While this guy was mugging me, he took off his mask and told me to wear it.

RODNEY HAD A "DUFFEL BAG FULL OF JOKES" AND ESTIMATED that he had written between 10,000 and 15,000 gags and used about one-third of those. Remarkably, he wrote most of his own material, though occasionally he would buy jokes—Dennis Snee, from Wichita, Kansas, was an occasional contributor, as was Alan Zweibel, later to find success as a writer on NBC's *Saturday Night Live* and on Showtime's *It's Garry Shandling's Show*. Rodney was known for paying handsomely for jokes, at least by a struggling comedian's standards. On one occasion, he coughed up $250 to Adrianne Tolsch for the rights to use one of her gags that he heard her use onstage at the Manhattan comedy club Catch a Rising Star.

Once, in San Francisco, Rodney was appearing at the Holy City Zoo nightclub when two aspiring comedians there, Mike Bizarro and Karen Warner, decided to write about fifty jokes for Rodney—which they brought to his hotel, unannounced, and cornered him outside the door to his room to give him the jokes. Rodney thanked them—and, the very next night, used four of their jokes in his act. He paid them a total of $200 and asked for more.[1]

Comedian and actor Robert Wuhl, who would later star in the HBO satirical series *Arli$$*, was a young hopeful when he approached Rodney with some material he thought might work for his act.

"I had just come out of college in the mid-'70s when Rodney's star was starting to rise. His appearances on *The Tonight Show* were must-watch TV for us in college," he said. "I thought I could possibly write some jokes that Rodney would like, and I met him at Dangerfield's when he was there performing. I talked to Tony Bevacqua and told him I had some jokes for Rodney, and he brought me downstairs, knocked on Rodney's door, and he's in there in his trademark bathrobe, naked underneath as usual, with the bathrobe pretty wide open. He said, 'Let me hear what you got' and I told him a couple of jokes. He said, 'Okay, kid, the jokes are good but don't do me.' He bought a few jokes and I continued to write for him and he'd say to me, 'You're a good writer, kid, but you're an even better comedy editor,' because I would get the fewest amount of words and syllables [in a joke] because this was an oral form—a one-liner, to Rodney, was the perfect art form: a beginning, middle, and end, a story in one line.

"So, I wrote for him, which gave me a leg up in the clubs," Wuhl said. "He was great to me. He was doing *The Tonight Show* in California, and he brought me out with him and introduced me to Mitzi Shore at the Comedy Store. I had Rodney's seal of approval at that time, which was really something.

"The thing about Rodney was you better have a point of view," Wuhl said. "He loved young comics who had something to say or had an edge. He'd say, 'You gotta piss off the squares.' He would go to the Improv and heckle young comics if they had nothing to say or did observational, banal shit. He would go, 'What are you telling me about this food? Next, you're gonna tell me where I buy my shoes.' He loved dangerous comics—he loved Bill Hicks, Sam Kinison, Andrew Dice Clay. He really loved [Andy Kaufman's obnoxious comic alter ego] Tony Clifton. We would go watch him perform at the Comedy Store. Rodney just loved to watch the effect on the audience, how Tony Clifton pissed them off. He had a hard edge."[2]

Rodney complained, often, that other comedians were stealing his jokes, but he could also be very gracious in making sure that a writer was compensated if he used one of his or her jokes—even paying for a joke twice, on at least one occasion.

Billy Riback, a successful producer (*Home Improvement*) was, at the time, a young comedy writer from Canada who was trying to break into the business. "I always wanted to write for Rodney, but I had no way of getting in touch with him. I have a friend, Steve Mittleman, who is a noted comic, who happened to be at Rodney's club, and he hears Rodney doing a joke and Steve knew it was my joke. (Here it is: 'I was playing a senior citizen's home, and the people were so old they were bobbing for applesauce.') The funny thing is, it's not even a great fucking joke and it's not even a Rodney-sounding joke, but he does the joke and Steve knew that I had written it. So, he went up to Rodney afterward, which is very hard to do, and he said, 'Hey, Rodney, that joke is my friend Billy Riback's.'"

Rodney told Mittleman that he bought the joke, "and Steve said, 'Well, that guy ripped it off from Billy and you should pay him,' which is incredible for Steve to say. And Rodney went, 'Okay, give me his address.' And two days later I had a check for $75 from Rodney after he had already paid for the joke once, which is insane and unheard-of."[3]

RODNEY TREATED HIS TELEVISION APPEARANCES SERIOUSLY, PARTICU-larly his visits to *The Tonight Show Starring Johnny Carson*, where he was a semi-regular on par with Don Rickles as one of Carson's favorites, appearing every three months or so. He worked feverishly to prepare for his eight-to-twelve-minute appearances with the King of Late Night and made sure he had a healthy reserve of new jokes with which to gift America. "Every time out, it's practically all new material," he said. "All new killers."

After writing his material for his upcoming visit to *The Tonight Show*, Rodney tried out the material at Dangerfield's, or maybe at the Improv, slic-ing out the bits that did not work and honing it down to the killers with surgical precision: "I know I'm ugly. While this guy was mugging me, he took off his mask and told me to wear it," or, "I started in this business with a ventriloquist. But I had to quit. I got too big for the guy's lap."[4] Carson once laughed so hard at one of Rodney's jokes that he fell off his chair.

Rodney also expanded his joke-telling empire beyond Dangerfield's, his other nightclub appearances, and his television guest spots. He signed a deal with New York Telephone for its new local service, Dial-A-Joke (999-3838. There was no area code needed in New York City, Nassau, Suffolk, and Westchester counties). The service was advertised in newspapers with a photograph of Rodney and the headline: With all due respect, Dial-A-Joke presents Rodney Dangerfield.

"Poor Rodney Dangerfield," read the ad copy beside Rodney's photograph. "He gets no respect. No respect at all. The least we can all do for him is listen each day and hear a different 60-second comedy routine on Dial-A-Joke." The work was easy—he recorded his spots at Dangerfield's—but it put an extra burden on Rodney to write even more jokes (with occasional assistance).

His association with Dean Martin resumed in 1974 when Rodney appeared on *The Dean Martin Comedy World*, a series of ten shows airing Thursday nights on NBC as a summer replacement for *The Dean Martin Show*. The series mixed new comedy acts (including Andy Kaufman in his first network appearance), interviews with comedians, and archival clips of classic movies in a fast-moving hodgepodge. Rodney taped his bits for *The Dean Martin Comedy World* in one marathon session at Dangerfield's. The show lasted six episodes and was canceled in mid-August.

Three months later, in November, he opened in the "Triple Treat Variety All-Star Review" at the Westbury Music Fair on Long Island along with singers Connie Francis and Enzo Stuarti. The show generated positive reviews but was tainted by tragedy when, on November 8, Francis was raped at knifepoint in the Howard Johnson Motor Lodge in Mineola after returning from the show and going to bed around 2:30 a.m. According to police, she was awakened three hours later by a young man with a knife who raped her, tied her to a chair with her hands behind her back, and stole her jewelry and a mink coat. Her rapist was never found, and Francis spiraled into a severe depression. Fifteen years later, in better times, Connie Francis and Rodney opened at Bally's hotel-casino in Las Vegas.

In June 1975, Rodney played Vegas for the first time in six years, opening for Tony Orlando and Dawn for two weeks at the Riviera while fielding offers for steady television work. (He later guest-starred on Tony Orlando and Dawn's CBS variety series, and his appearance at the Riviera blossomed into a few more weeks at the Thunderbird with singer Dick Roman.)

He was approached by, among others, Carl Reiner—who caught his act at the Riviera—Mel Brooks, Carol Burnett's husband, Joe Hamilton, and Norman Lear about starring in a comedy pilot based on his everyman/no respect schnook. He turned them all down. In early September 1975, he entered Mt. Sinai Hospital in Manhattan for a hernia operation, which he hoped would help him lose fifteen pounds in the process. Red Buttons filled in for Rodney at Dangerfield's for eight days in September while he recovered.

Rodney was turning fifty-four, an age where most comics are interacting with audiences their age. Rodney was a different breed—sure, he appealed to the fifty-and-over crowd—and voiced a public service announcement for the Arthritis Foundation while appearing on the Stop Arthritis telethon airing locally in New York City—but the younger generation comprised a large chunk of his fan base.

His albums could be heard blasting from dorm rooms on college campuses nationwide; he was named the best of all the "new hip standup comics" by the youth-oriented magazine *Crawdaddy*, and there was talk of Rodney hosting a radio show from Dangerfield's. "I have a whole new thing, now, kids," he said. "Colleges. The kids are into me now. I don't know why, dunno, dunno."[5] Dangerfield's catered to the high school kids, too—it offered an "After Prom Package" ($15 per person including the show, two drinks, cover, tax, and tip) that proved to be a moneymaker for the club.

"The prom kids would come in for like an hour or so and then leave and more prom kids would come in," said comedian Bob Nelson. "So, the show was constantly continuous, and you would go up three or four times a night. It was just brutal. But when I worked at Dangerfield's, there were times when I got to meet Redd Foxx and Jackie Mason and Gabe Kaplan. Rodney would have headliners come in all the time and hang out."[6]

The Ocean State Performing Arts Center in Providence, Rhode Island, banned Rodney, not because of his act but because of his audience—now mostly rock fans, who went wild and wrecked the place during one of his appearances there.

Rodney proved his generational bona fides by addressing the graduating class of Harvard University. "When they called, I asked, 'Who fell out?'" he said. "They told me the truth—that Woody Allen has been refusing for years and that Lily Tomlin stalled for a few days before saying no. I stalled for all of twenty seconds and said yes." He did, of course, tell the graduating class of 1978 that he got no respect.

CABLE TELEVISION WAS IN ITS INFANCY AND, IN THE SPRING OF 1976, Home Box Office, which had yet to morph into just HBO, signed Rodney, Myron Cohen, David Steinberg, and Freddie Prinze for its new stand-up television series, *On Location*. The nascent pay cable network, which aired commercial free, claimed it had 300,000 subscribers, roughly ten times larger than Johnny Carson's nightly viewership. It was a terrific, intimate showcase for Rodney's act, which he taped at Dangerfield's before a live audience.

That summer, Rodney relocated to Vegas, and to the Tropicana Hotel, where he opened a satellite club of sorts in the hotel's Blue Room. He was away from Dangerfield's for ten weeks, but he was in his element; he paid for all the musicians, advertising, etc. and hoped to earn about $250,000 from his investment that ran through early September. "No one ever financed their own show like this before," he said. "I like to gamble, but I gamble on myself . . . I'll be in one place ten weeks doin' my own number."[7]

(When Atlantic City opened for gambling in 1978, Rodney also took his act there for ten weeks, renting the ballroom at the Sheraton Deauville—and purchased a home in the city's pricey Chelsea residential area.)

While Rodney was in Las Vegas at the Tropicana, he flew to L.A. to tape a spot on his friend Redd Foxx's new ABC variety show and to film a week's worth of appearances on *Hollywood Squares*, then returned to New York to resume his busy stand-up schedule. There were stops at the Mount Airy Lodge in Pennsylvania's Pocono Mountains and, closer to home, he dropped in at Catch a Rising Star, a competing club on the Upper East Side, to do a 2 a.m. set for free.

Rodney celebrated his fifty-sixth birthday in November 1977 at Dangerfield's with a cake from Ann Meara, Jackie Mason, and Jerry Stiller. His slice of cake was, of course, promptly smooshed into his face by Meara as all four laughed for the cameras. It was not all fun and games in the competitive, cutthroat world of comedy, though; four months later, Rodney flew out to L.A. to tape a spot on *The Merv Griffin Show* and almost came to blows backstage with Shecky Greene over some slight, real or imagined. The fight was broken up before it could start by big Al Hirt, the trumpeter in Griffin's TV band. Perhaps their tiff was over a joke the other one claimed was stolen. Joke-stealing was one of Rodney's big bugaboos; he claimed that Henny Youngman stole his joke about visiting his psychiatrist: "My psychiatrist told me I'm crazy. I told him I'd like a second opinion. He said, Okay, you're ugly, too." "Phil Foster used to say, 'When people steal lines, it's like they're hitting your kids,' ya know?" he told one reporter.[8]

So indelible was Rodney's "no respect" line by the late 1970s that offers for television pilots arrived almost nonstop into his office. He was approached separately by producers James Komack, Rick Rosner, and Marvin Worth, as well as by comedian Johnny Yune, to headline potential series. One project was reportedly cocreated by Steve Martin. There was even an offer from the famous animation studio Hanna-Barbera. He turned them all down because he did not want to fly to L.A. and take time away from his club and his children. Money was not the issue. "I would not want to do 13 weeks of a lousy show," he told *Washington Post* television columnist Tom Shales. "That's not very gratifying. You do things for money, and you do things for art. We all love money, of course, but my thing is not to see how much money I can die with."[9]

One offer Rodney did accept was to play the foil opposite brawny ex-professional athletes in commercials for Miller Lite beer and its "Tastes Great. Less Filling" campaign that was the brainchild of Robert Lenz at the New York advertising firm of McCann Erickson, who had worked on the Miller Beer campaign since the early 1970s.

"We thought in the very beginning that if we were going to have basically talking heads [in the commercials] then they would have to be really interesting people, otherwise it was going to be dull," Lenz recalled. "So, we insisted there not be any actors or television personalities . . . we didn't really think yet that athletes would be the stars."[10]

The first Miller Lite beer commercial in 1973 featured recently retired New York Jets running back Matt Snell, a hero of the team's 1969 Super Bowl victory over the heavily favored Baltimore Colts. Snell shot his commercial at Joe Allen's, a bar in Manhattan. "He happened to be at the top of our mind, and we tried him out and he was great. It really worked out," Lenz said. "The second [commercial] was with [author] Mickey Spillane, who we thought would be appealing to beer drinkers. Then we started drifting around [from ex-athletes to personalities] and maybe by the fifth or sixth commercial we were locked into the athletes because they were big, they were beery and most of them had a self-deprecating sense of humor."[11]

The list of athletes and sports personalities starring in the Miller Lite ads proliferated as the campaign grew in popularity: from Bubba Smith, Frank Robinson, Ben Davidson, Boog Powell, Deacon Jones, and Ray Nitschke to Billy Martin, Bob Uecker, Tommy Heinsohn, Boom-Boom Geoffrion, Steve Mizerak, and Dick Williams. Actress Lee Meredith, who played Swedish secretary Ulla in the 1967 Mel Brooks comedy *The Producers*, and Miss McIntosh in Neil Simon's *The Sunshine Boys* in 1975, was the lone woman among the group. She was the "Doll" who first strolls past Spillane in a bar and appeared with him in his subsequent Miller Lite commercials.

The ubiquitous ads, directed by Bob Giraldi, became a pop-culture phenomenon and made stars of previously forgotten athletes, including onetime New York Mets first baseman and short-lived folk hero "Marvelous Marv" Throneberry, who was working as the general manager of an insulating company in Memphis, Tennessee, when he was tracked down and hired for his first commercial.[12]

"My partner, Bob Geary, and I tried to get someone who could be a foil to these guys—they were basically sort of the same in their presentations, even though they were from different sports—and that's the way we got to Rodney Dangerfield," Lenz recalled. "Although he didn't really fit the description we were set on, we thought he would be acceptable to beer drinkers; that he was the kind of a schlemiel in a bar.

"I remember the day I went to his apartment on the Upper East Side, way over on First Avenue, I was in a cab that stopped for a light and there he was, walking his poodle in a bathrobe on Second Avenue. I said to myself, 'Okay, we've got the right guy.'"

Rodney's role was to function as a foil to the jocks.

"He had this sort of funny, antagonistic attitude toward the big athletes, and they were poking him all the time," Lenz said. "We didn't expect how much the jocks loved him . . . They were always kidding him but loved the fact that he was around, and with them he was a great help because those guys were so unprofessional, in a sense, and Rodney was a professional and they respected that.

"He was definitely the straw in the drink, and he really kept things going. He was serious about his craft, I thought, but very funny and he semi-insulted [the athletes]. I remember we were shooting in a bar and Rodney came in and did some shtick—we were feeding him lines and he was ad-libbing as he went into the scene—and he came back and said, 'Was that funny?' He was serious about that."[13]

"It's good exposure," Rodney said of the commercials. "I like those fellas; I like those athletes and I hold my own pretty good in that crowd. I get the ballplayers in my own joint in New York—Joe Namath, Too Tall Jones, a lot of the ballplayers. It's a good crowd."

It was not easy work. On one occasion, Rodney spent eight hours and went through nearly 140 takes shooting a Miller Lite ad at the Lotos Club on Manhattan's Upper East Side, a few blocks from Dangerfield's, along with Bubba Smith, Happy Hairston, Deacon Jones, Boom-Boom Geoffrion, and seven others under Bob Giraldi's direction.[14]

The commercials' popularity spawned a quickie book, *Lite Reading*, authored by *Sports Illustrated* senior writer Frank Deford and published by Penguin Books in 1984. *Lite Reading* was presented in high school or college yearbook fashion, with colorful anecdotes about the stars and behind-the-scenes stories about the filming of the ads—including tales about the Miller Lite "All-Stars," who held an annual (mostly scripted) "banquet" every year in the form of a commercial, with Rodney as the emcee.

Deford wrote how Rodney was not quite a member of the Miller Lite

All-Stars—"he keeps too much distance"—and how his "special treatment" when filming the ads often antagonized his costars. "He suffers constant heckling and backbiting from them," Deford wrote. "Typical of the way the All-Stars respond to Rodney was when he showed up at the softball shoot this past year, hours after the others had come in a bus . . . You can be outgoing, private, noisy, quiet, profane, religious. About the only thing you can't be is a big deal."[15]

Rodney was not happy about how Deford portrayed him in *Lite Reading*; after it was published, he saw Deford in New York City, exploded at him in an expletive-filled tirade, and called him some nasty names. Bob Uecker was there. "Most of us thought Deford should have belted Rodney," he said.

"There is a pecking order here just the way there is in sports. There's also a hard core to penetrate," Deford said. "Rodney Dangerfield isn't really accepted in that sense. Part of it is his own fault for not riding the hotel bus with everyone else, and part of it is because he's never been a ballplayer."[16]

Even former baseball manager Dick Williams, a latecomer to the Miller Lite fraternity, took his shots at Rodney: "He sort of keeps to himself. When they break for lunch, everybody goes out together, except Rodney goes out with other people. That ticks the guys off. When they were shooting the tug-of-war a few years ago, Rodney came back from lunch an hour-and-a-half late. They were so mad, they heaved him into the ocean."[17]

Lenz recalled one occasion when the All-Stars were staying at the Waldorf-Astoria hotel in New York City while shooting a commercial at Silvercup Studios in Long Island City in Queens. "They had to get up at six a.m. and they all got in the bus and got to Silvercup Studios probably around seven a.m. and started going into makeup and wardrobe and feeling quite miserable," he said. "And around 11:30 Rodney pulls up in a white limo. I thought they were going to beat him up. But that was the relationship he had with them."[18]

When word got out that Rodney parlayed his Miller Lite celebrity status into personal appearances—at $10,000 a shot, compared to the $1,400 appearance fee commanded by Marv Throneberry—one of his costars grumbled, "That guy was a washed-up comic before he started working with us."

But the chemistry worked—so much so that, according to Lenz, there was nearly a big-screen movie from Universal Pictures starring the Miller Lite All-Stars . . . and Rodney. "It went pretty far in that world and then [Miller Beer owner] Philip Morris shot it down," he said. "It was a funny script." The movie's plot was centered around the All-Stars trying to save one of their own, who was kidnapped and being held on a small, secret island, with Mickey Spillane coming up with the idea that he would get the guys together and they would all go and rescue their teammate.

"They did not know at that point in the plot that it was Rodney," Lenz said. "It was a caper kind of movie, where one All-Star would show up on a mountain and find Ben Davidson, who would find Bob Uecker somewhere else, and they would round up all the guys and try to find this island, with a legitimate actor getting them all together and explaining how they were going to sneak onto the island—and them all groaning like, 'Oh my God, you called us all down here for that?' when they find out it's Rodney," who was cracking jokes to keep his captors off-balance.

"The movie just got shot down," Lenz said. "Commercials have a life of their own, and I think they thought if we got into something else, like a movie, it may not have been as appealing to beer drinkers. Who knows?"[19]

Miller Beer's rivals took notice of the spots' popularity and Anheuser-Busch reportedly offered Rodney $500,000 to defect over to "their side" for its "Natural Light" campaign, following Miller Lite alums including Nick Buoniconti, Joe Frazier, and ex-Yankees teammates Mickey Mantle and Whitey Ford. Rodney turned them down and told them to stuff it when they asked for permission to hold their "Big Switch" press conference (touting the defectors) in Dangerfield's.

Rodney, though, was not contractually tied to Miller Beer regarding his appearance in other commercials, and he was a ubiquitous presence shilling all kinds of products. His voice emanated from a gas tank in ads for "new Mobil super unleaded gasoline" ("I tell ya, with my higher octane I fight engine knocks and pings") and Bonanza Family Restaurants ("I tell ya, some restaurants. One place they charged me extra for a tiny salad—what a rip-off!") He pitched the Massachusetts State Lottery, adjusting his tie and swiveling his head on promotional material and proclaiming that "The instant casino games give everyone a lot of respectable ways to win—even me" and appeared in a thirty-second television ad for the board game Twister ("I tell ya, nothing goes right," he says after bringing Twister to a party and not being allowed to play by the teenagers twisting and turning and getting entangled in each other).

Soon he was seen in print ads hawking Pilot pens with a lobster ("Get your claws off my Pilot pen. I don't get no respect!")

Chapter Nine

The other night I was in a place and I felt like having a few drinks, ya know? I went over to the bartender and said, "Surprise me." He showed me a naked picture of my wife!

T EN YEARS EARLIER, RODNEY DID NOT HAVE MUCH LUCK WITH his big-screen debut in *The Projectionist*. But now, a decade later, he was back in front of the movie cameras for his second big-screen endeavor.

It was an Orion Pictures comedy called *Caddyshack*, and filming began in early September 1979 at the Rolling Hills Country Club near Davie, Florida. First-time director Harold Ramis cowrote the script with Douglas Kenney and Brian Doyle-Murray, and they were hoping to replicate the smashing success of *National Lampoon's Animal House*, the rollicking 1978 summer comedy written by Ramis, Kenney—a cofounder of *National Lampoon* magazine—and Chris Miller and featuring *Saturday Night Live*'s John Belushi as carefree, slovenly Delta House frat brother John "Bluto" Blutarsky, the movie's breakout star.

Animal House was, by Hollywood standards, a low-budget affair, which made its breakout success—it turned food fights and toga parties into national crazes—all the more astounding in its rowdy depiction of life at (mythical) Faber College in early 1960s Pennsylvania. (The movie was filmed over thirty-two days in the fall of 1977 at the University of Oregon in Eugene.) *Animal House* initially grossed over $120 million, rocketed Belushi into the stratosphere, and was the highest-grossing comedy film of all time until *Ghostbusters*—written by two of its stars, Ramis and *Saturday Night Live* alum Dan Aykroyd—came along in the summer of 1984.

Caddyshack was considered, by most, a sequel to *Animal House*, in spirit if not in its plot. "What we're trying to do is take *Animal House* and make it a little more coarse," Kenney explained, tongue planted firmly in cheek. The story arc centers around the personal lives of the caddies toiling at the highfalutin' Bushwood Country Club near Chicago. Its members' hubris is embodied by arrogant club cofounder Judge Elihu Smails (Ted Knight, so brilliant as dimwitted newscaster Ted Baxter from *The Mary Tyler Moore Show*). The role of Smails was offered to Bob Newhart, but he turned it down to shoot the big-screen movie flop *The First Family*.

"As for the *Caddyshack* part, I didn't think there was much real humor there," Newhart said.[1]

Rodney was cast as brash, boorish, foul-mouthed Al Czervik, an uncouth real estate developer/blowhard. Don Rickles was initially considered for the role—"he had the right obnoxiousness," Ramis said[2]—"but at the time Rodney had an amazing run on *The Tonight Show*, he was killing every time, he was just hysterically funny and we said, 'You know, maybe Rodney's the guy.' We didn't know if he could act, but even if he couldn't act just being himself would work for us."[3]

Caddyshack producer Jon Peters recalled how Rodney materialized at his office on the Warner Bros. lot for a meeting to discuss his role in the movie. "We brought him in, and he comes to the studio in a big black limo," he told author Chris Nashawaty. "He comes into my office in this aqua-blue leisure suit and takes out a plastic bag and does two lines of coke on the table. He sniffs the coke, undoes his shirt, and says, 'Where's the pussy?'"[4]

The setup of *Caddyshack* had *Saturday Night Live* stars Chevy Chase and Bill Murray playing preppy club playboy Ty Webb and Bushwood's mumbling, semi-psychotic groundskeeper, Carl Spackler, who spends his screen time trying to hunt down and kill a pesky gopher—that is digging up his beloved golf course—by any means necessary (including the use of a high-powered rifle).

The caddies were led by Michael O'Keefe in the role of rebellious Danny Noonan. O'Keefe had garnered critical acclaim as the teenaged put-upon son of Marine pilot Lieutenant Colonel Wilbur "Bull" Meecham, played by Robert Duvall, in the 1979 film drama *The Great Santini*. Cowriter Brian Doyle Murray based *Caddyshack* on his memories of working in an Illinois country club; he played gruff Lou Loomis, who is in charge of Bushwood's caddie corps.

Rodney's role as Al Czervik was not a throwaway; Czervik, the comedic antagonist, is central to the *Caddyshack* plot, particularly in his relationship with stuffy Judge Smails and life, in this case, imitated art since Knight was said to be annoyed with Rodney's scene-stealing.

Mark Canton, the executive in charge of production on *Caddyshack*, remembered some friction between Rodney and Ted Knight. "I don't think they really got along," he recalled. "I think Ted was very serious, a *Mary Tyler Moore Show* television-established kind of guy, and Rodney was a wild child, let's face it.

"We decided to go get Rodney, which some people thought was insane, but personally I think he was one of the funniest humans. When I watched him on Carson I laughed myself to sleep. I remember he was more of a gentleman, one-on-one, than you might expect based on his humor. But his humor came from a very deep place."[5]

Cindy Morgan, who played Judge Smails's niece Lacey Underall in *Caddyshack*: "Ted was trying to do his job and he's holding the script in his hand, and meanwhile Rodney is just running around saying whatever the heck popped into his head and Ted's trying to follow him. Ted was really angry."[6]

Rodney, though, was not an actor; he was a nightclub comedian who thrived off the energy of a live audience. Initially, he had trouble adjusting to the rhythms of both moviemaking, with its tedious downtime, and his on-screen alter ego. Chris Nashawaty, in his book *Caddyshack: The Making of a Hollywood Cinderella Story*, described Rodney's first scene before the cameras, when Al Czervik visits the pro shop with his shutterbug sidekick, Mr. Wang (Tsung-I Dow, who was, in real life, a history professor at Florida Atlantic University).

"On the first take," however, it did not go quite as planned. Not even close. When Ramis rolled the camera, hit the clappers, and called, "Action," Dangerfield just stood there like a redwood. Ramis got up from his chair and walked over to Rodney and asked if there was a problem. Was he ready to do the scene? "Sure," Dangerfield replied. Ramis returned to his chair, sat down, and again called, "Action." Nothing. Ramis went back over to where Dangerfield was standing and said, "Rodney, when I call 'Action,' that's your cue to come in and do the scene."

"You mean, do my bit?"

"Yes, do your bit."

Ramis again went back to his chair and called, "Action." Crickets. Ramis laughed incredulously, and said, "Okay, Rodney, now do your bit!" Dangerfield barged into the room and nailed it, even shoehorning in a hilarious line that he improvised on the spot: "You buy a hat like this, I bet you get a free bowl of soup."[7]

Michael O'Keefe was not in that scene, but he watched it being filmed. "Rodney was kind of hiding behind the little return in the wall that was being used as an entrance into the pro shop. And all of our cues when we do movies is ACTION! So they are setting up to do the scene, the camera rolls, the clapper comes out, does the clap, steps behind the camera and Harold Ramos goes 'Action!' Nothing happens. Rodney is right there. I can see him. Harold goes, 'Rodney?' Rodney goes, 'Yeah?' Harold says, 'Rodney, when I call 'Action!' that's your cue. And Rodney says, 'Oh, you want me to do the bit?' And Harold says, 'Yeah, do the bit,' and Rodney comes around the corner and nails it one take."[8]

Chevy Chase remembered it a bit differently. "Rodney couldn't act," he said. "I remember we shot a master shot on the eighteenth green with five or six of us standing there, and you have to do your lines the same every time. And he had some joke he put in there and then when they did the close-up, he said something different. You can't do that! It has to be cut together. He was not familiar with how movies are made."[9]

Rodney took some time to hit his stride in the acting department and was convinced he was bombing. "He was very, very nervous," recalled Cindy

Morgan. "I remember we had lunch together one day, just the two of us, and he was tugging at his collar just like he does in his act, saying, 'How am I doin'? How am I doin'? And I said, 'Rodney, you're stealing it.' He wasn't getting that instant reaction, and it was throwing him completely. Hearing people laugh was how he'd always gauged his timing. People who are funny are the most insecure people in the world."

On the nights before Rodney was scheduled to film a scene, Ramis would set aside some time to go over his lines with him to make them funnier. "Rodney needed every word, every syllable in place, every comma, every period," Ramis said.[10]

The *Caddyshack* set was notorious for the recreational drug use among its cast and crew, save for Ted Knight, who went to bed early every night and had just been diagnosed with the cancer that would kill him in 1986 at the age of sixty-two. Rodney, by this time, had added cocaine use to his everyday pot habit. "I did coke for a while," he recalled. "What a mistake that was. Coke is easy to start, and hard to stop . . . Coke makes you do stupid things . . . You do things on coke you wouldn't normally do, and you say things you wouldn't ordinarily say . . . The next morning you're beat, your heart's racing, you can't breathe, and you feel terrible."[11]

During the *Caddyshack* shoot, though, he stuck mostly to marijuana.

"Rodney smoked more pot than anybody," recalled cast member John Barmon (who played Smails's grandson, Spaulding). "He would get really stoned and walk around the halls of the hotel in his bathrobe with a towel wrapped around his neck and he'd see you and say, 'Hey, I want you to come listen to some of my set.' And you'd sit there in his room, and he had one of those old cassette players and he'd be really interested in your reaction . . . He was so paranoid it wasn't funny."[12]

"All the stories are true," O'Keefe said. "I was definitely partaking at the time. Rodney definitely enjoyed the party with us. He went, as we would say back in the day, 'toe to toe' with us. So, I'm not going to deny any of that. I don't want to give you the impression that we didn't show up to work and we didn't come with an agenda, and we didn't accomplish that agenda. We did. Somehow it was all part of the move in the '70s and we were all caught up in it. *Caddyshack* was not the only movie that had this issue and [that had] the 'cocaine budget,' as we used to refer to it. If you go back and look at the stories of *Lenny* with Dustin Hoffman and James Caan making *Thief*, that was the era, and everybody was partaking."[13]

Peter Berkrot, who played caddie Angie D'Annunzio in *Caddyshack*, recalled how much Rodney loved his weed . . . and other substances. "I was on my way back from someone's room; it must have been around eleven at night," he said. "Back in 1979, there were basically only three kinds of pot. If you had enough money you got Thai stick, but we mostly got stuck with the stuff where you had to break it apart and clean out the seeds. And I had a tray with weed walking through the lobby and saw Rodney and quicky went and hid my weed in my room. When I came back he said, 'Was that weed? You don't have to hide that. I love weed. You know what I love more than weed? Coke.' I thought he was doing a bit, but we found out he wasn't. The only person who didn't take drugs on the movie was Ted Knight."[14]

"It was a bunch of funny fucking people and some great actors like Bill Murray who were all thrown together in Florida at this hotel in Fort Lauderdale where nothing really worked," Mark Canton recalled. "Rodney had the room next to mine for a period of time. I was tossing paper basketballs into the wastebasket while I was watching TV late one night and I missed, and when I went to throw it in the garbage can, I sat up and hit my head on one of those hotel coffee makers . . . right on the part of the scalp that bleeds profusely.

"So, in a panic, as a Jewish kid from New York, I went next door with all this blood on me and I knock on Rodney's door. I go, 'Rodney, I need your help.' He came out in a silk robe which he was always wearing, even to the set. A silk robe and slippers. He goes, 'I'll be right back,' and he came back with a six-pack of Budweiser, and it was cold. He didn't have any ice and he wrapped the six-pack around my head, and we went to the emergency room. He was the guy who came through."[15]

Michael O'Keefe: "I show up in Florida on set, the first day, and I get introduced to Rodney and I said, 'Rodney, it's such a pleasure to meet you, you know, my father thinks you're the best comedian in the world.' He said,

'Hey, kid, great to meet you. Let me tell you, your teeth are really a mess, and my nephew is a dentist. I think maybe he can help you out.'

"And I'm like, 'Holy shit, Rodney, I'm about to go on camera with you and now you made me feel self-conscious about my teeth. Why did you say that?' He goes, 'Yeah, Florida, it's like a sauna with gnats, isn't it?' I'm like, 'Oh my God, what am I going to do?' He wasn't wrong. I ended up getting my teeth fixed later in life. But they weren't fixed then. But I was like, 'Now I can't smile.' I had to get over all of that to get on camera with him. But it was hilarious and there was not a day that I didn't laugh with him. He was really fun to be with – he was not unlike his act, but in person [he was] much more vulnerable. He was kind of open about himself and his capacities or what he considered to be his lack of capacities . . . and humble enough to know that he needed help when he didn't know what to do and when given the opportunity, he hit it out of the park.

"I loved him immeasurably."[16]

Caddyshack wrapped filming in Miami in mid-November, roughly ten weeks after shooting began and just before Rodney turned fifty-eight years old. He earned $35,000 for his work on the movie, which took his career to the next level and opened another rich revenue stream . . . though he later claimed he lost $150,000 on his *Caddyshack* deal due to missing a month's work in Las Vegas.[17]

A month after filming his final scene for *Caddyshack*, Rodney returned to television. He was shooting a special for ABC in Burbank, which was scheduled to air in the fall, when he took a spill off a four-foot-high ledge while taping a spoof of his Miller Lite beer commercials. He was taken to St. Joseph's Medical Center, then transferred to another hospital. "He just wanted everyone to know it's not serious," said his manager, Estelle Endler, and that was that.[18]

Rodney checked another pop-culture milestone off his list on March 8, 1980, when he hosted NBC's *Saturday Night Live*, with the J. Geils Band as that week's musical guest. *Caddyshack* was set to open in July and already the promotional engine was revving up: Rodney's *Caddyshack* costars, Ted Knight and Chevy Chase, hosted the show in December and February, respectively, Bill Murray was one of *SNL's* stars—though he left at the end of that season—and Brian Doyle-Murray joined the supporting cast as a featured player in January.

One of the show's trademarks was its opening monologue, and Rodney, who felt right at home in the clubby atmosphere, delivered a classic two minutes and started firing off one-liners as soon as he took the small stage in Studio 8H in Rockefeller Center. "I tell ya I can't relax you know?" he said, tugging at his requisite red tie and shrugging his shoulders nervously. "The other night I was in a place I felt like having a few drinks, ya know? I went over to the bartender and said, 'Surprise me.' He showed me a naked picture of my wife!"

"I was an ugly kid, too, I had plenty of pimples. One day I fell asleep in a library, I woke up and a blind man was reading my face!"

"Yesterday was a beauty, too. I asked a cab driver where can I get some action—he took me to my house."[19]

The following week, at Dangerfield's, he recorded a new album, *Rodney Dangerfield: No Respect*, delivering a monologue to the live audience that lasted seventy-five minutes and resulted in a five-minute standing ovation. Sample: "My fan club broke up. The guy died." In late March, he opened for nine nights at the Riviera Hotel in Las Vegas, where he welcomed a reporter to his suite wearing opera slippers and a knee-length navy blue bathrobe: "His voice is more than usually adenoidal. His nose droops mournfully between triple bullseyes of sleeplessness ringing his bulging blue eyes. It is 2 p.m."[20] He returned there in April to open for Canadian singer Anne Murray.

Rodney Dangerfield: No Respect was released by Casablanca Records in July with an advance sale of 250,000 copies. "On his new album, several one-liners are actually vintage Dangerfield as a consequence of previous exposure on shows hosted by Johnny, Merv and Mike," *The Boston Globe* noted in its review. "However, there are so many boffo lines, despite an excess of typically blue nightclub material, that *No Respect* deserves a place in your comedy album collection. The 'Poor Soul' of the '80s verbalizes numerous contretemps . . . There are the obligatory I-was-so-fat putdowns, too, as in: he was so fat that when he got his shoes shined, he had to take the guy's word for it."[21]

The *New York Daily News:* "It is laced with a wonderfully rich sense of humor. However, it is not for family listening . . . a closer listen shows the man to be as bright and witty as any comedian. This album is a real gas. And so is Rodney."[22]

". . . His vulgarity is pointed, not aimless in the chic Steve Martin mode," noted the *Fort Lauderdale News* critic. "He's also funny as hell . . . Dangerfield is hardly a feminist, for instance, but there's a kind of innocence behind Rodney's most derogatory laughs that wipes out your qualms."[23]

IN LATE JULY, RODNEY HOSTED A PRESS CONFERENCE AT DANGERfield's to promote the premiere of *Caddyshack*. He was joined by costars Ted Knight, Chevy Chase, and Bill Murray. It did not go well. Doug Kenney greeted the assembled journalists—"Glad you can all be here"—before turning his ire to one reporter and cursing him out. Rodney and Ted Knight were "aghast," at Kenney's bile, while Murray continued to munch on his pizza, seemingly oblivious to what was going on around him. Kenney later had to be removed from the press conference after repeatedly "shouting a biological obscenity" to a reporter who had exchanged barbs with Murray, who felt ignored by the journalists and, at one point—when quizzed about his role as Carl Spackler, a Vietnam vet—snapped at the reporter, "You're real perceptive. Takes brains to figure that out."

Rodney, for his part, said he was surprised at how he looked on the big screen. "I thought I was younger and better-looking," he joked. Knight said he could not tell if the movie would be received kindly after attending the previous night's preview.[24]

"I remember the premiere was a fiasco in New York," Mark Canton recalled. "We went to Dangerfield's the night before, Rodney performed and he brought everyone up. Nobody was passing on the substances at Dangerfield's—which was like a hallowed ground for comedians in New York—or at the premiere. It was kind of a shit show."

Caddyshack opened July 25, 1980 to a mixed reception. Rodney, for his part, was singled out by critics for his memorable performance as Al Czervik. The *St. Louis Post-Dispatch:* "Rather raucous, not-very-funny comedy as

Chevy Chase, Rodney Dangerfield, Ted Knight and Bill Murray take turns trying to upstage one another with their old nightclub routines (sic) while the minimal plot line drifts away."[25]

The *San Francisco Examiner:* "The only life in this film is provided by Dangerfield, who plays a loud-mouthed, fast-quipping real estate developer . . . It's too bad the whole film wasn't fashioned around him, since he makes mush out of the other comics. He has a certain electricity; let's hope he makes more films."[26]

Newsday: "The new Orion Pictures comedy . . . is a loosely woven fabric of caricatures and burlesque situations that is enhanced by a cast of heavyweight performers . . . The chief subverter is played by Rodney Dangerfield, impeccably cast as a maddeningly noisy, cheerfully vulgar multi-millionaire visitor who violates every taboo of the smug club members."[27]

The *New York Times:* "'Caddyshack' is a pleasantly loose-limbed sort of movie with some comic moments, most of them belonging to Mr. Dangerfield, who predates 'Animal House' by a number of years."[28]

The *New York Daily News:* "'Caddyshack' is, by anybody's standards, the bottom of the barrel . . . There is no plot. Three writers are credited with the execrable script, but the actors seem to be making up the vignettes as they go along from old nightclub routines and scraps of scratch-pad paper from the garbage cans at *Saturday Night Live.* What you get is sewage-faced Bill Murry as a sub-mental cretin who mumbles his way through the movie blowing up gopher holes and playing with himself. You also get Rodney Dangerfield, spouting filth in yellow shirts, purple pants, and plaid coats while he O.D.s on jokes that depend heavily on flatulence and other bathroom activities."[29]

The *Atlantic City Press:* "Master comics Rodney Dangerfield and Chevy Chase are the films only saving graces . . . Dangerfield, with his obnoxious attitude, always injects humor into the film, using many of the one-liners that made him famous. Even though the jokes are as old as the dirt on which Dangerfield stands, they are still funny."[30]

When all was said and done, *Caddyshack* earned nearly $40 million at the box office and a loyal cult following that exists to this day. Singer Kenny

Loggins, too, benefited from the movie's success. *Caddyshack* launched his soundtrack single, "I'm Alright," into the Top Ten.

"At the end of the day it's all about the results," said Mark Canton. "When I started playing golf years later, at the age of forty, I became the legend because, no matter what movies I had been responsible for afterward—*Batman* to *Lethal Weapon*—all the guys would want to know from me is, 'Tell me the *Caddyshack* stories.' So it really stood the test of time. Rodney was a big reason because he was funny. All of his routines that he pulled out were fantastic. And he was very serious about his comedy, about every line, and so he did question Harold [Ramis] all the time. He wanted to be great, and I think, in a way, by being himself, he was great."[31]

Caddyshack also paved the way for Rodney's newfound movie career, which was in solid shape by the time they got around to making *Caddyshack II* in 1988. Rodney demanded $7 million to reprise his role as Al Czervik but eventually dropped out of the project, which went through various iterations and directors. He was replaced by Jackie Mason playing a boorish Al Czervik type named Jack Hartounian, with Dan Aykroyd recruited to play an ex-Marine food truck vendor who runs afoul of the gopher (a la Bill Murray's Carl Spackler). Robert Stack was cast in the Ted Knight role as the elitist president of Bushwood Country Club. *Caddyshack II* bombed out of the gate, grossed only $12 million, and sank like a stone.

COMEDIAN DENNIS BLAIR JOINED RODNEY'S INNER CIRCLE SHORTLY after *Caddyshack* opened. He eventually opened for Rodney on the road and became a close friend and professional collaborator for several years before a falling out ended their relationship.

"I was a musician/singer and kind of did double duty with a guitar/comedy act for a couple of months and we [he and his wife, Peg] moved to Manhattan. We were four blocks from Dangerfield's," Blair recalled. "I went on an open mic night to try my little act and it went over really well, and they hired me to open for Jackie Mason. One of those nights, Rodney came in—I had never met him before—and I got a good reaction from the crowd.

"That night when I came off stage, Rodney is standing there. He said,

'They obviously like what you do. What do you do?' I told him, 'Well, I do song parodies and songs and stuff.' He goes, 'Oh, I'm going to watch you.' So he watched the second show and really liked it and then, the following week, he had me open for him at the club. So that's how it all began."[32]

Rodney was on a career roll. That fall, in November, he opened as a headliner in Las Vegas for the first time at the Sahara Hotel, just as the news broke that he was working on a screenplay for an Orion movie—subject unknown—and was preparing another special for ABC to air during the 1981–82 television season. Still, his self-awareness and expectations, tinged with world-weariness, reared their heads. "What keeps me going is anticipating new projects," he said. "It's exciting to see how they'll turn out. Unfortunately, the anticipation is usually better than the realization."[33]

He was in a philosophical mood in that immediate post-*Caddyshack* period. In an interview with *The Desert Sun* in Palm Springs, for which he sat while performing at the Sahara, he talked about his nearly lifelong devotion to marijuana and said he thought that pot should be legalized.

"Well, if booze is, marijuana should be, too," he said. "You find more accidents and problems with booze than with pot." The man who made a living by getting no respect was asked if smoking pot made him laugh at life, at least just a little. "No . . . it just gives your head a little change, you know what I mean? Makes you hungry. You can be in a good mood and smoke pot and be in a worse mood. Who knows where it'll take you? If you're nervous, it'll calm you down a little bit. How can you be in show business this many years and not be familiar with pot? I've smoked pot many times"—even after his live appearances at venues such as the Westbury Music Fair on Long Island or in Atlantic City.[34]

"I would get high with him right after the show. First thing he would do," recalled Rodney's booking agent, Dennis Arfa. "I would walk back in the room and get high and he would go, 'You high, man? Good shit, man.' Actually, he needed the marijuana because he was depressed and angry. The marijuana mellowed him. I could tell if he was smoking or not. It was a good medicinal thing for him. He didn't do it before he went onstage because he didn't want to forget his lines."

Arfa entered Rodney's orbit around this time. He was an agent at William Morris and was representing Billy Joel and the Beach Boys, whose manager introduced him to Rodney's trusted manager, Estelle Endler. "The meeting was set up for me to meet Rodney," Arfa recalled. "I think it was at the Westbury Music Fair. I took Billy Joel with me. Rodney and I seemed to kind of hit it off. I think the vibe was right; I was thirty-one and he was about fifty-nine.

"He really hated William Morris. He felt that they took advantage of him during the Catskill days. Rodney was a big provoker years later when I was looking to leave William Morris. When Estelle died he said, 'Listen, you stay here, I'm leaving. I can't give these fuckers any more commission.' He had a hatred for them. Like in the guts. It was primal. They were old school. He would call them more like 'square fucks.'"

When Arfa decided to leave William Morris in the mid-1980s to start his own company, QBQ, Rodney was there to help him establish himself in many ways.

"I thought, 'What the fuck am I still doing here?'" Arfa recalled. "So I picked up with another associate, found office space and left—and Rodney advanced me $43,000 for future commissions to be able make the move. I had Rodney, Billy Joel, the Beach Boys, John Cafferty, Ted Nugent. I loved Rodney in my way. I had a real affinity for him. I was working with the best. I believed that. I believed I was working with The King. I worked with some very big artists, and I still do.

"But Rodney was very special, right from my heart."[35]

Rodney was scheduled to close out 1980 with a New Year's Eve performance in Orlando, but fate had other ideas. He was driving near Fort Lauderdale on Christmas Eve, where he had just played the Sunrise Theater, when his car skidded on the wet pavement. He dislocated his shoulder in the ensuing accident and was forced to cancel his Friday and Saturday night shows at the Lakeland Civic Center.

In late February 1981, Rodney performed at the Grammy Awards, joining music luminaries including Barbra Streisand, Dionne Warwick, and George Jones—and waltzed off the Radio City Music Hall stage in New York City with a Grammy for his comedy album *No Respect*. "There's a guy in my neighborhood who wants to melt it down," he joked after winning the award, but he was thrilled with the honor.

In March, he began work on his next album, for Polygram, and, in May, he won "Entertainer of the Year," joining Dolly Parton, Carol Burnett, ABBA, Diana Ross, Barbra Streisand, and several others. The awards were handed out in a syndicated broadcast that aired on over one hundred stations in June and July and was hosted by Mike Douglas, one of Rodney's early television benefactors. Rodney also performed on the telecast, which was taped at Caesars Palace in Las Vegas.

Shortly thereafter, Rodney was onstage at the Aladdin Hotel in Las Vegas, about to segue into his encore, when he was surprised by host David Frost for an NBC television special celebrating thirty years of *This Is Your Life,* the series made famous its by creator, Ralph Edwards, who last hosted the show in 1972. (It returned briefly in 1983 with host Joseph Campanella.) Edwards would surprise celebrities and notable personalities, armed with his "Big Red Book" and proceed to recount their lives and achievements by bringing out friends, family, and colleagues to share stories about the stunned honoree and reminisce about the good old days.

Now, it was Rodney's turn. The cameras followed Frost as he walked onstage. "Look who's here," a flustered Rodney said, shaking Frost's hand. "David Frost, ladies and gentlemen, how about that? What are you doing here? I haven't finished my bit." He was wearing his trademark dark suit, white shirt, and red tie and mopping the sweat off his face and brow with a white handkerchief as Frost went into his spiel: "Rodney Dangerfield, comedian, actor, father of Brian and Melanie, the man who, from coast to coast, gets no respect, This Is Your Life!" They walked to the side of the stage and sat on facing chairs in front of a television monitor as the next twenty-plus minutes unfolded. Rodney lit up a cigarette and could not resist joking about it: "I have a crazy doctor—told me to keep smoking if I want to stop chewing gum."

Frost gave a brief biographical introduction of Rodney's early years as Jacob Cohen in Queens and mentioned his job working before and after school at a candy store called Giskin's. "Yeah, I used to mind a newsstand every morning there," Rodney said. "I got a buck a week for that for five days, you know?"

There followed a bevy of guests, each introduced by their offstage voiceover narration as Rodney tried to guess who each person was before they materialized on the stage. First in line was Charlie Burke, a childhood friend from P.S. 99 and Richmond Hill High School who talked about their baseball team, the Kew Gardens Giants, and their big rivals, the Forest Hills Ravens (Rodney laughed aloud when hearing that). Charlie told a story about how Rodney would sneak into the movies for free—and then, when he was an usher in that same theater, would let his friends in through a backstage door.

Charlie Burke was followed by Rodney's *Caddyshack* costar, Chevy Chase—who delivered a taped message from the set of his latest movie—and then a clip from Rodney's monologue on *Saturday Night Live*. Frost showed Rodney's photo from his high school yearbook, which included the caption "He sleeps by day," and then it was on to Sally Marr, Lenny Bruce's mother, who recounted meeting Rodney when he was a singing waiter at the Polish Falcon ("He didn't have much of an act but he sure had a lot of nerve"). "Rodney and my son hung out for a long time, they did a lot of crazy things," she said. "They used to work on their bits back in New York in the '40s." Sally was followed by Robert Klein, a taped message from Rodney's friends Jerry Stiller and Anne Meara, and his housekeeper and cook, Thelma Gopi.

Frost closed out the show by bringing out twenty-year-old Brian, who was a student at New York University, and sixteen-year-old Melanie, who attended the Dwight School in New York. Robert Wuhl came out as Rodney's supposedly long-lost son, Rupert Dangerfield, and the president of the Rodney Dangerfield Fan Club was there, along with many of Rodney's costars from the Miller Lite beer commercials including Happy Hairston, Bubba Smith, Boom-Boom Geoffrion, Lee Meredith, Jim Honochick, and Norm Snead.

Rodney spent the bulk of 1981 working on his act, touring, and making what seemed to be his weekly visits to *The Tonight Show Starring Johnny Carson* and other television appearances (Merv Griffin, Mike Douglas, Dinah Shore, et al.). On December 31, he left Dangerfield's for a few hours to star in Radio City Music Hall's annual New Year's Eve bash, where he was supported by comedians Michael Davis and Dennis Blair.

"*Caddyshack* came out and he became, like, this huge superstar, the hottest comic in America, and he couldn't fit into his own club—there were too many people who would come and they would be wrapped around the block," Blair recalled. "So he had to start doing theaters and he brought me along with him.

"Pretty soon after he started doing the theaters . . . he realized that so many gigs were like four hours away from New York, so if there were any gigs like that, he would just rent a rock-star bus, you know, those touring buses . . . and my girlfriend, who was now my wife, Peg, would come with us. It would be Rodney, me, and Peg in the bus and it was hilarious because he'd stop every once in a while at a gas station to get cigarettes or something and this tour bus would pull up and all of these people going, 'Who's that? The Eagles? The Who?' And this old Jewish man would get off to get cigarettes."[36]

RODNEY WAS SIXTY YEARS OLD NOW AND, OCCASIONALLY, THE CRACKS started to show in his stand-up performances. The reviews were not always laudatory. *Los Angeles Times* critic Lawrence Christon went to see Rodney's act at the Dorothy Chandler Pavilion—home to many of the Academy Awards ceremonies—in February 1982.

"However well-honed his act is, he's distractible," he wrote. "We saw him meander, and lapse into fits and starts, as though he had other things on his mind besides what he wanted to say and how he wanted to say it . . . Dangerfield is a curiosity. He's a quintessential old-time nightclub comedian, with brisk one-liners that snap out like left jabs at targets you would think are unfashionable to vilify these days . . . Women are objects of sexual chance that always spell trouble; gays are simply exotic and incomprehensible . . . He overstayed his welcome on stage; his act began to trail off limply. He doesn't ad-lib well, and sometimes his crudeness doesn't have the smartening effect a low remark will have when well placed. Occasionally toward the end he seemed a little thuggish, out of his element. It was like seeing a good club fighter finding himself overmatched."[37]

His appearance on NBC's *The Tomorrow Show* did not go well when he accused beetle-browed host Tom Snyder of breaching an agreement not to ask him personal questions. He was not always welcoming to reporters, if only because they asked the same questions over and over again—and they always harped on the "no respect" shtick. It had to be tiresome. "In real life he has corrected that situation through a policy of controlled access based on self-interest," a reporter for the *Miami Herald* observed. "His management emphasized, and Dangerfield reiterated, that he strongly dislikes interviews. He is granting them now only to obtain advance publicity for the television special. Rodney himself voiced his displeasure with the critics. "Every review, 40 jokes," he said. "It's ridiculous."

Still, the occasional bad night and bad press clipping did not slow him down. *Caddyshack* was still fresh in the minds of the public, as were Rodney's Miller Lite beer commercials, which were voted the top ad campaign of 1981 by a New York research firm called Video Storyboard.[38] He was later named "Star Presenter of the Year" by *Advertising Age* and was reportedly earning more than $250,000 from his television commercials.[39]

Rodney used the windfall to buy a $2 million mansion in the tony Connecticut town of Westport, fifty-five miles northeast of Manhattan. He enjoyed walking the local beaches, getting away from the grind and, occasionally, dropping in at the local comedy club, unannounced, to do a set. Westport was his home away from home; in 1985, he donated $4,000 to the community to buy flags to commemorate the town's 150th birthday.

The roomy house had an indoor pool in a wood-paneled room with a skylight, another room with a Jacuzzi, and some exercise equipment. A small study housed Rodney's showbiz mementos. Stafford Borg, Rodney's Man Friday, did the cooking and managed the house; he also accompanied Rodney on the road.

It was at the Westport house that Dennis Blair's friendship with Rodney took a yearslong detour.

"I would go to his house all the time to write," he said. "He lived in Westport, and this was really taking up most of my time. My wife Peg and I said, 'Can we bring our dog from Port Jefferson because we have to leave her alone?' and he said, 'Sure, but don't take her swimming in my pool.' We weren't planning on it. The long short story is that Rodney goes to take a nap and Peg and I are in the Jacuzzi in his house and my dog comes over, licks my face, and falls into the Jacuzzi. Rodney wakes up, sees this wet dog, and is convinced that we took the dog in the pool. And he would not be talked out of it. I tried to say, 'Rodney, this is what happened,' 'No, no, you're horrible people,' that kind of thing. But he didn't fire me right away. He also knew that I had some disagreements with Estelle Endler, and the third thing was that Joan Rivers's people had reached out to me, and he hated her because he felt that she was stealing jokes from him.

"So, I told him that they called me, and I said I couldn't work for Joan because they knew how Rodney felt and I turned them down. Rodney said, 'No, no, you got to do it, she cohosts *The Tonight Show* sometimes.' So I signed the contract in ten days. Three days later, Rodney says, 'I don't want you to do it.' I'm going, 'I signed a contract.' So those three things put the kibosh on me and Rodney for a while. But we semi-made-up years later, so it was kind of a happy ending."[40]

HOLLYWOOD BECKONED. RODNEY WAS SCHEDULED TO START SHOOTing his next movie, *Easy Money*, in Chicago that summer and was reportedly in the running for a remake of the W. C. Fields classic *My Little Chickadee* (that project never came to fruition—one can only imagine Rodney in the title role). He had another ABC primetime special on tap, *It's Not Easy Bein' Me*, which he taped in August 1981. It was scheduled to air in November, then was moved to February, and now was finally going to see the light of the television screen.

If Rodney needed any more validation that he was now a national treasure, he received it in spades when the Smithsonian Institution announced that it asked him to donate a white shirt and red tie, along with a black suit, to be displayed in its National Museum of American History in Washington, D.C. "It is very flattering, I guess," he said. "But I'm sixty years old, so I can't do cartwheels. They'll put 'em in there somewhere, so when I'm dead, they'll remember me, huh?"[41]

Rodney wore an open-collared green shirt with a black suit for the presentation ceremony and was pleased to learn that his iconic shirt/tie/jacket combo would hang alongside Jimmy Durante's hat, Irving Berlin's piano, Judy Garland's ruby slippers from *The Wizard of Oz*, and Archie Bunker's armchair from *All in the Family*. "I have a feeling you're going to use this shirt to clean Lindbergh's plane," he joked to the museum's curator, Carl Scheele—who assured him that "Your shirt and tie may get no respect, but we've given them respectability."[42]

It's Not Easy Bein' Me (finally!) aired on May 12, 1982 and the critics deemed it worth the wait. Bill Murray, Rodney's *Caddyshack* costar, was his guest—he resurrected his *Saturday Night Live* lounge crooner, Nick—along with actress Valerie Perrine and the Queen of Soul, Aretha Franklin, who belted out "Respect" as Rodney boogied in the background with Franklin's backup singers. "It's not off-color and it's not sophisticated—it's just funny," opined the *New York Daily News*. "And it keeps being funny through skit after skit, which by today's comedy standards is a surprise. But Dangerfield has been on the comedy scene a long time and he has learned the secret of comedy—and good timing."[43]

It's Not Easy Bein' Me finished in twelfth place for the week in the primetime race—sandwiched between *The Love Boat* and NBC's *Quincy*—helping to lead ABC to its third consecutive primetime ratings victory.

That summer, Rodney lost weight . . . and gained a new love.

He needed to slim down and to quit his heavy (tobacco) smoking habit, walking around as he did with filtered, unfiltered, and menthol cigarettes in his pockets: "Sometimes I'd quit for a whole day. Then I'd give myself a reward—a cigarette."[44]

In an effort to shed the extra pounds, he returned to the Pritikin Longevity Center, a well-known weight-loss center in Santa Monica where he sweated, exercised, revitalized, and tried to lose weight and quit smoking. Rodney had spent time there before and once encountered his celebrity friend Buddy Hackett, who was there with Hollywood producer Arthur Friedman.

"Picture putting Rodney Dangerfield into this place," Friedman said. "The backdrop of it was that it was some kind of historical landmark . . . and it was right on the beach in Santa Monica. It was a place where it was very expensive to go, like four thousand dollars a week. You had princes and royalty and very popular people coming from all over the world. It had a big dining room facing the ocean, but your rooms were nothing.

"Buddy Hackett and I walked into the dining room one evening about six o'clock and there is Rodney sitting at a table, alone. All the chairs were pushed up against the table so no one else could sit there. He sees Buddy, Buddy sees him. 'Hey, Rodney, how you doing? You want to sit with us?' And the next thing Buddy says to him is, 'Say hello to Arthur Friedman. He owns movie theaters.' And Rodney's first words to me were, 'You steal money, right?' And my response to him was, 'Only from your movies, Rodney.' Which he actually laughed at. And he didn't laugh very much.

"We became a threesome there—Hackett, me, and Rodney," Friedman said. "We would do the treadmill together; we would take a walk on Ocean Avenue together. One of the funny things I noticed about Rodney was that the moment he had any kind of conversation at the table, he would do that thing with his neck, even though he was wearing a jumpsuit, where he would, like, adjust his tie, which wasn't on. He would do that in conversation. But he was kind of quiet. He was a normal guy.

"Rodney would say, 'You come here to do this shit? This is fucking terrible. Walking. All this eating cardboard shit.' He would just hate it. He was there for . . . a booze thing, cocaine, and he had the pot. He was not very serious about it."[45]

It was at the Pritikin Center, during Rodney's stay there in 1993, that he met Joan Child, a thirty-year-old Utah-born businesswoman who grew up in a Mormon household and now owned a flower shop in Santa Monica. The two opposites attracted—in a big way.

"He lived in New York but was in town staying at the nearby Pritikin Longevity Center trying to lose weight and get healthier," she recalled. "Part of their program included taking morning walks. Being a diehard fan, I recognized Rodney immediately. I was sixteen when I first saw him on *The Tonight Show* and suddenly there he was, fourteen years later, walking towards me, the funniest man in the world."

Rodney and Joan struck up a conversation and Rodney began dropping by her shop to watch her arrange flowers.

"For me, it was love at first sight, the Holy Grail of encounters," she said. "He was fascinating and had those soulful azure-blue eyes, the color of the sky on a clear day. I couldn't look at him without smiling."[46]

"Joan was amazing, and she really loved him," recalled Fabio, who was a mutual friend of Rodney and Joan's. "I mean, there was a point when Rodney was drinking really heavily. He had a drinking problem. He met Joan and suddenly he was sober. He lost tons of weight when he was in L.A. He was doing great. You could see he was back to normal. As soon as he met Joan, she was the light with him. She was so good to him and loved him so much. She turned his life around. When Rodney moved to L.A., he looked much younger [and] his face looked younger. You could tell he wasn't drinking anymore."[47]

RODNEY'S NEXT MOVIE, *Easy Money*, LOOKED LIKE A WINNER ON PAPER. The movie, written by Rodney, Dennis Blair, Michael Endler, and P. J. O'Rourke, would be helmed by Joe Sedelmaier, the renowned director behind a collection of hilarious television ads including spots for Federal Express, starring fast-talking John Moschitta, Jr., and Wendy's hamburger commercials that turned senior citizen Clara Peller into a short-lived phenomenon ("Where's the Beef?!").

Dennis Blair remembers that he came up with the original idea for *Easy Money* shortly after he began his association with Rodney in the immediate aftermath of the *Caddyshack* tidal wave.

"We're talking in his dressing room and he says, 'Hey, Orion Pictures just came to me and they want to do a movie starring me since *Caddyshack* was such a big hit,' and he goes to me, 'So if you come up with an idea for a movie, let me know.' I run back to my apartment and pace the floor until I come up with an idea about a guy who has to quit smoking and drinking for one year so he can get ten million dollars. I told Rodney the idea and he said, 'Oh, it's pretty good.' So he submitted it to Orion, they approve it. He wrote part of it, and he got two other writers, P. J. O'Rourke, and Michael Endler and—this is the greatest story—he calls me up and goes, 'I read the script and it's a piece of shit. I'm going to send it to you and I want you to tell me what you think of it.'

"So he sends me the script, I read it. It's a first draft. Not bad. It needs some work. I tell him, 'Rodney, I read the script and it needs some work' and I couldn't get in, 'it's okay' and he cuts me off and goes, 'That's what I thought, it's a piece of shit.' He calls his manager, Estelle Endler, who's Michael Endler's wife, and says, 'Dennis agrees with me, it's a piece of shit. I want Dennis writing on the movie.' So now I'm suddenly a writer, but the first week of writing sessions was horrible because [O'Rourke and Endler] are glaring at me . . . but I straightened that out immediately."[48]

Orion was hoping for lightning to strike twice for Rodney following the success of *Caddyshack*. He was cast in the lead role as loutish photographer Monty Capuletti. Joe Pesci, hot off his Oscar-nominated turn opposite Robert De Niro in *Raging Bull*, was hired to play Monty's best friend, Nicky, in a cast that included Oscar nominee Geraldine Fitzgerald, veteran actress Candice Azzara as Monty's wife, Rose, and Jennifer Jason Leigh as their daughter, Allison.

"I auditioned on tape with a different hair color and I didn't get the part," recalled Azzara. "The director wanted someone funny-looking, and Rodney didn't want that, he wanted me. He saw me in *Fatso* and in *House Calls* and he said, 'That's my wife, that's the one I want.'"[49]

The project got off to an inauspicious start when production began in Chicago in the early summer of 1982. First, Rodney was out of action, suffering from a bad cold, and then he clashed with Sedelmaier, who was working on the script with *Saturday Night Live* writer Tim Kazurinsky.

"When we met I said, 'Rodney, I don't want to be held down by the script that way it is, a hodgepodge of gags and one-liners. I want to be free to make changes,'" Sedelmaier recalled in *Point of View*, a documentary about his career. "When a thing is too good to be true, it is . . . I spent the next few months back and forth between L.A., New York, and Chicago, casting, scouting locations, and hammering out a script with Rodney. But each meeting was getting more and more contentious. He wanted to add more gags. And now I was getting this thing about not being a team player, aside from the fact that I was a 'control freak.'

"Then, after a lot of wrangling back and forth, Rodney said he wanted to go back to the original script. And Rodney made it easy. He decided we'd be codirectors—he'd direct his scenes and I'd direct those scenes in which he didn't appear. No way. We took a meeting with the studio heads and I was given a choice: 'Go with Rodney or else.' I picked 'or else.'"[50]

Sedelmaier, and Chicago, were out. The parties reached a financial settlement, citing "creative differences," and agreed not to publicly discuss Sedelmaier's exit from the movie, an agreement that Rodney initially adhered to . . . until he did not. "He told me he didn't want me to have any jokes," he said in August.[51] Rodney's agent told the *Chicago Tribune* that Sedelmaier "rewrote the script and wrote Rodney right out of the picture."

Rodney and Orion pivoted to James Signorelli, a film segment producer for *Saturday Night Live* since 1976. Signorelli was hired to replace Sedelmaier, and shooting finally got underway, in New York City, in the fall of 1982.

Billy Joel, who was a friend of Rodney's, read the script and liked it so much he contributed a song, appropriately entitled "Easy Money," which was included on his new album, *An Innocent Man*. Rodney returned the favor by appearing briefly in Joel's video for "Tell Her About It," which was set at a fictional episode of *The Ed Sullivan Show*, where Joel walks off the stage and greets Rodney, who is waiting in the wings. The video went into heavy rotation on MTV, the twenty-four-hour music video network that sprung to life the previous year, further growing Rodney's younger audience.

"They respected each other as artists," Dennis Arfa said of Billy Joel and Rodney. "Rodney always had a high respect for Billy as a musician, and Billy thought Rodney was amazing. They had a mutual collaboration."[52]

"THIS MOVIE, IT'S KILLIN' ME," RODNEY SAID AS SHOOTING ON *Easy Money* got underway. "I'm a nightclub comic. I can't go to sleep until 3:30 in the morning. On this picture, they get me up at 4:30. I don't want to be the star no more. I want to maybe write a movie and appear in a few of the scenes. You know, just enough scenes so I'm in the goddamn thing, but not enough so I'm busting my ass every day."[53]

Rodney was not serious, of course—though the hours were brutal, and he was in every scene. But he could relate to parts of Monty Capuletti's life. Monty is a pot-smoking, heavy-drinking, hard-living baby photographer in Staten Island who loves to gamble and dresses loudly. He is married to Rose (Azzara) and, when the movie opens, their daughter, Allison (Leigh), is engaged to Julio (Taylor Negron) and getting ready for her wedding.

Lili Haydn, who was eleven at the time, played Monty's youngest daughter, Belinda. Haydn was an extremely talented violinist; *Easy Money* was one of her few acting roles (including the *Columbo* spin-off series, *Mrs. Columbo*, and the syndicated television show *The New Gidget*) before she fashioned a career as a renowned musician and social activist.

"He was super-nice," she said of Rodney. "My job in the film was to basically make fun of him and he was really cool with that, and I think he was really amused by how wicked I was as a child. We sort of sparred a little bit, like fun in that way. I would mimic him. That was my gig in the movie. I yelled at him and scolded him for not eating right . . . which was basically not a stretch for me because that's how I lived my life.

"I remember there was one scene at the breakfast table where we were all taking food from the center of the table and they directed me to take the sausages and then take one more—and Rodney thought that was hilarious."[54]

The setup for *Easy Money* is that Monty does not have a good relationship with his wealthy mother-in-law, Kathleen (Fitzgerald), who runs a chain of department stores and looks down on her slovenly son-in-law. She dies unexpectedly in a plane crash after Allison's wedding and, in her will, she leaves $10 million to Monty, with the proviso that he lose weight and surrender his vices—smoking, drinking, and gambling—for one year.

Monty struggles mightily but he comes through in the end with the help of Nicky and lives up to his end of the deal . . . just as Kathleen returns from the dead. As it turns out, she faked her own death just so Monty would reform his bad ways. She lets him keep the $10 million and he buys a mansion into which Kathleen moves—and, once again, she makes him miserable. But Monty has a secret hideaway for when the going gets tough, and he has the last laugh—hanging out with Nicky and his friends, eating pizza, drinking beer, and playing poker. All's well that ends well.

"Rodney was a very gentle soul and that's what I loved about him," said Candice Azzara. "He was terrified of doing our 'love scene'—all we did was talk—but it was like he was terrified of showing his emotions. That scene was very painful for him. He was kind of shy and a gentleman. I just saw the sadness in his eyes—even though he made a lot of jokes, he seemed like the saddest man I knew.

"He and Joe Pesci were very good on camera—they had very good chemistry together—but it didn't seem like they connected in person," she said. "There was nothing there, like a friendship or anything, yet on camera they looked like the best of friends."[55]

Dennis Blair: "Pesci wanted to hang out with Rodney in character, you know, like, 'Let's go to the track and hang out' and Rodney said, 'I don't do that. Here's what I do. You throw a line at me, and I throw a line at you. That's what I do.' I see Pesci's eyes going, 'Oh my God, can I get out of this?'"[56]

Easy Money was rated R for some brief nudity and opened in theaters in mid-August. You can call it Rodney Dangerfield's sophomore slump at the age of sixty-one; the movie was almost universally panned, with most of the critics' ire reserved for Rodney (Joe Pesci's performance was praised by many). "Dangerfield may have a gift for stand-up comedy, but he lacks the acting ability and variation to dominate a full-length picture," the *Dayton Daily News* opined. "The shallowness of Dangerfield's routine becomes evident during longer stretches, and in the case of *Easy Money* it's impossible to overlook the transparency of his character."[57]

The Detroit Free-Press was more succinct: "Let's get it over with: *Easy Money* and co-star-writer-star Rodney Dangerfield deserve no respect."[58]

Janet Maslin, the renowned film critic for *The New York Times*, gave the movie a barely passing grade. It could have been worse. "Mr. Dangerfield has some funny moments here, but he also has a screen presence that's decidedly strange," she wrote. "He won't stand still, being given to constant jerking motions, and neither will he refrain from eye rolling and mugging at the slightest opportunity. Almost never, during the course of a very long 95 minutes, do these tics have anything to do with what is ostensibly going on . . . A number of performers, also including Joe Pesci as Monty's buddy and Candy Azzara as his wife, take an earnest approach to roles that hardly seem to warrant one."[59]

The *Hartford Courant*: "Awful, awful, awful . . . The film idolizes slobbery and loutishness. It's skimpy in the joke department and flabby in every other way."[60]

The *Chicago Tribune*'s critic Gene Siskel liked the movie. "The big discovery in the comedy *Easy Money* is that Rodney Dangerfield, unlike most stand-up comics, does not need dialogue to be funny. He is funny standing still—or his version of standing still . . ."[61]

The critic for Newhouse News Service disagreed with Siskel. "If Rodney Dangerfield really wants our respect he'll have to do better than *Easy Money*, which plumbs new depths of the comedy of slobishness . . . It's a good comic premise, but even with the help of three other writers Dangerfield can't really squeeze much genuine humor out of it . . . A taste for Rodney Dangerfield, like a taste for raw oysters, must be painfully acquired. The only difference is that comedy as gross as Dangerfield's is never in season."[62]

Easy Money might have been a major misstep in Rodney's movie career on a metaphorical screen level; in real life, two months after the movie's release, he took a literal misstep by falling off a four-foot-high platform while filming his next ABC special, *The Rodney Dangerfield Special: I Can't Take It No More*. The special opened with a sketch in which Rodney pleads that he wants to get his own special—before he "jumps" off a window ledge.

Dennis Blair, who cowrote the special, remembered "he jumped, and he fell on a mattress, and didn't move for like a minute. We go, 'Rodney?' And finally, after a minute or so, he slowly starts moving and he goes, 'I think I need to go to the hospital.' He had a sprain or some kind of pinched nerve. We were scared for a long time."[63]

Rodney was rushed to St. Joseph's Hospital across the street from ABC's studios; he was then transported to Cedars Sinai Medical Center in West L.A. He suffered torn ligaments and a neck sprain. "He was doing a sketch in which he was on the ledge of a building and threatening to jump," said his longtime manager, Estelle Endler, who was also an executive producer on the special. "He did jump off the ledge as he was instructed by the director, and he took a bad fall. It was only about four feet but on a very thin mattress."

Rodney spent a few days in Cedars Sinai and was back at work a week after the accident. The specials' producers left the fall in when it aired in late November with guest stars Angie Dickinson, Donna Dixon, *Vega$* star Robert Urich, and Andy Kaufman (Rodney being a major fan of Kaufman's work). Explained Endler: "We can't very well make him try the jump again."

The Rodney Dangerfield Special finished a respectable thirty-fourth place for the week in primetime, just behind NBC's *Cheers* and ahead of ABC's *Monday Night Football.*

RODNEY'S FLEETING APPEARANCE IN BILLY JOEL'S VIDEO "TELL HER About It" sparked an idea: why not make his own video in which he would star? That resulted in "Rappin' Rodney," a rap-song compendium of Rodney's "no respect" one-liners within the framework of his imaginary alter ego's trial, death-row prison sentence, execution, and visit to heaven (where he is banned from the heavenly gates).

The catchy "Rappin' Rodney" tune was written by J. B. Moore and Robert Ford, Jr.—who worked with legendary rapper Kurtis Blow—with an assist from Dennis Blair. "I put a lot of his jokes in song format, and I think I collaborated on the chorus as well," he said.[64] The video featured backup singers, dancers, and cameo appearances from Don Novello in the guise of his *Saturday Night Live* character, Father Guido Sarducci (who delivers, and eats, Rodney's last meal), and rock star Pat Benatar as Rodney's black-masked executioner. The song was included on Rodney's new RCA comedy album, called, appropriately enough, *Rappin' Rodney*; the other tracks captured Rodney during a stand-up performance at Catch a Rising Star in Manhattan.

The "Rappin' Rodney" video, released right after Rodney's sixty-second birthday, was picked up by MTV, which aired it three times a day in its rotation, and it was shown on a large screen before a selection of Rodney's shows for the benefit of his younger fans. The song rose to number eighty-three on the Billboard charts and was nominated for a Grammy Award as Best Comedy Recording. The *Rappin' Rodney* album charted at number thirty-six—twelve spots better than its Grammy-winning predecessor, *No Respect.*

Chapter Ten

I'm an earth sign. She's a water sign. Together, we're mud.

RODNEY DANGERFIELD WAS, BY THIS TIME, HAULING IN OVER $1 million for his appearances in Las Vegas and Atlantic City as one of the highest-paid performers on the casino circuit. He performed regularly at Resorts Casino Hotel in Atlantic City for three years running and was reportedly pulling down more than $25,000 per show.

In December 1984, he was lured away by the Sands Hotel & Casino, signing an exclusive, two-year contract, and opening in its Copa Room in Atlantic City for the first time in February 1985—returning that summer for a week's worth of shows and intermittent performances in the fall months. The Sands, said Estelle Endler, made Rodney "an extremely lucrative offer."

"We had a very good reason for signing him," Sands Vice President Tom Cantone told *The Atlantic City Press*. "He's the perfect example of the use of entertainment as a casino marketing tool. What it boils down to is Rodney brings in the [casino] players." A Resorts spokesman put it more bluntly, saying that The Sands "offered Dangerfield a lot more money, which we did not want to pay . . . Dangerfield's not strong with the high rollers. He's very strong with the youth market."[1]

The Sands advertised Rodney's inaugural appearance in newspaper ads adorned with his *Rappin' Rodney* alter ego (holding a boom box and jauntily clenching a cigarette in his teeth): "Show Some Respect. See and hear this hilarious Grammy Award–winning star in the Sands' Copa Room." He performed a vignette from "Rappin' Rodney" in his new act, backed by a trio of local musicians (sax, drums, piano).

Rodney's two-year deal at the Sands in Atlantic City expired in August 1986 and he moved to the Golden Nugget, owned by Steve Wynn, in a new deal . . . that lasted for one weekend engagement. The two parties broke up "by mutual agreement," with Rodney's camp insisting he was only signed to appear for a "one-shot deal" over a weekend in early October. A Golden Nugget spokesman countered with a different story. "He was under an extended signed contract with us," he said. "But it was mutually agreed that his presentation was not what our audiences had come to expect from us." (Read: he was dirty.) The contretemps did not impact Rodney's drawing power in Atlantic City.[2]

"We had plans to play the Golden Nugget in Atlantic City," said Rodney's booking agent, Dennis Arfa. "Steve Wynn asks to see me. So, I go to see Steve and he tells me, 'You know, I hear Rodney is on heavy drugs. Cocaine.' And I go, 'That's not true. That's not what's going on with Rodney.' For me, it was not a good way to start a relationship.

"Then Rodney went to the [Golden Nugget] room and the room was big. Like a bad Catskills room," Arfa recalled. "So, he didn't want to work there. So, I had two parties that were not really happy with each other. Steve's saying that Rodney was into drugs. He dabbled, but he wasn't into drugs. He was into pot, but not heavy drugs. So, Steve's assessment was wrong. But Rodney didn't like the room, so we got out. Didn't play."[3]

Television continued to play a starring role in keeping Rodney front and center on the public stage.

The nightclub dates helped, of course, but his appearances on *The Tonight Show Starring Johnny Carson*—which grew to over sixty late-night visits—were burnished into America's consciousness as they were for fellow comedian Don Rickles. (Rickles, like Rodney, had an open invitation to sit on Johnny's couch whenever the spirit moved him. He also lived in L.A., which made the trip to "beautiful downtown Burbank" a bit easier for him. Rodney had to schlep out from the East Coast.)

Doing the Carson show was demanding work for Rodney, who prepared thirty or forty jokes beforehand and tried them out in front of a live audience at Catch a Rising Star or the Improv or at Dangerfield's before his *Tonight Show* visits. "You've got to know it completely, like you know your own name," he said about his jokes. He outlined each of his *Tonight Show* routines beforehand—two pages for each guest shot, one headed "STAND" for his stand-up bits and the other labeled "PANEL" for the jokes he used when sitting next to Johnny on the couch. Each page contained subheadings with titles including "Open, Girls, Sex"; then, with lightning speed, he would finesse his lines depending on the direction in which Carson took their interactions. There were pre-interviews with Carson's staff, but Johnny often eschewed his notes depending on that night's vibe . . . and its guest.

"I start three months ahead of my *Tonight Show* appearances accumulating jokes and writing jokes," Rodney said. "Sometimes people send me jokes and I'll pay them $50 if I use it, but most of my stuff I write myself. I try for perfection. I try to get thirty or thirty-five lines which all always get a laugh . . . nothing mediocre. My old man once told me, 'If you go in with something that's just fair, the thing that's fair turns out to be nothing, and the thing that's great turns out to be fair. So at least make everything great.'"[4]

"That whole thing looks like I'm ad-libbing on the panel, looks like I'm just kidding around, right?" he told another reporter. "That's all prepared. It's a play. Word-for-word I know where I'm goin' every second. The magic is to make it look like it's effortless."[5]

ABC, too, kept Rodney in the minds of television viewers with his semi-annual primetime appearances, and his next special for the network, *Rodney Dangerfield: Exposed*, aired in March 1985 with guests Morgan Fairchild, Harvey Korman, and his Miller Lite compatriots Dick Butkus and Bubba Smith. "It's a silly but fast-paced hour," noted the *New York Daily News*. "Dangerfield strikes us as a comedian who's surprised by his own popularity. He sticks to a tried-and-true formula—monologue, skits and one major musical number—the latter a takeoff on 'Top Hat' backed by an ensemble of dancers." Rodney was anything if not reliable; *Rodney Dangerfield: Exposed* was the week's thirty-fifth most-watched show, a solid finish for a primetime special.

And then there was cable television, which appealed to a younger demo-graphic—the sixty-three-year-old comic's core audience. Rodney's association with HBO (still routinely called Home Box Office at the time) paid dividends with the young comics who idolized him—including Robert Klein, Andy Kaufman, Roseanne Barr, Tim Allen, Sam Kinison, and Carol Leifer—and in the spring of 1985, he signed a deal to host *The 9th Annual Young Comedians Show*, to be taped at Dangerfield's.

"To be on Rodney's *Young Comedians* special was really kind of the Holy Grail," said Carol Leifer, who, in 1983, appeared on HBO's *The 8th Annual Young Comedians Show*, hosted by John Candy. "It was like doing *The Tonight Show*, and every comic of my generation really wanted to get that spot. Rodney was a master joke writer; I mean, even if he bought somebody's jokes he knew about the economy of jokes and he knew what made a great joke, and that's the character he created to sell those jokes. I just thought his whole act was brilliant."[6]

For *The 9th Annual Young Comedian's Show*, which aired in August 1985, Rodney assembled a roster of up-and-coming comics including Louie Anderson, Harry Basil, Sam Kinison (a former Pentecostal preacher), Rita Rudner, Bob Nelson, Bob Saget, and Maurice LaMarche, all of whom went on to bigger and better things after appearing on the special.

"I had been Rodney's opening act for a year and a half by that point," Maurice LaMarche remembered. "I took over from Jim Carrey. What happened was, I subbed for Jim once when he wasn't available; we had the same manager, and I was suddenly thrust into a four-thousand-seat theater-in-the-round and that's where I met Rodney. He was so generous and his reputation among the then-young comedians . . . we all loved him."[7]

"I always admired him because I'm somebody who loves jokes and he was a consummate joke writer," Rudner recalled. "And when I started to hang around Catch A Rising Star, when I decided to try to become a comedian, Rodney was always there. And one day I got up enough nerve—because he used to buy jokes from some people—and I thought of a joke that I couldn't use . . . and I went up to Rodney and I told it to him, and he laughed and wrote out a check for fifty dollars and I was very excited."

One night, Rita did her five- to six-minute routine at the Improv. "After I got off the stage, Rodney said, 'Rita, come over here.' He said, 'I think you're really good and I want you to be on my [HBO] special.' And I couldn't believe it, I was like, 'Oh my God, how is this happening?' And I got on that special . . . and it was the first time that people started to recognize me. Sam Kinison, Louie Anderson, Bob Saget—I was the only woman on it. People still, to this day, talk about me holding the dress up. That little show really resonated with people. It was a big deal for me."[8]

Bob Nelson was tapped by Rodney for the HBO special while he was working at the Comic Strip in Fort Lauderdale, Florida. "Rodney used to go to Florida a lot . . . and he was looking for a bunch of guys to have on the show with him. I'm onstage at the Comic Strip doing my thing and I walk offstage and, alongside the wall as I'm walking off, Rodney is walking toward me. I'm like, 'Oh my gosh, this is Rodney Dangerfield!' And he says, [in Rodney's voice] 'Hey, Bob Nelson, very funny, very funny. I gotta tell ya, how would you like to be on an HBO special with me?' And I go, 'Seriously?' He goes, 'Yeah, do you wanna be on a special?' I go, 'Yes!' And he says, 'Okay, you're in! So far it's me, you, and Sam Kinison. Let's take a ride, take a look at some of the other clubs and see what's around here, you know?'"[9]

Harry Basil took a different route with Rodney before he was hired for *The 9th Annual Young Comedians Show.*

"Rodney's manager, Estelle Endler, was looking for opening acts and Rodney always liked variety acts because he's up there talking for an hour and he didn't want somebody up there being a talking head before him," Basil said. "He wanted somebody with music, a guitar, impressionists . . . a variety act to do something different for a half hour."

Basil went over big at Mitzi Shore's Comedy Store in L.A. and Shore, who was good friends with Endler, set up a showcase for Basil. "I killed it. I got a standing ovation," he said. "And I'm thinking, 'Wow, this is great, I'm going to open for Rodney.' This was before the special. And I didn't get it. Estelle passed on me. And I said, 'Mitzi, what happened?' 'You were too fucking strong,' she said, 'Who wants to hire somebody that gets that reaction?'" Nonetheless, Rodney hired Basil for the HBO special.

"He would bring each one of us down into his dressing room he had at Dangerfield's," Basil said. "I remember there was a bed down there and Rodney had myself, Louie Anderson, and Yakov Smirnoff come in . . . you know, his robe was open, and he is hanging there like the bottom of a grandfather clock, you know what I mean? Nobody knew how big this special was going to be. I mean, there had been eight of these Young Comedian specials on HBO already and they had hosts like John Candy, Carl Reiner. But this one wound up becoming really big.

"It was just insane . . . all of us standing in the back of this little club and watching each comic go up and then watching Sam Kinison just blow away the room."[10]

Kinison, a brilliant comedian who would make a memorable (screaming) appearance in Rodney's next movie, *Back to School*, was seven years into his stand-up comedy career when Rodney tracked him down and invited him to do the HBO special. Kinison was reluctant; he had avoided coming to New York since being beaten up there by two guys once before and steered clear of the city as much as possible.

According to Kinison's brother, Bill, Rodney, who was at the Comedy Store, bumped another comic from the special to make room for Kinison. Sam got a standing ovation on the *Young Comedians Show* and, a few days after taping his spot, he called Rodney to thank him. Rodney asked him why he did not play Dangerfield's more often, and Sam told him he had been frightened to return after getting knocked out by those two guys—who, the following week, materialized in in L.A. and apologized to Kinison behind the Comedy Store.

Seems like Rodney made a few calls.[11] Or not.

In his memoirs, Rodney mentioned how Sam and Bill Kinison came to see him and were worried because Sam had "pissed off some Mafia guy" who, he thought, was now out for his blood. "I was pretty sure Sam had nothing to fear. So I told him. 'You got nothing to worry about. Concentrate on your show. The guy's just trying to scare you. I'm telling you, nothing's going to happen.' Sam said okay, and he felt better. And of course nothing happened to him. But because I had been so sure that nothing was going to happen, Sam and his brother got the idea that I had made a phone call to someone in the Mafia. Sam and Bill were now under the impression that I was connected, that I was 'mobbed up.'"[12]

Rodney had a special place in his heart for Sam, "one of the most talented guys I ever saw," he wrote in his autobiography, *It's Not Easy Bein' Me*. According to Rodney's recollection, the two comics first met in the early 1980s in Houston, at a theater-in-the-round called the Arena. "The show was Sam and two other comics. He was young, raw, but had something wild that I liked. After the show, I asked the club manager, 'Can I meet the guy who went on second?'

"They brought Sam over to our table and we talked for about fifteen minutes. He told me he was struggling with his act, but I told him, 'You'll be fine. You're great' . . . Sam didn't hold back. He was raw, honest, and very funny."[13]

In Rodney's memoir, he claims to have watched Sam's act that night in Houston and, after the show, offered him a spot on *The Young Comedians Show*.

Maurice LaMarche remembered it differently and recalled that he was responsible for getting Kinison on to the HBO special.

"I'm going to tell you a story that, unfortunately, is going to contradict Rodney's story [in his autobiography], but I swear to you this story is one hundred percent true," he said. "Sam and I had been friends for a couple of years. I had a signing account at Art's Deli [in Los Angeles]; I could sign for my meals. Sam had nothing—he was sleeping on the stage at the Westwood Comedy Store. So I said, 'Sam, this is my account number at Art's. If you're ever hungry or don't have money, just go in and sign my name.'

"So, we were on the tour bus coming home from one of the New York State jobs and my now-wife was sitting beside me. Rodney said, 'Hey, Maurice, man, I got one slot left on the *Young Comedians Show*. You're in, don't worry, but who else do I put in there? I got Bob Saget, Louie Anderson, Bob Nelson, you know?' I said, 'I think Sam Kinison is ready. I think he would be fantastic.' And Rodney said, 'No, man, Sam can't cook in five minutes. I love

Sam, don't get me wrong, but he alienates them and spends twenty minutes trying to get 'em back on his side.' I said, 'I'm telling you, he's got a brand-new hunk [of his act] about a 7-11 that just has them eating out of the palm of his hand. You gotta take another look at him.'

"My wife will swear to it on a Bible: I said, 'If I had to give up my slot on the show to get Sam on, I would do it.' Rodney goes, 'Oh, wow, okay, man, I'll take a look.' And Sam called me up the following week and he goes [in a Kinison voice]: 'Maurice, Rodney told me what you said, what you did, and I'm on the *Young Comedians Show*. We're gonna be in New York together, *OH, OH, OHHHHHH!!!*'"[14]

Comedian/actor Pauly Shore, the son of the Comedy Store's founder, Mitzi Shore, was a longtime friend of Rodney's. He recalled Rodney's blossoming friendship with Sam Kinison.

"I remember Sam was hot at the Comedy Store and he brought Rodney in because Rodney was very big on helping young comics," he recalled. "I remember Rodney being there and everyone freaked out because Rodney Dangerfield was there and . . . it was pretty amazing. Because he had been on Carson so many times and it was like Jesus Christ walking in, this iconic figure. My mom had all the best comics and Rodney knew that. And Rodney was in awe of Sam."[15]

BOB NELSON'S ASSOCIATION WITH RODNEY DID NOT END WITH THE HBO special. He toured with Rodney as his opening act for eight years, was invited by Rodney to appear on the 1981 NBC television special *The Stars Salute the President*—which aired in March and honored the new commander in chief, Ronald Reagan—and, later, worked on Rodney's first animated movie, *Rover Dangerfield*. "He had a whole stable of guys he used to have open for him," Nelson said. "He enjoyed me because I didn't curse. I was a pretty clean act and he liked the fact that I would go on and I would work clean. And then he would go out and shock them.

"He loved marijuana. It was very funny because I would sit backstage with him and it was kind of a strange relationship. He would say things to me like, 'So how long you married?' I was married, like, five years. And he goes, 'Five years? I don't understand how you can stay with somebody for five years. After twenty minutes, you know her whole life story.' He would be sitting backstage smoking marijuana, and we would just kind of stare at each other. I wasn't sharing [the pot] with him. It's like two o'clock in the morning. I remember one time we were sitting there and didn't say anything for like forty-five minutes. I'm just hanging with him, he's hanging with me . . . and he takes a puff of his marijuana and goes, 'So, Nelson. What are you thinking?' I go, 'Nothing.' And he goes, 'I believe it.'

"If it wasn't for Rodney, I wouldn't have played the Greek Theater or Broadway or Radio City Music Hall," Nelson said. "He gave me the HBO specials. I am very grateful to him for making all that happen for me."[16]

Harry Basil: "The cool thing about the HBO specials were this: they were all good, and they helped a lot of comedians, but Rodney's was the hottest. His was so highly rated they gave him his own special and he wound up doing more of them. They were paying him something like two million a special."[17]

"My attitude is all young, my following is all young," Rodney said. ". . . [G]uys my age, I don't think like them. I don't particularly care for them. Guys my age are all worried about insurance and how everyone else is doing. The guys I like, the guys I think are funny, are all young—Steve Martin, Dan Aykroyd, John Belushi, Bob Klein. They're all young. I never grew up, I guess. My head is young. People my own age, most of them bore me."[18]

Dennis Arfa, Rodney's booking agent in the mid-1980s, spoke of Rodney's love and, yes, respect for the younger-generation comedians.

"He loved Sam, he loved Dice. He loved all the young comics. They were like his children," he said. "He would do these HBO specials and he was a guy who hated most people and many things. But he loved the young comics. They were all important to him. He was like the godfather of young comics. And he was comfortable enough with where he was in the world. He was a young guy in his head. He was an old guy, but he wasn't in that crowd. He was in their crowd. They all believed he was the fucking godfather.

"He was the first rock and roll comic. He wasn't just doing comedy; he was a fucking rock and roller, which is what led all these giants and all these artists in the music space to be into Rodney Dangerfield."[19]

* * *

ORION PICTURES REMAINED UNDAUNTED IN THE WAKE OF *EASY Money*, despite its mediocre reception and oft-savage reviews. In the fall of 1985, the studio geared up for its next Rodney Dangerfield movie, *Back to School*, in which Rodney played Thornton Melon, a successful businessman who dumps his gold-digger trophy wife and enrolls at Grand Lakes University to join his son there and experience the campus life he never had.

The movie's premise consciously catered to Rodney's younger fans— which did not go unnoticed by its star.

"At first the rock groups got into me, seven or eight years ago. They used to tape my Carson spots and play them on the road with them, things like that," he said. "The kids have been into me for a while—they just got younger and younger. I guess that's my general thing now, kids twenty years old being into me."[20]

The *Back to School* producers scoured the country for a "progressive, politically aware" college campus on which to film the bulk of the movie (some interiors were shot back in L.A.) They considered Southern Methodist University, the University of Illinois, and twenty other schools, and ultimately settled on the University of Wisconsin-Madison, located in the state capitol. By mid-October, more than four thousand University of Wisconsin students turned out to audition for four hundred roles as extras and background players—and the chance to be in a Hollywood movie, however fleetingly, starring their hero, sixty-four-year-old Rodney Dangerfield.

The movie boasted four screenwriters (Steven Kampmann, *Caddyshack* director Harold Ramis, Peter Torokvei, and Will Porter) and an $11 million budget. Rodney chipped in on the script, writing with Kampmann et al. in Atlantic City and Las Vegas during the day while he performed in both cities at night. He made a surprise appearance at a press conference held on the University of Wisconsin campus to promote *Back to School* and claimed that he loved the city—and that he considered the University of Wisconsin after graduating from Richmond Hill High School back in Queens (doubtful, but it made for a fun anecdote). A wire service photograph that ran in newspapers nationwide in mid-October showed a smiling Rodney, clad in a white bathrobe with matching white slippers, walking through campus as a gaggle of students followed him around.

The good vibes were shaken, but not stirred, when word broke in the press that Rodney filed suit against the Bahia Mar Hotel in Fort Lauderdale, Florida, claiming that, the previous January, he fell and injured his left knee on the hotel stairs on the way from the swimming pool to his room. He was asking for $5,000 compensation. The case disappeared quickly and was likely settled out of court.

Alan Metter, who directed the "Rappin' Rodney" video, was hired to direct *Back to School* and was thrilled at the prospect of working again with Rodney. "Rodney Dangerfield is going to go down in history," he said. "Rodney Dangerfield, Jack Benny, W.C. Fields . . . that's how I look at Rodney Dangerfield. I looked at him that way before I ever dreamed I'd have the opportunity of working with him."[21]

Rodney was the indisputable star of *Back to School*, and the studio surrounded its big investment with a solid supporting cast including Sally Kellerman, Burt Young, Paxton Whitehead, Adrienne Barbeau, and Keith Young, who played Thornton Melon's son, Jason—a role that Rodney originally offered to Harry Basil.

"I get a call and he wants me to go up to *Back to School* to play his son. I was given an early draft of the script . . . and it wasn't the script that it became," Basil recalled. "Rodney's character wasn't really rich. His wife was rich, and he was more of a blue-collar guy. The son was a bastard. The son was like his mother.

"Then Harold Ramis got involved and he said, 'You should make Rodney rich.' I had a couple of readings and screen tests, and I didn't get the part. Rodney said, 'Hey, man, it's not up to me. It's the studio and the director.' I think if I had become as close as I was with him years later he would have said, 'Give Harry the part.' I was a little depressed, but on the same day I got cast in *Peggy Sue Got Married* and I got to work with Nicholas Cage and [director Francis Ford] Coppola and that was kind of cool."[22]

In the finished script for *Back to School*, Jason is unhappy at Grand Lakes

University and wants to drop out until Dad arrives on the scene. Thornton, born Thornton Meloni to Italian immigrants, is a self-made millionaire who owns a string of plus-sized clothing stores, among other business ventures. When his party-girl wife, Vanessa (Barbeau), throws a big party, Thornton decides that he had had enough of her and files for divorce.

He decides to visit Jason at school and discovers that his son has a C-average and wants to drop out because he feels he does not fit in. He has been rejected by the school's fraternities and is the towel boy for the diving team, where he is picked on by its star athlete, Chas Osborne, played by William Zabka, later to costar in *The Karate Kid*. Thornton bribes university administrator David Martin (Ned Beatty)—aka Dean Martin—to let him enroll in classes by donating a generous sum of money for a new campus building.

"Originally, I went back to college as a poor guy trying to help his son get through and embarrassing him by working in a car wash, things like that," Rodney said. "It was Harold [Ramis] who suggested we change it to a rich guy. I think [the change] made more of a human touch. No matter what, the father and son stay close. Melon is a right guy, not like the character I played in *Caddyshack*, who was not me. I had my hook in Melon. He was generous, fair; he was all right. He didn't turn bitter with success or his bad marriage."[23]

(Thornton sums up his marriage to Vanessa thusly: "I'm an earth sign. She's a water sign. Together we're mud.")

Once he settles in at Grand Lakes U., Thornton breaks all the rules, clashes with Dr. Philip Barbay (Whitehead), the highfalutin' dean of the business school, and develops a romance with Barbay's girlfriend, Dr. Diane Turner (Kellerman), an English professor in whose class Thornton reads Dylan Thomas's "Do Not Go Gentle into That Good Night" to her—igniting the flame. Off camera, Kellerman and Rodney met twice before she was hired for the role. "I had no idea what he was going to be like because I had seen his Lite Beer commercials, and that was it," Kellerman said. "That's one of the things I'm real proud of, is that the relationship we have is believable in the film. You actually do believe that we love each other."[24]

Future Oscar winner Robert Downey, Jr. plays Jason's punk friend, Derek Lutz, and the movie featured a cameo from author Kurt Vonnegut. (Thornton, who is too busy partying to deal with his classwork, hires the famous author to write a paper on himself for Thornton's literature class.) Vonnegut was paid $25,000 for his eight-word walk-on role—talk about easy money.

Rodney also found a part for Sam Kinison, who was sandwiched into the movie at the last minute. Jim Carrey, another one of Rodney's favorites, was reportedly considered for the same role but was deemed too young to play the part (he was twenty-three; Kinison turned thirty-two in December).

Kinison shot his bravura, scene-stealing performance over two days in Santa Monica. He plays Professor Terguson, a seemingly soft-spoken, rational, contemporary American History teacher who holds his history "sacred" and asks his class, in which Thornton is his oldest student, why the U.S. pulled out of Vietnam in 1975.

One of his students, a young blond woman, robotically regurgitates a politically correct textbook answer that enrages Terguson—he smiles, grits his teeth, and launches into a voluminous, screaming tirade (Kinison's trademark) that scares the shit out of his class and reduces the young woman to tears: *"I was up to my knees in rice paddies, with guns and ammo, going up against Charlie!"* When he's done, his face beet red, his voice hoarse from yelling (*"OHHHH! OHHHH! OHHHH!"*), Thornton tells Turguson to calm down. Bad mistake. Turguson pivots to him and asks him—dares him—to explain why, during the Korean War, "we didn't cross the 38th parallel and push those rice eaters back to the Great Wall of China . . . and nuke them back into the fucking Stone Age forever!" "All right, I'll say it!" Thornton fires back. "Because Truman was too big of a pussy wimp to let MacArthur go in there and blow out those Commie bastards!"

"Good answer, good answer," the now smiling and calm Turguson says to Thornton. "I like the way you think. I'm gonna be watching you."

By all accounts, there were no insurmountable hiccups during the shooting of *Back to School*. Rodney managed to overcome a case of gout, while shooting a scene with Ned Beatty (Dean Martin), by putting his aching left ankle on a chair next to him as the cameras rolled. Beatty, in character, says, "Mr. Melon, if you don't mind," and Thornton says, "I'm sorry, Dean Martin," as Rodney lifts his foot off the chair and puts it on Dean Martin's desk.

It was unscripted. "I did that to keep my foot elevated, but it looked so funny we had to keep it in the movie," Rodney said.[25]

"The first thing I remember is arriving on the set and Rodney had a trailer," recalled Adrienne Barbeau. "It was a free-standing trailer and there was a line of women standing outside the trailer. And I said to the producer, 'What's going on?' and he said, 'Oh, they're all here to see Rodney.' He was a real chick magnet, a real sex symbol. And I thought, 'Rodney?' He was absolutely lovely, a real sweetheart. I thought our director, Alan Metter, should have won an Academy Award just for getting Rodney to stand still and to say the lines in the script, because he would just start a scene and suddenly he would start riffing with all of his stand-up stuff and it was hysterically funny. Alan would say, 'Rodney, it's great, but I don't think it works here.' He just needed reining in."[26]

Sadly, Rodney's longtime manager, Estelle Endler—who was so instrumental in opening up his movie career—passed away in September 1985 at the age of forty-two. She was an executive producer on *Back to School* (as she was on *Caddyshack*) and the movie was dedicated to her memory with a message before the end credits:

"For ESTELLE. Thanks For So Much."

Back to School opened on June 13, 1986, and the verdict was swift: Rodney and Orion Pictures had a hit on their hands. This was no *Easy Money* disappointment, and while not all the critics registered their enthusiasm, word of mouth spread quickly and the movie opened strongly at the box office, earning nearly $9 million in its first week. By the end of July, it was among the summer's Top 7 box-office earners. When all was said and done, the movie grossed over $91 million and earned a hefty profit beyond Orion's $11 million investment.

"A big belly laugh of a comedy . . . sure to be cherished by his fans," the *Los Angeles Times* proclaimed. "Dangerfield seems to be setting the film's brisk pace and flawless timing himself."[27]

The New York Times: "Aficionados will be delighted with his performance as Thornton Melon, a self-made millionaire who goes back to college with his son . . . The film is a good-natured potpourri of gags, funny bits, populist sentiment, and anti-intellectualism . . . Mr. Dangerfield's characterization uses many of the bits that made him famous and also adds an appealing warmth."[28]

The *Tampa Bay Times:* "I like him. But not enough to watch 93 minutes of Dangerfield playing a self-made millionaire who acts like a middle-aged Bluto. Remember *Animal House*? *Back to School* is not a great movie. It's simple-minded and simplistic. But it works as a dramatic vehicle for Dangerfield."[29]

Roger Ebert in the *Chicago Sun-Times:* "Dangerfield has been looking for a movie style for a couple of years now. The problem with his last movie, *Easy Money*, was that he wanted to seem like a basically nice guy. He isn't a nice guy. Or at least, when he is nice, there is nothing simple about his niceness. The interesting achievement of *Back to School* is its ability to make those contradictions part of the character."[30]

The movie put Rodney front and center in the minds of Hollywood executives now that he had a bona fide hit, of course, following the relative disappointment of *Easy Money.*

"I was at United Artists and we're sitting in a meeting. It was right after *Back to School* was a hit," producer Doug Draizin recalled years later. "Somebody said, 'Who knows Rodney Dangerfield? We should be in the Rodney Dangerfield business.' We had an idea to do what Leslie Nielsen was doing, kind of a movie spoof. I knew Rodney and I called him up and he said, 'Come over, kid.' So, we go over to the hotel where he was staying, a small place on San Vincente Boulevard. I was with the head of the studio, Tony Thomopoulos. So, we walk into his hotel room and he's sitting there, the bathrobe is wide open and he's hanging out and he says, 'Come in, guys.' Tony looked at me, I looked at Tony, and there we were, trying to pitch him a movie and we were laughing so hard. It was hard for us to concentrate with the robe open."[31]

The good vibes from Rodney's performance in *Back to School* carried over into his next HBO special, *On Location: Rodney Dangerfield: It's Not Easy Being Me*, which was shot in late July and aired in September with comedians Jeff Altman, Roseanne Barr, Sam Kinison, Jerry Seinfeld, Bob Nelson, and Robert Townsend. Rodney met Barr for the first time in Las Vegas when he was working at Caesars Palace and his opening act, Pam Madison, introduced him to her friend Roseanne. "And he goes, 'I think you're the wife I've been looking for,'" Barr said. "I thought he'd forget. A month later he called me and said, 'I've got the script.'"[32]

The special was filmed mostly at Dangerfield's. Rodney opened the show with his tried-and-true stand-up routine. In-between, he introduced his guests and appeared in filmed interstitials with Barr playing his wife.

"Rodney had come into the Comedy Store scouting for some people to put on that show and those were the days when I was pretty strong there," said Jeff Altman. "I remember we had a talk about who should go on in what order. He said, 'You'll go on first, you know.' I thought I was strong enough to bat cleanup, but he said, 'Go on first, believe me, they'll love you.' So, I did okay.

"Let me say this about Rodney: I never saw anybody come into a club and just wipe the place out in nine minutes of being onstage. He could really light up the room when he wanted to like nobody else."[33]

"You had to be careful what you said to him," recalled Bob Nelson. "We get to the second [HBO] special, *It's Not Easy Being Me*, and we were sitting at a table at the Comic Strip and he says to me, 'So what do you think you're going to do on the HBO special?' I said, 'Well, you know, I got this piece, the duck piece, I think I might do that. It's sort of a pantomime thing.' And he goes, 'Do the football. That's your killer piece, what's wrong with you? Do your best thing.'"[34]

RODNEY AND HIS "NO RESPECT" PERSONA WERE NOW SO INGRAINED IN American pop culture that a bar in Washington, D.C., held a Rodney Dangerfield look-alike contest. In 1984, Rodney Dangerfield, a three-year-old gelding, made its horse-racing debut in upstate New York. Rodney's voice was easily impersonated in radio ads throughout the country, which did not please the real deal.

There were lawsuits.

He went to court in L.A. when he sued the Park Inns hotel chain in Dallas for using a mimic to impersonate his voice in radio commercials. The ads carried a disclaimer that said the voice was an impersonation of Rodney; Rodney's lawyers countered that the disclaimer was followed by the actor, saying Dangerfield-style, "You mean this guy ain't a real announcer? He really had me fooled." The case was settled out of court.

He filed suit in Fort Lauderdale, Florida, accusing a local car dealership, Hollywood Honda, of using his face and voice in radio and television commercials without his permission—and without paying him. He claimed he was "greatly humiliated and embarrassed, subject to public ridicule, caused loss of sleep and severe mental and emotional anguish" and demanded at least $25,000. Then, Rodney's lawyer in that case turned right around and sued Rodney, claiming he owed more than $24,000 in legal fees.

In 1988, Rodney was sued by a car dealership in Connecticut that claimed he owed them $51,000 on a customized van he bought for nearly $62,000— and that the van was delivered to Rodney, who wrote a $10,000 check before stopping payment on it. Rodney's attorney said he never bought the van.

There would be more serious legal filings in his future but, for now, it was an annoyance he could live without.

In September 1987, two months shy of his sixty-sixth birthday, Rodney signed an exclusive, two-year deal with Caesars Palace in Las Vegas and, shortly thereafter, 20th Century Fox and Orion announced that he would star in *The Scout* as a down-on-his-luck baseball scout who discovers the world's greatest ballplayer.

There were red flags all around; Peter Falk was originally hired for the role and then, in 1982, was paid over $1 million *not* to make the movie when Fox executives decided his name no longer had the drawing power to carry a big-screen movie (his NBC series, *Columbo*, ended four years earlier after a ten-season run). Orion vice president Mike Medavoy said Rodney would start shooting *The Scout*, to be directed by former *Happy Days* star Anson Williams, after he finished filming *Caddyshack II*—a role that, as mentioned earlier in this book, never materialized when Rodney backed out of making the movie . . . just as his starring role in *The Scout* was announced.

There was more to the *Caddyshack II* story: In November, Warner Bros. filed suit against Rodney for $10 million, claiming he entered into a "binding contract" the previous January to film the *Caddyshack* sequel, and that he was guaranteed a $7 million salary, including a $5 million cash advance. It also stated that it had agreed to all of Rodney's demands, which allegedly included the stipulations that the movie be shot exclusively in L.A.—to "minimize travel"—that he be provided with a sauna on the set, and that he have a "short-day" shooting schedule. The suit dragged on into 1988 and Warner Bros. sought a court order to keep Rodney from making other movies until this case was resolved. It disappeared when Warner Bros. hired Jackie Mason—who was on Broadway with his one-man show, *The World According to Me*—to replace Rodney.[35]

The Scout ran into trouble when, in June 1988, Mike Medavoy announced that the story was undergoing a major overhaul. "We have no script," he admitted. By the end of 1988, Anson Williams was dropped as its director, as was his successor, Alan Myerson. "Rodney wants a team player he can work with creatively," his representative said in a read-between-the-lines statement. "After all, he has a lot of ideas of his own."

The movie dragged along into 1989. In January, Rodney hired veteran director Michael Ritchie (*The Candidate*, *Semi-Tough*, *The Bad News Bears*) to go behind the camera to film the script—written by Rodney and Andrew Bergman—and a mid-April start date was targeted for shooting to begin in New York City. Rodney's camp said that Sam Kinison would play the general manager of the New York Yankees (Kinison was noncommittal).

Then, in April, Rodney fired Ritchie—and, in July, fed up with the whole business, he threw in *The Scout* towel for good.

"They were about to go into production and the studio had Michael Ritchie say to Rodney, 'You know, we're kind of overbudget. If you really want to do this movie, you'll do it for six million instead of eight million,'" Harry Basil recalled. "And Rodney is like, 'What the fuck? Who the fuck says that to somebody? Fuck you—I'm not doing the movie.' Things like that would piss him off. So here he walked off *The Scout*, and now he's walked off a picture from Orion, and he's walked off *Caddyshack II*. So, his career is taking a little bit of a hit here."[36]

It took another five years, but *The Scout* did make it to the big screen in

1994, with Albert Brooks as scout Al Percolo and a young Brendan Fraser as pitching phenom Steve Nebraska.

It was around the time that the nonsense with *The Scout* was dragging on that Rodney moved into a new apartment in the Promenade, a luxury high-rise on East 76th Street overlooking the East River that had its own dry cleaner and travel agency. Other celebrities lived in the building including Luther Vandross, the president of Mitsubishi, and the manager of the Rolling Stones. Rodney's neighbor across the hall was Fabio Lanzoni, better known as Fabio, the Italian-born model and businessman who, at the time, was forging a career as a romance novel cover model.

Fabio: "He was my neighbor for many, many years. I opened the door, and right in front of my door was Rodney Dangerfield's apartment and we became good friends back in the '80s.

"We saw each other pretty much every day or every other day. It's funny because sometimes I would crank the music up just to get ready to go out after a shower and he would knock on my door and say, 'Fabio, I can't believe it, you're having a party and you're not inviting me?' I'm like, 'Rodney, I'm not having a party. I'm just cranking up the music. Actually, I'm going to a party if you want to come.' He was always in his bathrobe, so it was like, 'You can't go like that.' He would say, 'Are you sure you're not having a party?' So, he would come into my apartment and look in every room to see that I'm not having a party.

"There was a time in life, back in the late '80s and early '90s, where he kind of isolated himself," he said. "When he was living in New York at that time he was very unhappy. He was not going out much. Sometimes—it happened a couple of time when I came back from the clubs at, like, four or 4:30 in the morning—the elevator doors would open and I would find Rodney sleeping in the hall, totally passed out. I would have to bring him back to his apartment. Sometimes he would lock himself in the apartment for an entire week and not go out. Like a lot of comedians, through their lives, they are not very happy people. It's funny, because they make a living out of making people laugh, but most of the time they are not happy themselves.

"He used to go to the store, buy a bunch of liquor, and then lock himself in for an entire week. He would run out of alcohol, and then go out again. It was really sad. He was such a talented, intelligent person."[37]

Rodney was still a big enough draw for Broadway, and on February 2, 1988, he opened in a one-man show at the Mark Hellinger Theater on West 51st Street. The limited-run performance was called *Rodney Dangerfield on Broadway!* and unfolded in the spirit of the one-man Broadway shows staged by Mort Sahl and Jackie Mason before him, with one significant difference: there were no press previews and Rodney did not sit for any interviews to promote the show. Perhaps that soured some of his critics in the press—one of them anonymously sniped that "He doesn't want everyone to know it's nothing but a nightclub act."[38]

Bob Nelson was Rodney's opening act and Night One went well. Rodney's audience, most of them less than half his age, ate it up. *The New York Times*, in a glowing review, called the crowd "raucous" and noted that they "greeted him with the sort of enthusiasm normally reserved for respected aging rock stars."

"Onstage, Mr. Dangerfield is a verbal boxer who dances lightly around a theme, then closes in for the kill, delivering a barrage of one- and two-line punches in an accelerated rapid-fire delivery that becomes an orgiastic flurry of jabs," wrote *Times* critic Stephen Holden. "The pleasure in watching Mr. Dangerfield perform comes more from his delivery than his material . . . as he lands his often smutty punches in a virile drill-instructor's growl that deepens and expands as the action speeds up."[39]

Village Voice writer Laurie Stone was also there on Rodney's opening night and wrote in her book, *Laughing in the Dark*, that "Sadness rises from Rodney Dangerfield, surrounds him, wafts across the footlights of the Mark Hellinger Theater. He's sad because he's clumsy and fat. He feels isolated and inept. No joke. And because the sadness is real—because the tie-touching and squirming come from his gut—the comedy he spins from it is rich and conscious. His machine-gun delivery and dancer's timing share much with Henny Youngman's but Youngman's manner is typically Borscht Belt: sunny and masked. Dangerfield's material grows from inside, and it's no wonder so many young, confessional comics credit his influence."[40]

Rodney Dangerfield on Broadway! closed, as planned, on February 12 after twelve performances on the Great White Way.

That summer marked two years since Rodney's last big-screen role in *Back to School*—an eternity in Hollywood—and he turned his attention to *Rover Dangerfield*, an animated movie that was in the works with Rodney voicing the lead character, a hip Las Vegas canine.

He was also talking to NBC about a nascent animated series called *Oh, Rodney!* produced by cartoon kings Hanna-Barbera. That eventually morphed into *Young Rodney* and then *The Rodney Dangerfield Show*, a live-action sitcom.

The original idea for the sitcom was about a young boy who idolizes Rodney and tries to model himself after him—Rodney shows up occasionally to lend some advice. That approach was scrapped in the fall. It was rejiggered to have Rodney play the lead role as the owner of an Italian deli/restaurant, a widower with a teenage son . . . but only if he agreed to the script changes. He did not.

He returned to HBO in the spring to host the R-rated *Rodney Dangerfield: Opening Night at Rodney's Place*, an *On Location* special filmed in Rodney's second Vegas nightclub, called Rodney's Place. This one was located in the Tropicana Resort and Casino—close to the El Rancho Hotel, the site of Rodney's first nightclub endeavor in Sin City.

Rodney, who opened the show in an F-bomb-laden sketch, also did his stand-up routine and appeared in taped sketches throughout. His guests included Sam Kinison, Jeff Foxworthy, Heather Thomas, Tim Allen, John Fox, and Thea Vidale, among others. Rodney's friend from *The Projectionist*, Chuck McCann, played Ed McMahon opposite Rich Little's Johnny Carson in a *Tonight Show* sketch, and Kinison was featured in a sketch that had Rodney drinking his sorrows away over his broken relationship with busty, dim-witted "Laverne" (a running gag throughout the ninety-minute special). It was not for the faint of heart, with racy, expletive-filled material . . . but, hey, it was cable, right? The club, Rodney's Place, enjoyed only a short shelf life: it closed in August, six months after opening, when Rodney and the Tropicana could not agree on a new contract.

* * *

IT SEEMED LIKE THE WORM IN RODNEY'S LIFE WAS TURNING NOW, JUST a little bit, and not for the better. He had not made a big-screen movie since *Back to School* and his micromanaging of scripts—which eventually killed off his starring role in *The Scout* after all the dithering and fired directors—had, for now, nipped his NBC sitcom in the bud.

Rodney took immense pride in his work and cared—perhaps a little too much. His uncompromising approach toward the movie industry, which, for better or worse thrived on compromise in order to get projects off the ground, was starting to encroach on his success. He was, in short, being branded as "difficult" to work with, at least by the Hollywood executives with whom he sparred. That he did not care what they thought, and marched to the beat of his own drummer, was both admirable and troubling regarding the ongoing arc of his career.

His proposed NBC series was now in the hands of mega-producer Aaron Spelling and Hanna-Barbera. It had become a live-action sitcom called *The Rodney Dangerfield Show* and was projected as a midseason replacement premiering on the network in January 1990. Spelling ended up ordering several rewrites.

"If NBC and Rodney like it, then we'll shoot a prototype of the show, and plan for a fall debut," he told the press.[41] In the latest iteration, Rodney would play the owner of an Italian deli/restaurant who is a widower with a teenage son. Then word broke that Rodney and NBC were at an "impasse" over plans for *The Rodney Dangerfield Show*. Rodney favored returning to an earlier version, in which a young boy named Rodney turns to the real Rodney Dangerfield for advice, but NBC was not sold on the concept, having scrapped an earlier pilot in that same vein.

Rodney got his wish for the earlier version of the show, and he taped a pilot for the new series. It was now called *Where's Rodney?* Jared Rushton, who starred opposite Tom Hanks in *Big*, played twelve-year-old Rodney Barnes, the kid who is obsessed with Rodney Dangerfield and turns to him for advice, being able to summon his idol with unexplained magical powers. The pilot finally premiered as a special at 8 p.m. on Monday, January 15, 1990—sandwiched between *The Magical World of Disney* and *Ann Jillian*—then quickly disappeared. It reappeared on NBC five months later on June 11 as a onetime summer burn-off and then vanished forever.

RODNEY WAS MAKING HEADLINES NOW FOR ALL THE WRONG REASONS. In August 1989, he filed a lawsuit against Caesars Palace in Las Vegas, claiming that his eyes were burned in a steam bath accident at the hotel in March 1988, causing him to cancel a series of shows for which he earned $45,000 per show. Rodney was asking for $225,000 in disputed contract money, reimbursement for medical and legal bills, and unspecified punitive damages. Caesars filed a countersuit for $100,000 plus punitive damages, calling him a "malingerer" and a hypochondriac. It was not pretty.

The two sides tried to work out the disagreement in federal court but failed to reach an agreement, and the kerfuffle made its way back into the headlines in July 1990 when the case headed for a trial that was set to begin in late August. Before that could happen, though, events took a turn for the ugly when attorneys for Caesars Palace filed court papers claiming that Rodney smoked marijuana regularly, drank heavily (vodka), and often used cocaine—which, they claimed, was the real reason behind his cancellation of shows in March 1988 and had nothing to with his alleged steam bath accident.

"Anyone who knows me knows it's untrue," Rodney said. His lawyers then filed motions in U.S. District Court saying the allegations were untrue and without foundation—and that the allegations should be barred from the upcoming trial, which was postponed until September 10.[42]

"The chances of a settlement are almost nil now that Caesars has chosen to take the tack they have," said Rodney's lawyer, Barry Langberg.[43]

The trial got underway on September 10, 1990, and Rodney's lawyers rested their case after just three days—calling only Rodney and a hotel employee as witnesses. Rodney was described as "combative" and "contradictive" in his testimony, though he was able to wring some laughs from jurors and spectators when he told a joke to demonstrate how he used his eyes in his stage act: "My dog found out we look alike. So, he killed himself."[44]

Langberg said Rodney performed nearly 1,000 shows in Las Vegas without a cancellation until his eyes were burned in the accident—and claimed that Caesars tried to escape blame and refused to pay Rodney for the five shows he missed afterward. He described how Rodney's eyes were injured by a burst of "scalding steam" when he entered the steam room, alone, after a performance on March 16, 1988—and how he could now not cope with bright lights from the pain from the injury, particularly with the spotlights used in his act.

The attorneys for Caesars Palace countered that his eye injuries were self-inflicted; Caesars lawyer Louis Meisinger described Rodney as a "petulant performer" whose injuries were "a figment of his fertile, comedic imagination." A Caesars engineer testified that the steam bath was working properly before the alleged incident, but admitted it had no temperature gauge to measure how hot the water was before Rodney entered the room.

The defense rested its case on September 19. Nine days later, the jury awarded Rodney $725,000. "The truth won out," Rodney told reporters. "I wouldn't have gone through this unless I was right." Rodney was awarded $500,000 for pain and suffering and $225,000 for the missed shows. He also criticized the Caesars attorneys for the allegations of his drinking and drug use. "I'm surprised they went to that level to degrade me falsely like they did," he said. "All they did in this entire trial was to try to degrade my character. I wasn't concerned with the amount of money. Money is money. I was concerned about the truth."

But it did not end there.

In October, the Caesars lawyers contended that the jury was "starstruck" when it awarded Rodney the $500,000 for pain and suffering. They filed a motion in federal court asking for a new trial. That did not happen but, in August 1991, Judge Roger Foley ruled that Rodney should receive only $50,000 of the $500,000, calling it "grossly excessive." He gave Rodney the option of taking the $50,000 or face a new trial. Finally, in December—after meeting behind closed doors—Rodney settled the case. There was no word on the settlement.

Chapter Eleven

The truth is, as you get older your depression gets greater because you realize this is what it was. And it's not what I thought it would be.

R ODNEY DID NOT LET THE DRAMA OF THE CAESARS COURT CASE get in the way of his professional career. There were movies to make.

While the case was being played out in public, plans were set in motion for *Rover Dangerfield* and a film Rodney was calling *A Dream Come True*, in which he would play a man who finds a "certain cologne" triggering a string of unexpected events. "Rodney worked at an ad agency, and he discovered this cologne that made him irresistible to women," Harry Basil recalled.[1] When that idea apparently died on the vine, he shifted his focus to *Serenade Café*, "a fairy tale about a guy who has to learn to sing to win the hearts of the woman he loves," he told gossip columnist Marilyn Beck. "I got the idea, and I wrote the script fairly quickly. I just finished it, in fact, and now I'm obsessed with it."[2] We will revisit *Serenade Café* a little later. "They were both kind of far-fetched ideas," Basil said.

Rodney initially pitched *Rover Dangerfield* to Hyperion Pictures. "Rodney funded the first phases of the production entirely himself," said Hyperion cofounder Thomas Wilhite. "That's well over a million dollars, and that included the character and the production designs, songs and screenplay—all of the basic work that convinced Warner Bros. to fund the picture."[3] David Newman composed an original score for the film and Billy Tragesser collaborated with Rodney on writing the songs (yes, Rover sang a few tunes).

Rodney then returned to Warner Bros. for *Rover Dangerfield*, a full-length animated feature he wrote with help from his *Caddyshack* director Harold Ramis and an uncredited assist from Bob Nelson and Jeff Schimmel, the brother of comedian Robert Schimmel. He envisioned *Rover Dangerfield* as an R-rated movie, incorporating elements of his stage persona, but Warner Bros. wanted a G-rated movie in order to appeal to the kiddies. It was targeted for a release in the summer of 1991.

"I got no credit for [*Rover Dangerfield*] because Rodney was writing it. I was kind of like a ghostwriter," Nelson recalled. He said, 'I would put you guys as writers, but Harold Ramis doesn't want that.' It was fun, writing a movie with Rodney. Oh my God. He would pay me five hundred dollars a day, which was really awesome, and I would go into the city and go to his apartment, and we'd sit there and the first thing he says is, 'What are you guys going to want to eat for lunch?' He goes, 'Here's what you do, Bob, go down to David's Chickens, okay? On Third Avenue. Go in there and get some chicken but tell them you want it boiled and tell them it's for Rodney.'"[4]

One day, Bob and Rodney were working on *Rover Dangerfield* when Rodney had to run to a dentist appointment. "He had a Subaru station wagon in the garage in his building, a beat-up old thing. He'd say, 'Why have a good car? People are going to hit it anyway.' So, we're driving in this car through the city and we're writing *Rover Dangerfield*, double-parked . . . while he was in the dentist, with our papers on the roof of the car. He goes, 'I'll be down in maybe twenty to thirty minutes, okay? So just stay here and write some stuff. If a cop comes by, just tell him it's Rodney and he'll let you stay here.' Things like that would happen all the time."[5]

Rodney voiced the lead role of Rover Dangerfield, a basset hound who gambles with bones and hangs out with showgirls. He lives with Connie, a Vegas chorus line dancer, and eventually, after she leaves him with her no-good boyfriend, Rocky, he ends up on a farm where he meets and falls in love with Daisy (Susan Boyd), a beautiful collie who lives next door. Ronnie Schell, Shawn Southwick, and Rodney's *Back to School* costar Paxton White-head were among the cast members who lent their voices to the endeavor.

Harry Basil recalled that "Rodney financed *Rover Dangerfield*. He put his own money into it. He wrote the songs and he got all of the animation. And then Warner Bros. paid him; they did a negative pickup and they paid him back what he spent on the animation, the drawings, and the songs, which was like $2.5 million or $3 million. And then they financed the movie . . . and that's why Rodney was so mad when they released *Rover Dangerfield* because he didn't get anything for it."[6]

Rover Dangerfield opened in limited release in early August in a handful of smaller markets including Orlando and Atlanta, and garnered solid reviews. *The Sacramento Bee*, giving it four stars, called the movie "a revelation . . . It can be enjoyed on two distinctly different levels, with the novelty of its delightful visuals for children in the audience and the trademark malicious wit of Dangerfield for their parents . . . it's an honest delight."[7] The *Orlando Sentinel* raved that *Rover Dangerfield* was "consistently amusing."[8] The hype did not make a difference. The movie played for a few weeks and disappeared from view, spurring rumors that it was about to open nationwide, that it was not going to open at all, that it was being reedited, or that the soundtrack was being rerecorded.

"It is probably not going to find a broad national release," a Warner Bros. spokesman said in September. "As of right now, *Rover* will probably have a limited release around the country in the next couple of months." Instead, it went straight to video, where it languished in obscurity—or, as Rodney said, "They buried it like a bone."[9]

THERE WERE MORE LEGAL HEADACHES FOR MR. NO RESPECT THAT year.

In March, he filed a $10 million lawsuit against the *Star*, accusing the supermarket tabloid of publishing false and defamatory statements in its issue of September 11, 1990, in a story headlined "Vegas Casino Accuses Caddyshack Funnyman: Rodney Dangerfield Swills Vodka by the Tumblerful, Smokes Pot All Day and Uses Cocaine." The story detailed Rodney's alleged offstage activities in Las Vegas, among them shouting an obscenity at a fan who wanted his autograph, making a "vulgar suggestion" to a casino patron, and cavorting with two naked girls in his suite at Caesars Palace. Rodney's attorney, Barry Langberg, said the *Star* refused to print a retraction despite repeated requests.

The case dragged on for years. Rodney filed a libel suit against the *Star* and, in October 1993, a federal appeals court in San Francisco upheld a Los Angeles trial judge's order requiring the tabloid to disclose the names of its confidential sources. Then, in 1995, the *Star* was ordered to pay Rodney $45,002 in damages (including $1 for emotional distress and $1 for defamation) when U.S. District Court Judge Ronald Lew ruled that the article was false and was published "with at least reckless disregard of the truth." Rodney's lawyer called the ruling "ridiculous." Rodney wanted more money, and the case wound its way all the way up to the Supreme Court—which, in 1997, ruled that the $45,002 judgment would stand. It conceded that the article was full of lies, but that there was no evidence that the story caused Rodney any emotional distress or damaged his reputation.

"I did coke for a while," Rodney wrote in his autobiography, *It's Not Easy Bein' Me.* "What a mistake that was. When you're on coke, things can be going bad and you think you're doing great. I remember one night I was playing dice in Vegas, high on coke. I had lost $3,000—but on coke, I thought, *Man I'm doing great! I'm still here!*"[10]

In July 1991, following the demise of Rodney's Place in Las Vegas, Rodney opened another nightclub, this time in L.A. It was called Rodney's Place—The Outrageous Comedy Club and was a 170-seat venue located inside Twenty/20 at the ABC Entertainment Center in Century City.

The club opened June 27 to a capacity crowd with performances by Lenny Clark, Hugh Fink, and David Tyree, all of whom appeared in Rodney's upcoming HBO special. Rodney got up onstage and did fifteen minutes of stand-up. The place closed the very next day because it lacked the proper permits—or "operational difficulties," according to the club's booker.

Rodney's Place reopened in mid-October, with Rodney performing for an overflow crowd backed by Harry Basil, Dom Irrera, and Blake Clarke. Its entrance featured three pairs of brightly colored birds that "nuzzle each other in a huge glass case" and a black marble corridor papered with Rodney's publicity photos lining its walls. The club's interior featured low ceilings with white-and-black drapings covering the walls, flying saucer lamps, and tables with long red candles and a nice view of the elevated stage.

"Whether you enjoyed yourself Wednesday was a matter of, um taste," reported the *Los Angeles Daily News*. "With a few exceptions . . . the topic of the evening was body parts and bodily functions . . . Dangerfield, looking fit and relaxed in baggy, mismatched clothes, warmed to the appreciative audience with his usual self-deprecating remarks: 'I called up AT&T. They won't take me back. I went to a nude beach. They made me park in the handicap section.'"[11]

Rodney hoped for the best with the newly reopened Rodney's Place. "I'll have a place to go, meet people have friends and have a few laughs," he said. "And what the heck life's all about? It's better than doing nothin' at night. Movies are great, and I just finished one . . . but you don't get that immediate response 'cause I was brought up in nightclubs so I guess I'm partial to 'em."[12]

Rodney's Place closed two months later.

SOMEHOW, IN-BETWEEN HIS TOURING, TELEVISION APPEARANCES, legal worries, and his new club in L.A., Rodney found the time to make another movie.

In *Ladybugs*, for which he was reportedly paid $7 million, he played a salesman, Chester Lee, who, in order to earn a promotion, endeavors to coach a girls' soccer team called the Ladybugs. He knows nothing about the sport, of course—therein lies the comedy rub. He's helped by his assistant, Julie Benson (Jackée Harry), his fiancée, Bess (Ilene Graff), and Matthew (Jonathan Brandis), Bess's son, who dresses in drag as "Martha" to help the Ladybugs on the field (yep). The movie was shot in and around Denver, Colorado, from July through September and was directed by Sidney Furie. Harry Basil, who helped Rodney rewrite the script, was the associate producer and had a small role in the film.

The movie was originally going to be shot in Dallas, but it was too hot there in the summer; for the part of Matthew/Martha, Basil recalled that it came down to Brandis and Leonardo DiCaprio—whose on-camera experience, at that point, was limited to small roles on television, including twenty-three episodes of Alan Thicke's ABC sitcom *Growing Pains*.

"Rodney and I had their head shots taped up to the mirror at the Beverly Hilton," Basil said. "We had a final meeting when they came up to the suite and they both read. We thought Leonardo was terrific but when he played Martha, he did this high voice, he talked like a little girl and it was cute. He was adorable. But what we loved about Jonathan Brandis was that he had this deep voice, and he did [Martha] in his voice. And we just found that to be hysterical."[13]

Rodney was deeply involved in the casting process for *Ladybugs*; veteran actress Julie Kavner (*Rhoda*), who voiced Marge Simpson on *The Simpsons* and was one of Woody Allen's ensemble players (*Hannah and Her Sisters, Radio Days, New York Stories*), was in the running as Chester Lee's sidekick but Rodney thought her New Yawk-y voice did not make sense for a movie that, at the time, was set in Texas. That opened the door for Jackée to snare the part.

For the role of Bess, played by Ilene Graff, Rodney met with Dee Wallace of *E.T.: The Extraterrestrial* fame. "We just absolutely loved her, and she did one line reading and Rodney corrected her, like, 'Say it this way,' and she goes, 'Rodney, no disrespect, you're a fifty-something-year-old comedian and that's the way you would read it. As a mom, this is the way to say it,' and Rodney goes, 'She's right.' She was terrific and we wanted her, but Sidney didn't want her in the movie. He wouldn't give us a reason why."

Basil: "Rodney wanted to put Sam Kinison in *Ladybugs* and wrote a part for him . . . and said, 'Sam is going to be in this and you're going to pay him a hundred Gs, okay?' Sam was kind of straight at the time and Rodney was taping an HBO special at the Improv in Santa Monica and Sam didn't show up. It was one of those days where Bill, his brother, said 'I can't wake him up.' Rodney said, 'He'll be here. I know he won't let me down.' But he didn't come, and we wound up getting Fred Willard at the last minute, but Rodney still wanted Sam for *Ladybugs*. He was trying to get a hold of him, but Sam was so embarrassed that he let Rodney down [that] he didn't return his calls."[14]

Joe Ancis flew out to Colorado to visit Mr. No Respect during the shoot, as did Rodney's daughter, Melanie. Harry Basil was also there, and he recalled a dinner with Sidney Furie and his wife.

"We're all sitting at the table there and Sidney Furie's wife, a very lovely lady, she goes to Melanie, 'Oh, your father was so excited about you coming out here, that's all he could talk about.' Well, that's not Rodney, you know? He never acted that way. He would say, 'My daughter's coming out and Joe's coming out'; he was probably more excited by Joe. So, Joe looks over at Rodney when she says that and he crisscrosses his hands like he's playing the piano and he goes, 'They're playing you, man. They're playing you.' Rodney just loved that shit. That was Joe. He was the ultimate hipster. He would call people 'Jim' even if their name wasn't Jim."[15]

The *Ladybugs* script was credited to Curtis Burch—Basil, as pointed out earlier, contributed to the writing process—and it was released in March 1992. It did not move the critical needle in either direction. Its biggest distinction was its producer, Albert S. Ruddy, who also produced *The Godfather*.

"I think I came up with the tagline, 'He's coach, not first class,'" Basil said. "The movie opens big, like in fourteen hundred screens, and it comes out opposite *Basic Instinct* and *White Men Can't Jump*. It only did like five million at the box office and got some bad reviews. 'Grab the bug spray,' you know?"[16]

Rodney promoted *Ladybugs* on *The Tonight Show* in April 1992. It was his first appearance with Johnny Carson in nearly a decade due to a disagreement, but now that Carson was retiring after nearly thirty years he welcomed Rodney back to his late-night couch. The "feud," such as it was, seemed to be one-sided on Rodney's end. The story is that Rodney was angry at Carson because he helped the drunken talk show host get back to his hotel one night, following him in his car . . . and Johnny never thanked him. Rodney was insulted and refused to go back on the show. Until now. He did a minute and a half of stand-up, then sat on the couch next to Bernadette Peters, convulsing Carson with a string of one-liners for another six minutes before finally getting to the *Ladybugs* clip.

Rodney also made an appearance in support of *Ladybugs* on MTV VJ Pauly Shore's spring break special, *Chillin' with the Weasel*, which was filmed in Daytona Beach, Florida.

"MTV brought him down there on to my show to promote *Ladybugs*,"

Shore said. "It was time to rehearse with him and go over what we were going to do. So, we knock on his door and he's wearing his robe, of course. He's smoking weed and we go in there, me and the producers, and Rodney's like, 'All right, what the fuck is going on? What do you guys want to do here?' He's smoking weed and his dick is pretty much hanging out of his robe as he's sitting there.

"So, me and Rodney went over the bit, and I was in charge. He kind of disagreed. He knew I was hot, but he was being nice to me and being on my show and kind of going with it. That's why he was there, to promote his movie—you would go on MTV to promote it. We did a lot of bits together."

One of those bits involved Rodney and Pauly driving down to Daytona Beach in a convertible. "We're just doing this dialogue . . . it was pretty classic," Shore said. "Part of history, that moment; it felt like a feature film, to be quite honest. We were acting—there was a beginning, middle, and end—like we prepared a little sketch. It wasn't just improv. I remember in the middle of it I'm like, 'Fuck, I gotta do a movie with this guy.' I thought me and him together was really funny—him looking at me like I'm an idiot was great, you know?"[17]

All of the promotional stunts did not help much when *Ladybugs* opened at the box office.

"The new comedy runs as if it were composed of plastic joints and transplanted organs not in mint condition," Vincent Canby wrote in his review for *The New York Times*. "Even when the material is feeble, as it is here, Mr. Dangerfield can sometimes be funny, a gravelly-voiced comic confusion of emotional insecurities laced with aggressive tendencies."[18]

"'Bugs'? Fumigate The Theater" blared the headline in the *New York Daily News*: "In his tireless but tiring quest for respect, Rodney Dangerfield pops up again in movie theaters . . . The team and the film are called *Ladybugs* and it'll have you reaching for the Raid in five minutes."[19]

The Palm Beach Post: "This tired comedy—the actor's first since *Back to School* in 1986—has 'desperate' written all over it. Nothing in it is fresh, and even devoted Dangerfield fans may find it only moderately entertaining."[20]

Harry Basil: "If you look at the movie now, there is a lot of humor in it that you cannot get away with today. There is politically incorrect, #Me-Too stuff. Rodney flirting with one of the secretaries. We thought we were making this silly farce and we're writing these sex jokes. There are a couple of websites that are dedicated to going, 'I can't believe this movie got made.' So, the movie bombs and Rodney says, 'What are you going to do? I'll go back to standup.'"[21]

There was more bad news. On April 10, 1992, Sam Kinison was killed in a car crash in Needles, California. He was on his way to a show in Laughlin, Nevada, when his Trans Am was struck head-on by a pickup truck that swerved into Sam's lane. The pickup truck was driven by a seventeen-year-old who was reportedly drinking prior to the accident. Kinison was not wearing a seat belt and died at the scene; his wife, Malika, was injured but survived the carnage. The hard-living Kinison was sober at the time of his death. "He said, 'I don't want to die, I don't want to die,'" recalled comedian Carl LaBove, Kinison's best friend who watched the crash from another car and cradled Sam's bloody head in his hands.

Rodney, like everyone else in Kinson's orbit, was devastated by the news, which broke while he on a press junket for *Ladybugs*. "When you hear something like this you think maybe it was Sam's fault," he said. "But it wasn't, and that makes it worse. It's a big loss to people who want to laugh."[22]

In September, Rodney participated in *A Tribute to Sam Kinison*, a televised memorial concert that featured, among others, Robin Williams, Jim Carrey, Richard Belzer, Carl LaBove, Judy Tenuta, and Pauly Shore. It included clips of Sam's work, including *Back to School*, and aired in May 1993 on Fox.

THERE WERE HEALTH ISSUES, TOO. AROUND THIS TIME, RODNEY HAD surgery to repair an abdominal aortic aneurysm that, if not detected, could have killed him almost instantly as it did with Lucille Ball, John Ritter, and Albert Einstein. The surgery was kept on the down-low—there was no mention of it in the press—but Rodney pegged the year as 1992 in his book, *It's Not Easy Bein' Me*. "One day I woke up and had some pain on my right side. I went to the doctor and got an X-ray. As the doctor suspected, the tests showed that I had pancreatitis. But they also showed something the doctor really didn't like—an aneurysm." After the surgery, he recovered in the intensive care unit: "My torso was wrapped in bandages, and there was an IV stuck in my arm to feed me intravenously."[23] He eventually recovered but it left a big scar on his chest; the replacement aortic valve would come back to haunt him a decade later.

In May, Oliver Stone began filming the follow-up to his 1991 blockbuster, *JFK*, in Santa Fe, New Mexico.

It was called *Natural Born Killers*. *Cheers* star Woody Harrelson and Juliette Lewis played husband-and-wife Mickey and Mallory: ultra-violent, sexed-up serial-killer lovebirds—a modern-day Bonnie & Clyde—who embark on a killing spree that is being tracked by cynical, ratings-hungry tabloid TV reporter Wayne Gale (Robert Downey, Jr.), who works for the television show *American Maniacs*.

Stone had won an Oscar for directing the Vietnam War movie *Platoon*; he was, and still is, a controversial iconoclast who paid no heed to Hollywood traditions (or decorum). He was also a big Rodney Dangerfield fan and approached Mr. No Respect about the prospect of appearing in an extended cameo in *Natural Born Killers*. ("At first I thought it was a movie about my wife's family," Rodney said.[24])

It was a brave and strange casting choice. Rodney agreed—not quite sure what to think of it all—and turned in a bravura performance in six minutes of screen time that almost defies explanation.

"I thought of Rodney for the movie, and I always liked him," Stone recalled. "In New York City, where I grew up, he was a big deal. Rodney was very interesting, very smart, and who knows what complexes drove him. Obviously, he had inferiority complexes to the hilt.

"We had a lot of fun because Rodney was a big eater," Stone said. "I took them all to an introductory dinner before the film started and he and Woody and Juliette and Robert Downey, Jr. and Tom Sizemore and God almighty, he ate two plates [of food]. He ate his own plate and then he turned to either Robert or Juliette and said, 'If you're not eating it, can I have it?' So, he sure had an appetite."[25]

Stone framed Rodney's initial appearance in *Natural Born Killers* within the framework of a '50s-era sitcom called *I Love Mallory*, a play on *I Love Lucy*—complete with a laugh track and audience reaction—in a flashback to Mallory's childhood. Rodney plays Ed Wilson, Mallory's repellent, foul-mouthed father, who sexually molests his daughter—and brags about it—while his milquetoast wife (Edie McClurg) does absolutely nothing to stop him. "It was a dark, twisted role—completely different from what I'd done in my previous movies—but I was interested," Rodney said.[26]

"He was my first choice for Dad, because I just pictured the father as somebody who was partially insane, and also at the same time could operate within the confines of a sitcom," Stone said. "I brought Rodney this script and he thought I was crazy to want to cast him. He says, 'What's so funny about this?' I would say, 'But it's funny, Rodney, don't you understand?' I still have a vivid memory of sitting in this trailer in Arizona arguing with Rodney Dangerfield about what was funny."[27]

Rodney described Ed Wilson as "the father from hell, who uses language that can't be repeated anywhere," and even that does not do justice to the character, or to Rodney's riveting performance as this horrific specimen of a human being. In true *Natural Born Killers* fashion, Mickey and Mallory return later—this scene is shot in black and white—to seek vengeance on Mallory's parents. They bash in Ed's head and drown him in a fish tank and then they burn Mallory's mother alive as she lies, gagged, in bed. It is tough to watch. "I loved the part," Rodney said later. "It was a real challenge to do something deeper than one-liners."[28]

"He was perplexed about the role, and, to an extent, why I wanted him," Stone said. "He said, 'This is not me; this is hard for me.' Especially the scene where he goes up and eyeballs his daughter."[29]

Rodney claimed that, at Stone's invitation, he wrote the part of Ed Wilson himself with only a spare description of the character. "There's only one line that someone else wrote," he said. "Every other line of my talk I wrote." Stone disagreed and noted that Rodney "changed a couple of lines. That's a typical comedian. They say, 'Oh, yeah, I redid the movie, nothing was funny.'"[30]

"Those scenes were hard for him," Stone told the author. "He was great—

his eyeballs roll, and he does it right. He didn't understand the humor of it. I remember we had one interesting moment when we went back to where there were no cameras and we were talking and he says to me, 'I don't know what's funny about it.' And here I am, the director of serious films, trying to convince one of my actors that he's in a funny scene. It's hilarious. You can imagine trying to justify it to a guy that doesn't understand why it was funny.

"I thought it was funny and I still think it's funny and I love *Natural Born Killers*," Stone said, "but some people just don't get it."[31]

On December 26, 1993, after ten years of dating, Rodney, seventy-two, and Joan Child, forty-two, got married in Las Vegas at the Silver Bells Wedding Chapel. It was Rodney's second marriage (or third, counting his re-marriage to Joyce) and the first for Joan. "He started smoking marijuana in the limo, and I wasn't sure how serious he was," Joan recalled. "But he went through with it, thank goodness."[32]

Comedian Harry Basil was living in Burbank when he heard from Rodney the next day. "He called me up and says, 'Harry, I'm in Vegas with Joan. We came to Vegas last night and guess what we did? Are you sitting down?' He goes, 'We got married, man. I'm fucking married.' I got on the phone with Joan, and she said Rodney was like Al Czervik in *Caddyshack*. He had hundred-dollar bills and he's handing out the money: 'Hey, I just got married!'"[33]

Natural Born Killers opened nationwide on August 26, 1994, grossing a nationwide-best $11 million in its opening weekend, and triggering both outrage and praise from critics and moviegoers. "Shock artist Oliver Stone outdoes himself with *Natural Born Killers*," wrote veteran Associated Press columnist Bob Thomas. "By the time Woody Harrelson and Juliette Lewis as kill-crazy lovers end their shooting spree, the count is 52 cadavers. After the pair escape from prison, the number has risen to that of a Bosnian skirmish."[34]

"Both Harrelson and Lewis are overpowered by the editing, but you won't soon get over Rodney Dangerfield playing the profoundly perverse father against '50s-style canned laughter," noted *The Des Moines Register*. "He spawns, abuses and sends into the world the she-creature half of Mickey and Mallory Knox . . ."[35]

Roger Ebert in the *Chicago Sun-Times:* "As he shouts and threatens violence, as he ridicules Mallory's thoroughly cowed mother, as he grabs his daughter and makes lewd suggestions, we hear a sitcom laugh track that grinds out mechanical hilarity. Everything is funny to the 'live studio audience,' because Dangerfield's timing is right for the punchlines. Never mind how frightening the words are. Who really listens to sitcoms, anyway?"[36]

Natural Born Killers eventually grossed over $50 million in the U.S. and Canada and another $60 million worldwide, earning Warner Bros. a hefty profit of around $76 million, kudos for Rodney, and talk of a possible Oscar nomination for his portrayal of Ed Wilson—which was nipped in the bud by the dismissive letter he received from Roddy McDowall and the Motion Picture Academy of Arts and Sciences after applying for membership (as recounted at the start of this book).

Rodney might not have gotten any respect from his cinematic brethren, but it was not so in the world of television, his true mass-media métier. In 1995, he was honored with the Creative Achievement Award on *The 9th Annual American Comedy Awards*, which aired on ABC. The executive producer of the telecast, George Schlatter, noted that the honor was appropriate in the wake of Rodney's snub by the Motion Picture Academy.

Touché.

THE INTERNET WAS IN ITS INFANCY IN 1995—BUT IT WAS OLD ENOUGH for Rodney to get in on the ground floor and establish himself as a pioneer of the World Wide Web as the first celebrity to have his own official website. "That was largely due to the strategy of his wife, Joan, who was more in tune with what was going on digitally," said Kevin Sasaki, Rodney's publicist in the latter years of his career. "But it was the right time when websites started to become places where people went, and because Rodney was a very old-school entertainer, of course. But he was also very progressive in his thinking and was certainly very open to these kinds of innovations. And Rodney was very promotion-savvy. In his own mind, he was always looking for that new thing to do that would generate viewers or fans."[37]

Anyone could log on to Rodney.com (by modem, in those days) and listen to his joke-of-the-day, watch video clips of him performing, and even access photographs. The online service Prodigy hosted a chat with Mr. No Respect and his fans in June and, by the fall, Rodney.com was also selling merchandise—everything from Rodney's books to flowers from Joan's Jungle Roses business in Beverly Hills . . . and even a Rodney Dangerfield screensaver.

The site was bringing in over eighty thousand inquiries a day; it was voted the "Coolest Site of the Day," and was featured in the magazines *Rolling Stone* and *Entertainment Weekly*. It also was not immune from hackers and, in October, it was broken into by a group of online hackers calling themselves the "Chaos Merchants." They hijacked the homepage and left a picture of a naked woman.[38] That did little to slow the site down; Rodney eventually revamped Rodney.com to plug his new movie, *Meet Wally Sparks*, added a schedule of his talk show appearances, offered holiday wishes from him and Joan, and even posted a copy of the court's opinion in his victorious lawsuit against *Star* magazine.

Joan, meanwhile, worked hard on her Jungle Roses business, which counted among its clients Hillary Clinton, Elizabeth Taylor, and Helen Gurley Brown, all of whom were fans of the grapefruit-sized long-stemmed roses that were grown in the South American rain forests. The company helped preserve endangered rain forests by recultivating degraded land and creating an exportable business that boosted local economies; it was honored in 1993 as a Business of the Future by Earth Day International.[39]

In addition to his new website, Rodney branched out into the world of . . . romance novels? He put his own unique, very spicy spin on the genre by narrating *La Contessa*, an audiocassette recording for Dove Audio. Its cover artwork featured a version of Rodney's (much younger) face adorned with brown, flowing locks. Our hero's muscled body is ripped, brawny and bare-chested; he holds on to a bosomy, beautiful damsel-in-distress wearing a low-cut shirt; she, too, has long flowing hair. The twenty-five-minute audio book is ribald, lewd, chock-full of sexual innuendo, and, of course, replete with Rodney's self-deprecating humor. That is followed by another twenty-five minutes of Rodney performing his stand-up act at the Laugh Factory in Hollywood.

Rodney checked another pop-culture milestone off his bucket list when, in November 1996, he appeared in an episode of Fox's popular animated series *The Simpsons*, which was in its eighth season (and still continues to hum along nearly thirty years later). The episode was called "Burns, Baby Burns" and posits Rodney as Larry, the estranged, long-lost love-child son of Homer's boss, the decrepit Mr. Burns. Larry and his dad hit it off early on but, eventually, Mr. Burns realizes that Larry is just a big oaf, and they part ways as Larry returns to his wife and kids—after Homer convinces him to stage his own kidnapping in order for Mr. Burns to admit he loves his son. The episode was written by Ian Maxtone-Graham, and Josh Weinstein and Bill Oakley were the showrunners who worked closely with Rodney when he came in to record his part.

"Rodney Dangerfield was and is a hero of ours and of a lot of people on *The Simpsons* staff," Weinstein recalled. "We were told it was kind of early in the morning for him [to record the episode] and I think he came from not too far away. He seemed a little sleepy at first, but then he perked up while we were directing him. It seemed like he had to 'get going' and then he really jumped in. He was perfect in the episode.

"I have his script; it's one of my prized possessions from *The Simpsons*," Weinstein said. "I have the script that he used and that he wrote his better versions of the jokes we wrote for him. That's the thing: *The Simpsons* is really funny, it has great jokes, but writing Rodney Dangerfield jokes is especially hard. It requires a real talent that only Rodney had. And when we were writing the script, I think we knew that he would improve upon certain jokes or work on the places where he changed the phrasing slightly, so it sounds more like him."[40]

Weinstein remembered the episode fondly years later. "Rodney was a real gentleman. He was friendly, he laughed, he was jovial. He was not difficult in any way."

Rodney was fairly busy on the television scene now; in addition to *The Simpsons* he appeared opposite Brooke Shields in an episode of her NBC sitcom *Suddenly Susan*, guest-starred opposite Ernest Borgnine on his NBC series, *The Single Guy* (starring Jonathan Silverman), and lent his voice to an episode of Comedy Central's animated series, *Dr. Katz, Professional Thera-pist.*

Rodney turned seventy-five in November, and HBO, in conjunction with the American Film Institute, announced plans to fete him with a birthday toast at the U.S. Comedy Arts Festival in Aspen, Colorado. in late February 1997. *Rodney Dangerfield's 75th Birthday Toast* aired that spring on HBO.

"Rodney can't breathe because of the altitude, and he's got an oxygen tank," Harry Basil recalled. "I go up to his hotel suite and he's got an oxygen mask under his chin and he's smoking a joint. All over the tank it says 'FLAMMABLE.' 'Rodney! You're going to blow up the Ritz-Carlton!' It was wild. There was a *Saturday Night Live* reunion and all of the current *SNL* stars—Dana Carvey, Chris Farley, Adam Sandler, Norm Macdonald—were there, and Chevy Chase and Dan Aykroyd and Laraine Newman. It was just crazy. George Carlin was taping a special and the *This Is Spinal Tap* cast was up there. It was just a wild weekend."[41]

Rodney Dangerfield's 75th Birthday Toast opens with Rodney lamenting the fact that no one showed up for his birthday (Jay Leno hangs up on him from backstage at *The Tonight Show*). Rodney bemoans his fate to a papier-mâché Rodney puppet, who calls him a loser. But he makes a wish as he blows out the candles on his birthday cake . . . and . . . cut to the birthday toast, with guests including Steve Allen, Louie Anderson, Sandra Bernhard, Bob Saget, and Paul Rodriguez, and cameos from Roseanne Barr, Jerry Seinfeld, and Conan O'Brien.

The timing was serendipitous (or maybe it was not)—Rodney's first movie in three years, *Meet Wally Sparks*, was in the can and ready to be sprung on the American public.

Harry Basil had the original idea for the movie, which he based on *The Man Who Came to Dinner*, the 1942 big-screen comedy based on the 1939 stage play by Moss Hart and George S. Kaufman and starring Monty Wooley. It told the story of acerbic radio personality Sheridan Whiteside—Wooley reprised his role in the movie—who is in Ohio to dine with a local family as part of a promotional stunt. When he slips on the ice and breaks his leg, Whiteside insists on staying with the family and soon begins to dominate their lives and those of the townspeople. The movie costarred Bette Davis and Ann Sheridan.

"I was like, 'Oh my God, this could be a great idea for Rodney," Basil recalled. "Imagine having Rodney Dangerfield stuck in your house if he was a celebrity and taping a TV show? So, I start writing this movie with Rodney as a tabloid talk show host and I pitched it to [production company] Ruddy-Morgan, and they loved it. They want this to be the next Rodney Dangerfield movie. Rodney is like Jerry Springer, he's crass, and this governor's son invites him to this conservative Southern ball. Al Ruddy goes, 'Harry, you don't need to call it *The Man Who Came to Dinner*, you have a whole original twist on this.' So, I pitch the idea to Rodney, and he's really intrigued by it."[42]

Ruddy-Morgan produced *Ladybugs*, and Rodney was not enamored of Albert S. Ruddy and Andre Morgan at this point, since the movie did not do well, and he was convinced he should have been paid an extra $1 million for his work on the film. According to Basil, Rodney had shown the script for *The Scout* to Ruddy-Morgan before agreeing to star in *Ladybugs* and they were initially enthused about *The Scout* before the deal went south. Though the producers were interested in backing Basil's new movie, which was now being called *Meet Wally Sparks*, money issues came to the fore—namely a lower salary for Rodney. So, Ruddy-Morgan was out, for now, and Rodney took the script to Edward Pressman, who produced Oliver Stone's 1987 big-screen drama *Wall Street*.

"Rodney and Edward Pressman were going to produce it together," Basil recalled. "Edward Pressman gives it to Oliver Stone, who was a huge Rodney Dangerfield fan, and he loved *Ladybugs*. So, we're going to make this movie and Oliver Stone is going to direct it, and Rodney is shooting *Natural Born Killers* in New Mexico, and I'm going to fly to New Mexico and work on the script with Oliver Stone at night, right? And I'm going, 'Holy fuck, I can't believe this.'"[43]

The inevitable trouble arose when a contract was drawn up with Oliver Stone's name at the top. Pressman told Rodney that if Stone did not want to direct *Meet Wally Sparks*, he would remain as a producer. "And Rodney goes, 'Well what does that mean?'" Basil said. "'Well, sometimes Oliver gets attached to something and we get a green light, but there is always an out clause if he takes another movie job, but he stays on as a producer and the studio is still happy with that because it's an Oliver Stone production."

That did not sit well with Rodney, who was concerned it would look bad for him if Stone dropped out as the director. Pressman remained on the project and Basil rewrote the script with Neil Israel.

Harry Basil: "We're going, 'Jesus, a lot of these sex jokes are not going to fly if we keep them in. The daughter or the son is supposed to be a fan of Wally Sparks and Wally is like a cross between Jerry Springer and Howard Stern. So . . . I make this bad call and we just leave the jokes in, so Rodney does not get mad. Rodney knows we're writing the script and I kind of feel that he is a little jealous because he and I wrote together and he's like, 'Well, let's see what they do.'

"Well, the studio and Ed Pressman read the script and they love it. It's got great coverage. Rodney reads the script and he fuckin' hates it. He can't believe that we left all the sex jokes in with the little girl. And I'm trying to save it, and I'm like, 'Well, we can go back to it being a son.' It was Rodney's idea. And Rodney says, 'Harry, I can't believe you let these fuckin' sex jokes stay there.' I said, 'They're just jokes we'll take them out, I was afraid you were going to be offended if we took all the jokes out, right?' So now Rodney is turned off on the whole thing."[44]

Rodney dropped out of the movie altogether and Basil read him the riot act. "I said, 'Rodney, I don't think I can work with you anymore. You pulled this movie away three times. It was my original idea. Ruddy-Morgan wanted to make it, you got mad at them and pulled it away. Pressman was going to make it with Oliver Stone and then you got mad when he said he wasn't going to direct it, and you pulled it away. And then you pull it away from Neil Israel . . . I was counting on making $150,000 off this thing and it's originally my idea and now I can't do anything because you've written it with me and it's only for you.' And he gave me a check the next day for $150,000."

Rodney knew that Basil and his wife, Laura, wanted to buy a house in Encino and that the money would come in handy. "He goes, 'You're right, man, that's not fair. You know, you worked really hard on it.' So, he gave me that money and then he pitched his new idea to me, which was *My Five Wives*."[45]

In the meantime, though, Rodney called Basil out of the blue and told him that *Meet Wally Sparks* was back on, this time with producer Leslie Greif, with Rodney financing the entire project by himself to the tune of $6 million. "Rodney was confident that the movie was going to get sold and be a hit and we would get our money and he added his $7 million salary to the budget," Basil said. "He's thinking the movie is going to make $100 million and he'll get back his $7 million and points."[46]

Greif produced the 1996 movie *Heaven's Prisoners* with Al Ruddy, so they had a history together. They found their man behind the camera in Peter Baldwin, an Emmy-winning television director (*The Wonder Years*) whose long résumé also included *The Dick Van Dyke Show*, *The Mary Tyler Moore Show*, *The Bob Newhart Show*, *The Brady Bunch*, *The Partridge Family*, and *Sanford and Son*, the '70s-era NBC series starring Rodney's good friend, Redd Foxx.

Rodney was a big Jerry Springer fan—he and Joan visited *The Jerry Springer Show*—and his on-screen alter ego, Wally Sparks, bore a passing contextual resemblance to the popular, controversial daytime talk show host (sans the glasses). The movie revolved around Wally, who hosts a sleazy tabloid TV show so down-market that his viewers start abandoning him in droves. He is given an ultimatum by the network's president, Lenny Spencer (Burt Reynolds): clean up his show and goose the ratings or lose his job. Wally's producer, Sandy Gallo (Debi Mazar) hits on a scheme that should do the trick: lure Wally's most vocal critic, conservative Georgia governor Floyd Preston (David Ogden Stiers)—who is running for reelection on a platform of family values—on to the show as a guest.

(The Preston role was initially pitched to James Garner—he declined, it was too physical, and he had bad knees—and to Jonathan Winters, who said no, citing too many dick jokes in the script. Stiers, the former *M*A*S*H* star, accepted the offer. "A fine actor but he wasn't going to sell any tickets," Basil said.[47])

In an effort to get Preston to appear on his show, Wally agrees to attend a reception at the governor's mansion (the invitation was sent by the governor's son, Robby, a huge Wally Sparks fan) and then everything goes sideways. Wally plays strip poker with Preston's wife, Emily (Cindy Williams), and somehow gets involved in a plot to extort Preston—just as Wally's son, Dean (future *NCIS* star Michael Weatherly), romances the governor's daughter, Priscilla (Lisa Thornhill). The movie, shot in L.A., was rife with cameos, including Jerry Springer, Roseanne Barr, Michael Bolton, Tony Danza, Gilbert Gottfried, Bob Saget, and Lesley-Anne Down. When all was said and done, however, *Meet Wally Sparks* was met with a tepid public reception.

To promote the movie, Rodney visited Daingerfield, a small town in Northeast Texas (population 2,655), which held a screening at the Morris Theatre, one of the oldest movie houses in that part of the state. The town's mayor declared January 16, 1997, as Rodney Dangerfield Day and there was a downtown parade in Rodney's honor. Trimark Pictures, the movie's distributor, shelled out $20,000 for the world premiere in Daingerfield.

There was more, of course. "We've got ads airing during *Seinfeld*, we've got commercials during *ER*, we're on buses and taxicabs and billboards in Times Square," Harry Basil recalled. "I had this great idea for Rodney to appear live and do stand-up in Lincoln Center, like Dean Martin and Jerry Lewis used to do, performing live. I opened for Rodney, and it was really cool, and it was completely sold out."[48]

The movie opened January 31, 1997, and did not perform well at the box office, generating only $2.1 million its opening weekend in nearly 1,600 movie theaters nationwide. The critical reaction, though, was fairly positive, for the most part. "The humor may be spotty, but the movie is still engaging enough to remind us what's fun about trash television," wrote *New York Times* critic Stephen Holden. "If Dangerfield gets funnier as he grows older, it's because there is primal humor in the spectacle of a 15-year-old sex fiend trapped in the body of a 75-year-old clown."[49]

"The comedy is erratic, but the performances are surprisingly good," noted *The Boston Globe*. "Rodney is Rodney, and in his orbit are the zesty Mazar doing her street-smart-princess thing, David Ogden Stiers wisely playing it straight as the butt of many of the jokes, and Cindy Williams shining sweetly as the dingbat dowager."[50]

And . . . the not-so-enthusiastic: "Beyond a few guilty chuckles, nothing in this toilet-humor-drenched script, co-written by the star himself, sparkles enough to merit anything but an immediate box-office flush."[51]

"They spent $15 million on print and ads, which was big for a movie release, and we're at that big movie theater in Westwood [in L.A.] and there is the line for [the rerelease of] *Star Wars* just around the block," Basil said, "and there is *Meet Wally Sparks* with three ushers just standing in front and nobody is there. So Trimark pulls it after a week or two because it was just too expensive."[52]

There were also movies that Rodney did not make, although he came close on one project called *Buddy Cops*. TriStar executive Mike Medavoy sent him the script for *Buddy Cops* while Rodney was shooting *Meet Wally Sparks*, and its plotline piqued his interest.

"Rodney and I are reading the script and we're going, 'Oh, we can put all our jokes into this,'" Harry Basil recalled. "Rodney said, 'Okay, man, tell them we're going to do it; that we will rewrite it and they have to give us $200,000 for the rewrite and I'm going to get $8 million, okay?' They really wanted Rodney. So, Rodney says he is going to do it, he wants $8 million, and he and I are going to get $100,000 each to do a rewrite on the script and I'm going to be a producer."

Their enthusiasm was dampened when Rodney and Harry got to the last thirty-five pages of the script and felt that the story just fell apart at that point. "Rodney is going, 'This fucking sucks! This is terrible! I can't do this!' I'm going, 'Rodney, we can save this, trust me,'" Basil said, all the while thinking to himself that Rodney was right but also wanting to produce the movie.

"Rodney's lawyers said, 'Well, this happened to so and so and you might have to do the movie.'" TriStar was only willing to pay Rodney $6 million for *Buddy Cops*. "Where does he think a guy his age is going to get $8 million?" one of the studio's money men told Basil, who relayed the comment back to Mr. No Respect—who was not happy. "Tell them I'm out of the fucking movie, man," Rodney said. "This is great. This is perfect. A verbal commitment, and then he says that and insults me? I'm out." The studio then countered with $7 million for Rodney but he refused to budge. *Buddy Cops* was dead to him.

"Rodney had integrity and would rather spend $7 million and make his own movie that he loved and was passionate about," Basil said. But TriStar wasn't done. They flew one of their executives out to Las Vegas, where Rodney was performing, hoping to lure him back into the fold.

"So, this guy flies all the way to Vegas. Rodney gets his room comped, and the guy wants to talk to Rodney. Rodney's show is over, the guy saw the show, and is sitting there. Rodney is pristine, he looks great, he has his robe on with his towel, his hair is all wet and he's smoked a few joints. 'Okay, man, tell him to come in.' So, the guy comes in and he says, 'Rodney, I'm so sorry, I should never have said that, you're absolutely right, the studio wants to pay you $8 million. That was a very insulting thing for me to say and I'm hoping that you'll forgive me. But TriStar really wants you to make this movie and, of course, we'll pay you $8 million.'

"So, Rodney goes, 'Well, all right, man, let me tell you something. I appreciate you coming here, you know? Let me tell you, it's very insulting for you to insult somebody about their age.' And, again, Rodney wasn't really hurt, he just wanted to fuck with the guy. Then Rodney says, 'I'm not going to do the movie. I don't care if you offered me $10 million, I'm not fucking making this fucking movie and you're a fucking low man, you know? I don't know how you got in this position.' So, the poor guy has to back to L.A. with his tail between his legs."[53]

But TriStar *still* did not give up, and Rodney was invited to the studio to meet with studio chief Mike Medavoy. Rodney and Harry Basil pulled up to the studio in Rodney's big white Cadillac, reeking of pot smoke, and were told they would meet Medavoy, but did they first want to visit the set of *Hook*, directed by Steven Spielberg and starring Dustin Hoffman and Robin Williams? Rodney declined. In the elevator, on their way up to see Medavoy, agent Lloyd Bloom offered Rodney a breath mint. "I don't want to kiss him, I want to fuck him," Rodney said—and then turned down an offer of $9 million to make *Buddy Cops*.

"And that was that," Basil said.[54]

* * *

RODNEY AND JOAN WERE NOW LIVING IN L.A. FULL TIME WHILE, BACK in New York, Joe Ancis was hunkered down in the apartment on the Upper East Side. "He was retired. He was going to Lincoln Center and going to the ballet a lot," his daughter, Julie Ancis, recalled. "He made friends with these kids at Juilliard who played classical music and jazz and they were touring in the summer and called their band the Joe Ancis Jazz Band."

There seems to have been a falling out between Rodney and his best friend, and then Joe became ill with "this mystery illness," according to Julie. "My dad got very sick . . . and moved back in with my mother and then he was in New York Hospital," she said. "The reason that we lived so close to New York Hospital is because my dad wanted to be close to 'the best doctors.' My father was heavy into the 'best doctors.' He was diagnosed with prostate cancer, which is a very slow disease; it was not an aggressive cancer."

Joe's doctors, however, treated the cancer aggressively with radiation. "He was telling me he was going and getting 'zapped' with his radiation and sometimes the nurse would say, 'Oh, we have to do it again' and he's like, 'Are they double-zapping me? Did they make a mistake?' So, within a year he started to deteriorate. He lost an incredible amount of weight, he got very weak, and then he ended up in the hospital and they couldn't figure out what was wrong with him."

Joe Ancis died on December 9, 2001, at the age of seventy-five.

"Rodney called me when my dad died," Julie said. "He didn't come to the funeral, he didn't come to New York. I don't know what kind of physical state he was in. He called me and it was a weird conversation. He wasn't one to get emotionally expressive, you know what I'm saying? Neither was my dad, really."[55]

But, for Rodney, it was all a façade. He was diagnosed in 1995 with clinical depression and took a daily regimen of antidepressants to fight the black moods in which he often found himself. In August 1997, he gave an interview to *Parade* magazine in which he bravely and openly discussed his battle with depression—describing himself as having "a down head" that was eased, somewhat, by his medication. He found the right dosage that worked, he said, after suffering from increased depression for a year and a half and visiting "at least twelve" psychiatrists before finding the right one. "I only see him once a week," he said. "He helps me learn how to handle disappointments."

Throughout the interview, conducted in Rodney and Joan's L.A. condominium, Rodney talked about his life and his career—looking within his "oversized mahogany pill box" for his medication. "People think comedians are happy people," he said. "It's the reverse. When I was writing jokes when I was fifteen, it wasn't because I was happy. It was to escape reality. If I could go someplace and pay money for a laugh for an hour I'd love it. But there is no place for me to go.

"The truth is, as you get older your depression gets greater because you realize this is what it was. And it's not what I thought it would be. I pictured the golden years as The Golden Years: have money, go to all the shows you want, go out. I saw a much more relaxed, joyful life. But all of a sudden, nothing interests me. I have no desire to go out. I'm more comfortable at home."

He credited Joan with making him as happy as he could be: "She's a very easy person to be with, to talk to. She's fair. She's very sensitive. She treats me right."[56]

To producer Joseph Merhi, who grew close to Rodney in the last decade of his life, there were deeper issues nagging at the Dangerfield psyche. "I think he's a genius as a comic and as a human being he was struggling with a lot of issues. He would say, 'What does it all mean?' Rodney was obsessed with the Holocaust; he really thought, deep down, that this could happen again. It was like, 'Tommy is going to come back from the Iraqi War in a coffin and they're going to blame it on the Jews. They're going to round up the Jews and kill them again.'

"One time he was very sick, and he was supposed to perform in Salt Lake City. He had a fever of 101 and was sweating and was getting ready to go to the airport and I said, 'Rodney, for chrissakes, you don't need this gig, cancel.' And he goes, 'I don't know if they're going to reschedule it, I'm gonna make $60,000 or $80,000.' I said, 'Rodney, that's not your money, who gives a damn. This is your health.' He said, 'You don't understand, man, the Jews make this money in case we need to make a quick getaway.'"[57]

David Permut: "We spent a lot of time talking about a lot of things in the world—human behavior, politics, world affairs, being persecuted as Jews, the horrors of what people can do to other people. All of that affected him deeply. His favorite show was *The Jerry Springer Show*. He would watch it and go, 'They're all fucking maniacs.' He's smoking pot and watching it in disbelief and laughing at the guests and the absurdity of the fights breaking out.

"I think we're all products of our childhood, and when you look at Jacob Cohen and his early years they weren't happy years—growing up in an anti-Semitic neighborhood, being taunted in school, a father who abandoned him as a child, a mother who had some issues . . . he had no parental guidance and you think, 'How did this kid survive?'"[58]

Chapter Twelve

After this repair work, I'll be as good as new, but right now I'm in rough shape. I joined a weightlifting class . . . they started me with helium balloons.

THE LATE 1990S WAS A DEFINING PERIOD IN RODNEY DANGER-field's movie career in that he would never again reach the heights of *Back to School*. While he never lost interest in the movie production process and was intimately involved in the films he did make, particularly those with Harry Basil, he stumbled in his choices of big-screen projects and never recovered his box-office mojo.

In 1998 he costarred with Dom DeLuise in *The Godson*, a takeoff on *The Godfather* and *Scarface* in which Rodney played a mob boss named the Rod-father, with DeLuise as the Oddfather and Kevin McDonald as thug Guppy Calzone (of the Calzone Crime Family). The movie, which went straight to video, featured such luminaries as Lou Ferrigno, famous for playing *The Incredible Hulk* on television, and Joey Buttafuocco, he of the infamous "Long Island Lolita" headline-grabbing tabloid story. 'Nuff said.

Rodney also played God opposite Frank Gorshin's George Burns in *Angels with Angles*, which was shot in L.A. in the fall of 1997 but was not released until eight years later, after both Rodney and Gorshin were dead.

Then Rodney and Harry Basil turned their attention to a long-gestating script they wrote called *My Five Wives*. "Joan would tell stories about some of her ancestors who were polygamists; some of them had sister wives," Basil recalled. "Sometimes it would be two sisters or three sisters that were married to the same husband and about how they were attracted to older men. So, Rodney is telling me this idea, how this guy goes to buy some real estate and I said, 'You know what? You're going to buy some property and you buy it at a land auction and then you don't know this, but three wives come with it. And they're hot and really young.' We come up with this idea that [Rodney's character] likes to ski and wants to open a ski resort."[1]

"I was inspired to write the movie because my wife is a Mormon and I became fascinated with the whole polygamy thing," Rodney said. "One of the advantages of having five wives is, they can't all have a headache at the same time."

Basil sent the script for *My Five Wives* to producer Gray Frederickson, a longtime producer for Francis Ford Coppola, who won an Oscar as one of the producers of *The Godfather, Part II* (he was also nominated for *Apocalypse Now*). "He really loved it and said, 'You know, I showed it to Sidney Furie and Sidney is making all these movies in Canada,' so Sidney wound up getting the movie financed in Canada," Basil recalled. "Rodney didn't take a salary and he didn't have to put his own money into it."[2]

Sidney Furie directed the movie, now titled *My 5 Wives*, in which Rodney played wealthy L.A. land developer Monte Peterson, who, after his divorce, flies to Utah where he hopes to open a ski resort but finds himself battling a malevolent banker named Preston Gates (John Byner), who wants to build a casino backed by the mob (in the form of Andrew Dice Clay). Monte wins the bidding, but he has to join a church in order to purchase the land—and ends up marrying the three comely widows (Jud Tylor, Angelika Libera, and Kate Luyben) of the former owner. Later, he marries two other widows in his continuing battle with Gates over the land. John Pinette, Molly Shannon, and Jerry Stiller played supporting roles.

The critics were not pleased.

"There was, for a brief moment, hope for those laugh-starved souls who had worn out their VHS copy of *Back to School*. Could it be? A new Rodney Dangerfield movie? That moment ended during the first two minutes of *My Five Wives*," noted the *Los Angeles Times*. "Humor generally doesn't get any broader than Dangerfield's one-liners, but in his new film . . . each joke strikes like a creaky swinging barn door . . . It's hard to tell if *My 5 Wives* is so completely dumb that it's impossible to be offended by it, or so completely offensive that it's just dumb."[3]

My 5 Wives opened in late August 2000 in limited release and then went straight to video. On the night of the premiere, Rodney and Joan, married now for seven years, renewed their wedding vows in Santa Monica. Andrew Dice Clay led the ceremony; Adam Sandler, who had already filmed *Little Nicky* with Rodney, was the ringbearer, and Fabio was Rodney's best man. After the ceremony, Rodney and Joan cut into a five-tiered wedding cake and there were smiles all around.

Little Nicky did not fare much better than *My 5 Wives*, although it did open in theaters nationwide. Sandler, late of *Saturday Night Live*, was a big Rodney Dangerfield fan and was on a roll following the comedies *Billy Madison*, *Happy Gilmore*, and *The Waterboy*, but he whiffed with *Little Nicky*, another farcical comedy with a budget of $75 million in which he played Nicky, the youngest and kindest of Satan's (Harvey Keitel) three sons (his mother is the angel Holly), who is sent to Earth to stop his brothers from wreaking havoc. Rodney played Nicky's grandfather, Lucifer, Satan's father who created Hell. Like that. The movie premiered in November and finished a respectable second to *Charlie's Angels* in its opening weekend but did not please the critics.

Rodney turned seventy-nine in November and his health was becoming a concern. Eight months earlier, in March, he was hospitalized one day after wrapping up a six-night performance at the MGM Grand in Las Vegas after complaining of chest pains. He was flown back to L.A. where he underwent double-bypass heart surgery. "They cut my chest in half with an electric saw. It still hurts when I think about it," he said. "When the operation was over and they wheeled me out, Joan was waiting for me in the cardiac intensive care unit. She later told me I had tubes stuck in every imaginable place."[4]

RODNEY WAS ALWAYS WRITING AND WRITING. EVEN WHILE HE WAS shooting a movie he would be working on another screenplay. Over ten years earlier, in the midst of filming *Back to School*, Rodney was working on a treatment for a script he called *Serenade Café*. Here is the setup: his character owns a restaurant in Little Italy with singing waiters and falls in love with a waitress. But there is one major problem: She tells him that she can only love a man who sings opera—he has the voice of a toad—so, in order to win her hand, he journeys to Italy where he discovers a family of winemakers who stomp grapes that elicit magical singing powers. Rodney showed the treatment for *Serenade Café* to Harry Basil.

"It was kind of like *Moonstruck*. Even though it's set in New York City, it's this little block in Brooklyn and it's all about love and romance," Basil said. "It's a sweet little movie and people just don't see Rodney Dangerfield in that kind of story."[5]

They sent the script to New Line, and the studio was interested. Rodney was willing to split the cost of *Serenade Café* with New Line 50/50, and Ben Stiller was briefly attached to the movie in what would have been his directorial debut. The project collapsed when Rodney received the final contract from New Line and was not happy with its financial structure.

Fast-forward a decade and Rodney now wanted to revisit *Serenade Café* with Harry Basil. "He wants to make this romantic comedy at eighty years old. He is going to finance it and it is going to be my first directing job," Basil recalled. "Rodney hung out at Caffe Roma in Beverly Hills, and he knew Dick Van Patten. And he said, 'Hey, Dick, I want to make a movie and I just need a producer to make it for under $3 million. You know anybody like that?' And Dick says, 'Yeah, I know the perfect guy.' And he introduces Rodney to Joseph Merhi."[6]

Rodney personally delivered the script to Merhi's house—and bought Van Patten a Chrysler convertible for making the introduction.[7]

"I had a standing tennis game with Dick, Mel Brooks, and Ann Bancroft, so Dick introduced me to Rodney because he wanted to make a movie," Merhi recalled. "He was seventy-four or seventy-five at the time and the movie was a romantic story of a guy who wants to chase the girl and get the girl. Rodney was going to spend $6 million on the movie and Dick [Van Patten] was concerned."

Merhi, a self-made millionaire originally from Syria, lived in Las Vegas and fell in love with the movie business. His company, PM Entertainment, which he ran with partner Richard Pepin, specialized in low-budget action and exploitation films (*L.A. Heat, Bikini Summer, Cellblock Sisters: Banished Behind Bars*) that all turned a hefty profit on VHS and DVD sales with stars including Lawrence Hilton-Jacobs of *Welcome Back, Kotter* fame, Jeff Conaway, C. Thomas Howell, Lou Diamond Phillips, Wings Hauser, and Jim Brown. Merhi owned his own equipment and "a whole working studio . . . the action and stunts were absolutely amazing," according to Harry Basil. "PM Entertainment was huge."

"Having made over one hundred movies in my career, specializing in low-budget action movies that transformed into bigger-budget movies, I knew the foreign and domestic markets," Merhi said. "And I thought it was very dangerous to spend that kind of money, $6 million, and if it doesn't work then Rodney would lose it, so I advised him not to spend that kind of money. Maybe spend a couple of million on the project.

"Our first meeting was at the Playboy Mansion with Dick Van Patten and Hugh Hefner. Rodney was very easy to work with . . . every waking moment he was thinking about stand-up. He always had a pad and a pen and was writing down jokes."

Merhi then invited Rodney to his mansion in Beverly Hills for a meeting.

"He was a bit fascinated by my lifestyle, by my friends, by what I did, by my close relationship with my wife and my kids. The first time Rodney walked into my house—it's 12,000 square feet in Beverly Hills, $20 million—he was a bit shocked. He just looked around and said, 'Oh, I get it. I get it.'"[8]

Serenade Café, which was cowritten and directed by Harry Basil, was now called *The 4th Tenor* and retained many of the elements of its original incarnation.

Rodney plays Lupo, the owner of an Italian restaurant (the Serenade Café) with singing waiters who falls in love with star singer/waitress Gina (Annabelle Gurwitch). She is a wild child who insists that she will only marry a great opera singer, so Lupo goes in search of the world's best singing coach. He is dispatched to Italy by a con man, Ierra (Robert Davi), to study with Ierra's shady cousin, Vincenzo (Richard Libertini). It is there that Lupo meets a family who sings beautifully while they stomp grapes; the daughter, Rosa (Anita de Simone), falls in love with Lupo and tells him that their magical voices come from the wine they produce ("It makes you sing like the angels"). Lupo has a few glasses of the magical elixir and is suddenly crooning a la Pavarotti.

Harry Basil: "Rodney was absolutely adorable in it, and I remember we started shooting before 9/11 and we shot a scene with Rodney and Charlie Fleischer, who played his bartender and best friend. We shot it in Brooklyn, down where they shot *Moonstruck*, where the grandpa would walk the dogs, so we had the World Trade Center behind them—the Brooklyn Bridge and the World Trade Center. And then 9/11 happened and we were getting ready to release the film and we digitally removed the Twin Towers."[9]

The weekend before the 9/11 attacks, Basil and Rodney were in Las Vegas when Rodney pitched him the idea for their next movie, *Back by Midnight*, a lighthearted prison caper. But there was trouble in comedy paradise and Rodney was more depressed than usual: he forgot a joke onstage one night and suddenly developed a case of stage fright as he neared his eightieth birthday.

Rodney would have been appearing at the MGM Grand during the incident in question—he was booked there in 2001 over Labor Day weekend—and he was doing his usual act when an audience member shouted out "Canada!" and Rodney flawlessly pulled the trigger on his bag of Canada jokes: "Canada. They started a country, and nobody showed up, okay? Yeah, in Canada, they only have sex doggie style—that way they can both watch the hockey game."

Harry Basil was watching from the wings. "So now he's about to go on with his act, and he forgets where he is, because the 'Canada' jokes are from the end of his act. And I'm watching this and I'm going holy shit, where is he? He walks offstage to get a glass of water and he goes, 'I don't know where I am.' He goes to the end of the show and maybe cuts out ten minutes. Now he's doing the encore and he's killing. And he gets to the part where he is supposed to do the Canada jokes and he knows he did them already, and he completely forgets where he is again. So, he's like, 'Oh, fuck.'"

Rodney was very upset after the show and told Basil he might be through, that he did not think he could do it anymore. "We had these other two weeks coming up, back-to-back," Basil said. "He's going to the Laugh Factory and he's working on his act, and he keeps forgetting it. He said, 'I don't think I can do this anymore.' He was really scared. He wants to cancel the next two weeks in Vegas."

Rodney and Harry next appeared at the Hermosa Beach Comedy & Magic Club. Jay Leno played there every Sunday night. Rodney sold the place out, of course, and he performed his act flawlessly. Still, he had doubts about playing Vegas, Basil recalled. "Melanie and Joan were in the car with us, and he goes, 'I'm cancelling Vegas. I can't do it, man. I'm scared. I'm done.' I had to give him this big pep talk and he's smoking a joint, you know? He goes, 'Well, I guess we're going to Vegas, huh?'" He got through his shows without a hitch and, with a huge sense of relief, started working on the script for *Back by Midnight* with Harry the next day in the steam room at the MGM Grand.[10]

Rodney and Harry finished a draft of *Back by Midnight* in about three weeks and turned the script over to Joseph Merhi, who wanted to finance the movie. But Rodney, as usual, was impatient. "I don't want to wait, who knows how long I'll be around?" He figured he needed $3.5 million to make *Back by Midnight* and was set on financing the film himself, until Merhi was able to pull together a deal with a $2.5 million budget for a straight-to-video release and a cast including Kirstie Alley, Randy Quaid, Ed Begley, Jr., Harland Williams, Gilbert Gottfried, Paul Rodriguez, and Yeardley Smith, who voices Lisa Simpson on *The Simpsons*.

On November 21, 2001, Rodney visited *The Tonight Show* where he was feted on his eightieth birthday by Jay Leno in a salute that included taped birthday greetings from several of Rodney's friends.

Rodney came out, looking a little frail and wearing his trademark dark suit, white shirt, and red tie. He did about two minutes of stand-up in front of an appreciative, receptive studio audience ("I don't get no respect at all. When I was a kid, my old man didn't like me. He gave me my allowance in traveler's checks. My old man, are you kidding? When he took me hunting he gave me a two-minute head start") before walking over to sit on Leno's couch next to Jay, where he riffed for another two minutes: "And this girl was no bargain either, she was fat. She told me she'd love me 'til the cows come home. I told her leave your family out of this . . . She does charity work; I mean, she handles all the policeman's balls . . . Old is when the testicles tell you it's time to mow the lawn."

When the show came back from its first commercial break, Leno pulled up a video screen with birthday wishes from John Travolta, Rob Schneider, Tim Allen, Adam Sandler—and then Jim Carrey came waltzing out on the *Tonight Show* stage to hug Rodney, to take a seat next to the Man of the Hour, and to reminisce with him before they brought out a birthday cake.

But Leno noticed that something was amiss with Rodney that night. "I know Rodney and I know his act, and his movements were off," he said. "As he was doing his standup, I told our producer, 'I think Rodney's having a stroke or heart attack. Call the paramedics.'"[11]

It was a mild heart attack and Rodney spent the next day, his eightieth birthday, in the intensive care unit at Cedars-Sinai Medical Center. His publicist, Warren Cowan, told the press that when Rodney entered the emergency room with Joan, he asked the heart specialist, "Who gave me this present?" He underwent an X-ray of his blood vessels, and the angiogram revealed that he had good blood flow to his heart and that he did not need to undergo surgery.[12] He was discharged from the hospital after several days and felt well enough to work on his autobiography for HarperCollins and to begin planning for *Back by Midnight*.

In March, Rodney was honored with a star on the Hollywood Walk of Fame in L.A. Jay Leno and Bob Saget were on hand to lend praise to Rodney. "I appreciate the fact that he always took time to talk to all the young comics," Leno said.

Rodney was now filming *Back by Midnight*, in which he plays Jake Puloski, the put-upon warden of a privately owned prison catering to white-collar criminals that is owned by greedy Eli Rockwood (Quaid), who ruins Jake's plans to renovate the prison and is in the midst of selling his company to wealthy British businesswoman Gloria Beaumont (Alley). In retaliation, Jake sends out a crew of four prisoners (played by Phil LaMarr, Paul Rodriguez, Marty Belafsky, and Joe Nipote) to rob a sporting goods store owned by

Rockwood—provided they return by midnight before the security guard makes his rounds. The plans go awry, however, when, after stealing gym equipment from Rockwood's store, the men get a flat tire, and everything spins out of control from there with farcical results.

"There were a lot of funny people in it, and it was a lot of fun," said Harry Basil, who directed *Back by Midnight*. "But Rodney was getting a bit older, and he couldn't remember his lines. He was very impatient. He would show up at the set . . . and as soon as he would come onto the set he would go, 'Harry, when am I going to move?' I always tried to shoot him first. Sometimes I would save the scene where he didn't have much dialogue for the end of the day, so he didn't get high, because once he got high, he was like, 'Hey, man, this is fucking great!' He loved everybody. Sometimes I would release some of the other actors . . . so I could say a line to him and all he had to do was repeat it back to me. That is how we got all of his close-ups at the end. It was kind of tough, but we pulled through it.

"His memory was starting to fail, but he was still as funny as a motherfucker."[13]

The 4th Tenor was on its way to the home video market when Rodney celebrated his eighty-first birthday in November 2002. Joan threw him a party for the movie's "premiere"—"Rodney, in a gesture of solidarity, wore pants," the *Los Angeles Times* reported—and producer Joseph Merhi said that "Romania, of all places" was interested in closing a deal for the movie, which would help recoup its $4 million budget.

Several celebrities, including actor Gary Busey, Hugh Hefner (with six blondes) and Bob Saget attended the premiere party; Rodney and Joan arrived in a limousine. On the sidewalk, a group of musicians played string music and girls in Italian peasant outfits stomped grapes outside the theater. Later, at the Napa Valley Grille, they served Rodney's new line of wine, Rodney's Red, to the guests, though Rodney no longer drank, since alcohol impacted the medications he took for his dodgy heart. Rodney sat at a table with Joan, *Everybody Loves Raymond* star Brad Garrett, and a woman who, Joan noted, crashed the event. No one knows who she was.

Rodney's website, meanwhile, was going great-guns, and now there were even slot machines in Vegas that regurgitated Rodney's voice when their handles were pulled ("Thanks a lot! Your kids don't need college anyway!"). Regis Philbin and Gene Wilder also lent their pipes to similar one-armed bandits. What a town! In February, Rodney celebrated Valentine's Day when he surprised Joan with a redwood hot tub that he had airlifted up to their twenty-first-floor apartment on Wilshire Boulevard, in the Westwood neighborhood of L.A.

News photographers were there to cover the event; a photograph captured a helicopter hoisting the tub up to the apartment. On its side was a huge heart reading "I Love Joan" in a font reminiscent of the *I Love Lucy* title card. Reporters noted that the stunt shut down traffic on Wilshire Boulevard for an hour. Rodney did not care—he was celebrating the love of his life for the last eleven years and he was living in the moment.

In two months, he was undergoing brain surgery.

Rodney needed a heart-valve replacement. The brain surgery procedure, known as an extracranial-intracranial brain bypass, was necessary to improve the blood flow in his body for the new heart valve. It involved inserting the superficial temporal artery near the ear into the middle cerebral artery of the brain. "It's all being done because he does have to have heart valve replacement surgery," Rodney's publicist, Kevin Sasaki, told the press. "He needs to have his blood flow going for that."

The surgery was expected to take roughly eight hours with a ten-day recovery period; the heart-valve surgery was scheduled for three weeks later. "After this repair work, I'll be as good as new, but right now I'm in rough shape," Rodney said. "I joined a weightlifting class . . . they started me with helium balloons."[14]

The surgery was performed in early April 2003 at UCLA Medical Center. Dr. Neil Martin detoured blood flow by threading a tiny artery from Rodney's scalp through a small opening in the bone above his right ear and connecting it to another artery downstream from the blockage.

A day later, Rodney was reported to be in stable condition in intensive care from the twelve-hour operation—four hours longer than expected. He remained heavily sedated and, a week later, was breathing on his own and was eager to watch *The Jerry Springer Show*, his favorite television program. "He's not out of the woods yet, but they took out the breathing tubes today and he appeared thrilled and absolutely elated," said Rodney's publicist, Kevin Sasaki.[15] His surgeons were pleased with his progress; Jim Carrey and Jay Leno sent their best wishes and fans could do the same via Rodney's website, Rodney.com.

On April 18, he was moved from intensive care to a private room, with Joan by his side, and "is up and walking and looking younger and more rested than ever." Three days later, he was released from UCLA Medical Center and the heart-valve-replacement surgery was targeted for some time in June. He lost thirty pounds throughout the ordeal but was walking and looking better than he had in quite some time.

"I truly feel like a new man," Rodney said in a statement. In early May, he held a press conference to talk about the surgery and was in fine form, wise-cracking that his hospital food was "garbage" and, remarking, as he entered the room, that "I gave my wife a kiss on the way in. At my age, that's about as sexy as I can get." He wore a sweatshirt and sandals with white socks at the press conference (no robe this time) and a long scar was visible on the right side of his head. "Rodney looks so good, I think from now on he should only play romantic leads," Joan quipped. Said Rodney: "If you want to lose weight, do what I did. I went on the brain surgery diet."[16]

"He had that room packed," recalled Kevin Sasaki. "And he came out with the doctor and talked about his recovery. I mean, it was really something. But Rodney being Rodney, he was happy to talk to the press and kind of filled that little room. He was never the most physically fit person, at least in the years that I knew him. He would have trouble walking far distances. A lot of that could have been . . . hard living and party habits and all that sort of thing.

"He certainly didn't avoid smoking pot during all of that."[17]

Rodney took it easy as he recovered. He and Joan did not go out much, but they did attend the L.A. opening of Jim Carrey's new movie, *Bruce Almighty*, and were guests at Adam Sandler's wedding. Rodney was, once again, dropping in at the Comedy Store for unannounced appearances to work out new material, and he had a post–brain surgery voice coach to help get his speaking voice back to its familiar baritone. He expressed a desire to play himself in a planned biopic of Sam Kinison.

Less than a month after the surgery, he stopped in at the Laugh Factory. "Rodney looked fragile, and I walked him to the stage," club owner Jamie Masada recalled. "I remember after the first and second joke he got this rolling laughter. That audience gave him life, that laughter, applause gave him energy. It was amazing. I've never seen anything like it."[18]

"I've been cut up so much. I feel like I've been back in my old neighborhood," Rodney joked about the surgery, and said that, "If my progress is really good," doctors could avoid the looming heart-valve-replacement surgery for that much longer, "but I don't want to get too old."[19]

In mid-June, he announced plans to perform in July at the MGM Grand Garden Arena in Vegas . . . and, four days later, cancelled the engagement because he needed more time to recover from the surgery. "Rodney is in pretty good health," said his spokesman, Kevin Sasaki. "The doctor just feels that Rodney needs more time to recover before undertaking a big concert."[20]

At around the same time, Mr. No Respect announced in the press that he signed a deal with MGM to reboot *Back to School*, which had grossed $91 million at the box office seventeen years earlier. Rodney retained some rights to the movie when MGM bought the film library of Orion Pictures, the original distributor of *Back to School*. It was understood that Rodney would not star in the movie, but he was expected to make a cameo appearance and to likely receive a producer or executive producer credit. The deal never came to fruition. But there were plans to release a Christmas album of jazz standards that he recorded before his brain surgery and he was putting the finishing touches on his HarperCollins memoir, which was targeted for release in early 2004.

David Hirshey, an editor at HarperCollins, worked with Rodney on the book.

"One day in the spring of 2003, I received a call from my friend, literary agent Chris Calhoun. He was all abuzz about a manuscript his boss had asked him to look over," Hirshey told the author. "An hour later, a manila envelope landed on my desk at HarperCollins with the words 'For Your Eyes Only' written on the outside. I remember pulling just enough of the manuscript out of the envelope to glimpse the title and let out an audible groan. 'My Lifelong Affair with Swiss Cheese' was printed in large type at the top of the page."

Hirshey thought it was "another quicky book by some hack," but when he pulled the entire manuscript out of the envelope he saw the byline at the bottom of the page: Rodney Dangerfield.

The manuscript was only 160 pages long, "and half of those pages were seemingly taken up with his jokes," Hirshey recalled. He called Chris Calhoun back and told him there was not much in the book save for lines from Rodney's act, "but if we can dole out his personal story, which is both sad and moving," that it could work. The title would also need to be changed, of course; Hirshey and Calhoun met at a Hamburger Heaven located across the street from Hirshey's offices at HarperCollins and worked over the manuscript.

"We cut whole swaths of jokes and brought the autobiographical elements into higher relief. But at least we solved the problem of the title by changing it to *It Ain't Easy Being Me*. Next, we contacted Rodney's wife/manager, Joan, who proved a formidable presence. She immediately asked how much we were willing to pay for the book and Chris explained that we were prepared to make a mid-six-figure offer, while I blanched, but only if Rodney was willing to accept our edits and add some more personal stuff.

"Joan invited us to come out to L.A. the following week to visit Rodney, who, she said, was not in the best of health and tired easily."

Hirshey and Calhoun flew out to L.A. and met Rodney and Joan at a "swanky" Chinese restaurant near their apartment. "We got there a little early before them and watched as Joan valet-parked her red Mercedes," Hirshey said. "She went around to the passenger seat and extended her hand to Rodney to grab on to, and he slowly got out of the car. Though physically fragile, he was still quick-witted and remarked on my red-and-blue checked shirt: 'I didn't know they made those for men.'"

The party of four spent the next hour or so coaxing a few stories out of

Rodney about his early days of coming up in the business. "Among other things, he said of all the famous comics with whom he worked, the funniest person in the room was always a non-comic named Joe Ancis, who hung around with Lenny Bruce," Hirshey recalled—although, when asked to give an example of Joe's genius, Rodney could not remember a single line.

But, prompted by Joan, Rodney eventually came around and regaled the group with some fun stories, including one about opening up Dangerfield's in 1969—telling them how everyone said he was nuts for starting his own nightclub, how the mob would shake him down and the cops would turn a blind eye to any of the mob's strong-arm tactics. "Rodney said, 'I ignored them and opened it anyway and guess what? The mob loved the joint and the cops protected us.'"

Joan invited Hirshey and Calhoun to come over to the apartment on Wilshire Boulevard in Westwood the following afternoon. That was the time of day when Rodney was his most energetic.

"This is my most vivid memory of the whole six months working with Rodney," Hirshey recalled. "I will never forget the sight of Rodney the next day when he greeted us at the door to his apartment. There he stood, in his flapping, semi-opened silk robe that afforded us a panoramic view of his testicles. Personally, I couldn't believe it. And I didn't know what to do, what to say. 'Rodney, your robe is open, you might want to tie it?' I thought that would be disrespectful. He was in a fine fettle, having smoked some killer weed that he immediately offered to us.

"One hit later and I knew this would be an editing session like no other."

Hirshey remembers being led into the dining room where, on a table, was a container with Rodney's allotment of pills for the week, organized by Joan into the days of the week in which Rodney was to take them.

"Joan handed him his day's allotment, along with a glass of water to wash them down, and Rodney eased into an overstuffed chair without adjusting his robe—so we were careful not to let our eyes stray from his face."

To help jog Rodney's memory, Joan laid out dozens of photographs; Hirshey and Calhoun asked him to identify the people in the photos, hoping to spur a story or two and any other details he might remember. "At first this proved a useful exercise, but as Rodney kept passing the joint around the table, his focus and ours began to wander."

Still, Rodney did fire off a string of one-liners, almost as if he were seated across from Johnny Carson (and now Jay Leno) on *The Tonight Show*. Recalled Hirshey: "Here is this physically frail and sad-eyed creature sitting there, trying to remember details of the last fifty years, but once you asked him to tell a joke, the light goes on and it's as if he was standing onstage. I found that amazing.

"It just depended on the day you spoke to him," Hirshey recalled. "At times he was so stoned that he couldn't tell a coherent anecdote. He was either zonked out or he was able to tell us some stories which, of course, we had to go and fact-check. It was a struggle, but we dragged him across the finish line together. In the end, I was proud of the book and so was Rodney. So that is all that really mattered."

Rodney was adamant that he would not discuss his children, Brian and Melanie, at any great length in the book. "We pushed and pushed but he didn't want to go there," Hirshey recalled.

Rodney asked that Hirshey and Calhoun leave a copy of the edited manuscript for him and Joan to peruse and was told there would be additional edits once the new material he provided was added to the existing manuscript. "In the end, I only got him half of the $500,000 advance that Chris originally mentioned, but Rodney and Joan seemed reasonably happy with the $250,000 plus bestseller bonuses," Hirshey recalled.[21]

AND NOW CAME THOUGHTS OF MORTALITY. RODNEY WAS TURNING eighty-two and intended to work as long as he could, with no intent to retire. He would go as long as he possibly could before even thinking about hanging it all up, despite the touch-and-go inability to remember his lines or losing his place doing his stand-up. But his double-bypass and now the brain surgery were giving him pause. Could he clone himself for future generations? Perhaps. In the fall of 2003, Rodney and Joan met with the CEO of Clonaid. Earlier that year, the company announced that it had successfully cloned a baby girl named Eve, though the claim was never proven and there were doubters.

"Rodney and I are clone-curious," Joan told *The New York Post*. "I contacted Dr. [Brigitte] Boissselier, and she came to our home shortly after Rodney was recovering from brain surgery. They said they could create a clone of Rodney by taking a swab of cells from Rodney's cheek. When we asked how much it would cost, they said they wouldn't charge us anything . . . Rodney and I remain skeptical, but if the ethical and legal concerns could be met, I would start painting our spare room blue."[22]

Rodney was feted by Comedy Central on November 22, his eighty-second birthday, with a party and the network's first-ever Comedy Idol award. It was part and parcel of Comedy Central's inaugural Commie Awards, which bestowed bobbleheads of St. Genesius, the patron saint of comedians, to its winners. The event, hosted by Andy Richter, was taped in L.A., and aired December 7 on the cable network to little fanfare.

This was a low-key, very quiet time for Rodney, but the public silence and his lower profile got a boost in March 2004 when Fox Television announced it secured the rights to Rodney's upcoming memoir, which was now called *It's Not Easy Bein' Me: A Lifetime of No Respect but Plenty of Sex and Drugs*." "I'm excited that Fox is making a movie on my life story, but I hope they do it soon!" Rodney said in a statement. "I'm eighty-two years old. At my age, I'm looking for a one-night sit! I'm thrilled about finishing my first book. Now I'm going to read another one."

Dave Madden, the chief of movies and miniseries for Fox Television Studios, called Rodney's "no respect" catchphrase "fodder for a compelling biopic" and "more than just a glib line. Rodney struggled through a lot of menial jobs and a tortured personal life. It wasn't until he was 40 that he found his path."[23]

In April, word broke that Rodney's MGM reboot of *Back to School* would star Cedric the Entertainer, who was currently shooting the studio's *Be Cool*—the sequel to John Travolta's *Get Shorty*—and would be "loosely based" on its 1986 forebearer. It was yet another of Rodney's projects that never saw the light of day.

Rodney kept in the public eye via television, visiting *The Tonight Show Starring Jay Leno* and *Live with Regis and Kelly*—and, in late May, Harper-Collins released his 270-page autobiography. Shortly thereafter it landed on *The New York Times*'s bestseller list.

Respect.

Rodney dedicated the book to Joan "and to all the girls who let me sleep over." Jim Carrey wrote the foreword, recounting his relationship with Mr. No Respect and the role he played in fostering Carrey's career.

"Most people don't know this about Rodney, but he is also a very sweet and generous man," Carrey wrote. "We're talking about a guy who has dozens of people walk up to him every day of his life and say, 'Hey, Rodney, I'll give you some respect,' as if he's never heard it before, and not once has he cold cocked anyone. That alone is an incredible achievement."[24] Rodney wrote a short introduction and then it was off on a journey through his life and career over seventeen short chapters peppered with his oft-candid recollections—he did not shy away from discussing his sex life and his drug use, including co-caine—and his one-liners.

Rodney's hometown newspaper, Long Island's *Newsday*, published a lengthy feature in conjunction with the book's publication in which reporter Jeff Pearlman noted that Rodney was naked under his open robe when he was being interviewed: "His gut is large and his skin is wrinkly, and the fact that federal law prohibits fleshy, 82-year-old men from exposing themselves to strangers seems lost on him."

Pearlman noted Rodney's "regular sessions with a psychiatrist" and his medications: 137 pills, daily—ranging from antidepressants to Aleve—that required their own color-coded chart. "Truly, I don't want people to feel as bad as I have in life," Rodney told Pearlman. "If this book helps anyone im-prove their outlook, that'd be great."[25]

He spent the summer promoting the book, shooting an appearance for the CBS sitcom *Still Standing* and providing his voice for an upcoming epi-sode of Fox's animated series *Family Guy*.

He sat for a long interview with *Rolling Stone* magazine, in part to pro-mote his book and, inevitably—since these chats always seemed to head in that direction—to talk about his happiness, or lack thereof, within the context of his much-publicized life . . . and to smoke a joint with the reporter during the interview, which was conducted in Rodney's twenty-first-floor apartment. Rodney wore a robe, of course (blue), which slid open a few times revealing his private parts, "huddled between his legs, looking quite pleased to be out of the dark." He seemed to be tired and weary: "You know you're going to die. You just don't know how. So, what I'm doing now is hanging around, waiting—waiting to see when and how I'm going to die."

He talked about his love affair with marijuana dating back over sixty years—"It relaxes me. It allows me to cope with life"—and the "shit" he's just bought, $500 an ounce ("As a kid I bought pot for $25 an ounce. An ounce! Oh, everything's insane. Oh, everything's wild!"). He mentioned getting stoned at the White House in the Reagan years and lighting up in the intensive care unit after his heart attack.

In the lead photo accompanying the article, Rodney sits on a bed, wearing a bathrobe adorned with playing cards, Vegas-style, and dark slippers. The robe is open, with a visible scar running from his sternum up and over his protruding abdomen to below his belly button. His hair is white, his eyes staring straight ahead, plaintively. He looks resigned, and a little weary.[26]

It was around this time that Rodney called Dennis Arfa with some bad news.

"I remember the last time he told me he couldn't work," Arfa recalled. "He gets on the phone and goes, 'Man, I can't make it, man. I can't make it.' Just like that. Because he was starting to cancel some shows. I always read between the lines, but I knew he was slowly struggling. And when he said he was out, I was hoping he wasn't and it was just a feeling for a moment. But I knew basically the time was coming."[27]

On August 24, 2004, Rodney was hospitalized for the long-awaited, long-dreaded heart-valve-replacement surgery and was asked how long he expected to remain in the hospital: "If things go right, I'll be there about a week, and if things don't go right, I'll be there about an hour and a half."

"I was going to Bucharest, Romania to shoot a movie . . . and I just called Rodney out of the blue to see how he was doing," recalled Rodney's longtime collaborator, Harry Basil. "And he told me he was going to be going into the hospital the next day for surgery. He told some people, but he didn't tell me, and he didn't tell his kids, and if I didn't happen to call him I wouldn't have known. I was in San Diego, and I went to visit him at the hospital. David Permut and Bob Saget were there, and it was late at night.

"Rodney is telling me about his surgeon, a great heart doctor and he wants me to stick around to meet him. We heard Rodney snuck a little pot in [to the hospital] and he wasn't supposed to, and we talked and told him how much we loved him, and we'd see him later. We were telling him now great he is and how much we love him and then when I'm leaving, it was really late, like 12:30 in the morning, I'm leaving with Bob Saget and I said to Bob, 'I have a feeling I'm not going to see him again.' And Bob gave me a hug and said, 'He is going to be around. Don't worry.'"[28]

Rodney underwent a seven-hour operation on August 25 at UCLA Medical Center and was said to be "resting comfortably" in the hospital's intensive care unit. Depending on the progress of his recovery, his stay at UCLA would be about a week and, following a two-month recovery, he could return to focusing on his career.

Harry Basil: "I remember Joan called me and said the surgery was successful and that Rodney was still asleep. They gave him morphine. The next day I called. 'Is he up?' No, he's not. Then another day went by, and he wasn't up yet."[29]

On September 3, one week after the surgery, it was reported that Rodney remained hospitalized in intensive care and that he was on a respirator. He was listed in stable condition and his doctors were expected to release a statement sometime in the next week. Then, on September 7, came another Associated Press report: Rodney was expected to make "a full recovery" from the valve-replacement surgery but remained in intensive care.

September 16: "Rodney Dangerfield's recovery has been gradual in the three weeks since he underwent heart-valve replacement surgery, but his publicist says that's no cause for alarm."[30] Another report noted that "old friends" including Jay Leno, Jim Carrey, Roseanne Barr, Andrew Dice Clay, Louie Anderson, Bob Saget, and Adam Sandler stopped in to visit Rodney, who "is conscious and in stable condition" but still hooked up to a respirator.

September 21: "Rodney Dangerfield in coma after heart surgery. Rodney Dangerfield has been in a coma for a couple of weeks after undergoing heart surgery, but has begun to show some awareness, his wife said Monday. The 82-year-old comedian was stable and had been breathing on his own for 24 hours, Joan Dangerfield said in a statement released by the comic's publicist, Kevin Sasaki. Dangerfield had a heart valve replaced August 25 at the University of California, Los Angeles, Medical Center."[31]

September 22: "Rodney Dangerfield . . . fell into a light coma two weeks ago, but is in stable condition, according to a statement released by his wife. 'After recent visits from his family and close friends, Rodney is starting to show signs of awareness,' Joan Dangerfield said."[32]

"They pretty much let me try everything to bring him out [of the coma] and . . . they gave me permission to bring in beyond family other people that had strong connections to him," Joan recalled later. "I got on the phone and called a few comics, and they all knew the mission—try to say something that maybe Rodney would react to. I heard some of the best material in the world from Jay Leno, Jim Carrey, Adam Sandler. Louie Anderson came almost every day . . . Bob Saget, Andrew Dice Clay, Roseanne, and we just thought there was hope, there was a chance."

"I held his hand, I talked to him, I did all those things that you would do with any person that you loved," Louie Anderson said. "I just thought, shit, man, this guy should be alive."

Jim Carrey recalled how he tried to get a laugh out of Rodney in those final hours. "I said, 'Don't worry, I'll let everybody know that you were gay.' At that point, his eyes kind of shifted and his mouth started shaking like he wanted to say something to me. I could see there was a look of like joy and recognition and stuff, and all the machines lit up."[33]

RODNEY DANGERFIELD DIED AT 1:20 P.M. ON OCTOBER 5, 2004. HE WAS eighty-two years old. Joan, Melanie, and Brian were with him when he slipped away, along with Joan's father, Smokey, and his niece, Suzie. He was also survived by his two grandchildren, Melanie's sons, Joshua and Matthew.

Although he was in a coma for nearly a month after his heart surgery,

Joan said he emerged from it during the last week of his life. "When Rodney emerged, he kissed me, squeezed my hand, and smiled for his doctors," she said, paying kudos to Rodney's medical specialist. "To her, I will be forever grateful for giving me those moments."[34]

His family issued a press release noting that Rodney suffered "a small stroke post-operatively and developed infectious and abdominal complications from which he did not recover."

Within hours after his death, the Laugh Factory comedy clubs in New York and L.A. were paying tribute to him on their marquees: Rodney Dangerfield: May He Rest in Peace and Make God Laugh.[35]

His death made international headlines. *The Los Angeles Times, The New York Times,* the *Chicago Tribune, The Baltimore Sun, The Independent* in London, England, and other big-city newspapers recounted Rodney's life and career and, in the days following his funeral, published editorials and letters from readers praising Rodney and his comic genius.

The New York Times:

"With a rumpled suit and one hand perpetually loosening his trademark red necktie, Mr. Dangerfield took the stage as a hapless, self-deprecating Everyman slapped around by life and searching in vain for acceptance. It was a role that he had had some experience with offstage . . . Still, he remained a rarity among comedians in the late 20th century—he remained a one-liner comic of the old school whose best work was done before a live audience."[36]

The Los Angeles Times: "Standing on stage in his trademark black suit, the bug-eyed Dangerfield was always the picture of sweaty unease, nervously tugging at his red tie as he delivered his sharply timed, self-deprecating lines: 'My wife's a water sign, I'm an earth sign; together we make mud . . . I mean, she's attached to a machine that keeps her alive—the refrigerator . . . The other night, she met me at the front door wearing a see-through negligee. The only trouble is she was coming home.'"[37]

Tom Shales of *The Washington Post:* "Many labels were hung on Rodney Dangerfield during his long, frenetic heyday as the funniest joke-teller in America. His was 'the comedy of angst,' or 'the comedy of the loser.' What it really was was the comedy of funny. It was the comedy of laughter. His act wasn't conceptual or observational or stream-of-consciousness; it was a bunch of jokes."[38]

Harry Basil was in Romania, shooting his movie, when he heard the news. "I remember getting on the flight from Romania and somebody was reading *People* magazine, and it had a picture of Rodney and Janet Leigh, who died two days before Rodney. I flew back for the funeral on a red eye. The funeral was amazing. I was a pallbearer along with Jim Carrey, Adam Sandler, Rob Schneider, Bob Saget, David Permut, Michael Bolton, Rodney's son, Brian, and his son-in-law, David Friedman."[39]

Among the twenty-four honorary pallbearers were George Carlin, Roseanne Barr, Chris Rock, Tony Bevacqua, Andrew Dice Clay, Larry David, Jon Lovitz, Bob Nelson, Carl Reiner, and Dennis Arfa.

"It was a great service. I got there a little late with my wife and kids and I was sitting toward the back in an aisle," Basil recalled. "Those were the last seats. Larry David was there. There was one seat all the way at the end and Larry kind of stood and looked at me like, 'You're not going to slide down?' He has to sit next to my three-year-old son, and he's got his arms folded. The service is about to begin and Roseanne, who is up front, turns around and says, 'Larry, in here.' He kind of threw me a look."[40]

Rodney would have appreciated that.

The funeral took place at Pierce Brothers Westwood Village Memorial Park in L.A. and was held at dusk—since Rodney never liked to have appointments before 5 p.m. The entrance leading into the chapel was covered with white cashmere carpets, and candlelit chandeliers hung from trees that were covered in roses. A harpist played as those in attendance passed under an ornate iron gate in which Rodney's initials were intertwined with sterling silver roses. Joan had the ground covered in clouds of softly lit chiffon that were swept twenty feet into the sky. Flowers and candles hugged the pathways. Floral bouquets sent by those unable to attend—including Larry King, Jack Nicholson, John Travolta, Rita Rudner, Cindy Williams, and Byron Allen—were placed around the chapel and the grounds.

Bob Saget led the service; several of Rodney's family members delivered eulogies, including his daughter, Melanie, and his nieces Morgan and

SueAnn Reese. Jay Leno also eulogized Rodney—calling him "the greatest stand-up comedian of all time"—along with Roseanne Barr, Paul Rodriguez, Tim Allen, Jerry Stiller and Anne Meara, Michael Bolton, Dom Irrera, and Jim Carrey, who said, "I'll never forget how kind he was to my father. I remember watching Rodney on *The Ed Sullivan Show* as a child, and laughing, not because I got the jokes, but because my father was in hysterics."

The funeral service booklet was tied with Rodney's signature red tie; each guest was given a cookie with Rodney's face immortalized in icing. A memorial video, produced by David Permut, was said to bring the crowd of five hundred to tears. A caricature of Rodney could be seen behind his casket, draped in chiffon.

The coffin was led to the gravesite, accompanied by strolling violinists, just after sunset, to the tune of Frank Sinatra's "Come Fly With Me"—the song that played in Rodney's hospital room the day he died. A final "prayer of comfort" was delivered by Louie Anderson. Rodney's friends also contributed a memorabilia box that was buried with him. Afterward, guests were led to a feast of Rodney's favorite dishes. Shortly thereafter, Joan, Melanie, and Brian gathered at Rodney's star on the Hollywood Walk of Fame and adorned it with armloads of flowers.

"Although Rodney has transcended this physical plane, what he stands for—kindness, humor, humility, and heroic struggle against all odds—remains, and is the essence of the human experience," Joan said. "Rodney will always represent what it feels like for all of us to crave a little respect. That's a desire our life on earth will always evoke and Rodney Dangerfield will always be around, eternally, to epitomize the experience."[41]

Coda

THE LEGEND OF RODNEY DANGERFIELD CONTINUES TO LIVE ON, twenty years after his death.

Four days after Rodney's passing, on October 9, 2004, NBC's *Saturday Night Live* honored Rodney in a sketch starring Darrell Hammond as Mr. No Respect, who arrives at the Pearly Gates seeking admittance into heaven from St. Peter (Horatio Sanz). St. Peter asks Rodney about his childhood. "Oh, I tell ya, I had a rough childhood, all right? When I was a kid my parents moved a lot—but I always found 'em. I'll tell ya, I got no respect as a kid. I worked in a pet store; people kept asking me how big I would get!"

The skit continued with St. Peter asking Rodney about his wife and their sex life ("one night she used me to time an egg"). When all was said and done, Rodney said, "So whattaya say, St. Peter, do I get in or what?"

St. Peter: "Of course you do."

Rodney: "Then, what's with all the questions?"

St. Peter: "I just wanted to hear those jokes one more time."

Rodney: "Finally! A little respect!"[1]

IN 2005, ONE YEAR AFTER RODNEY'S DEATH, UCLA'S DIVISION OF NEURO-surgery named a suite of operating rooms after him and established the "Rodney Respect Award." Jay Leno was its first recipient; future honorees included Tim Allen, Jim Carrey, Louie Anderson, Bob Saget, Chelsea Handler, and Chuck Lorre.[2]

That same year, Joan sold the Wilshire condo she had shared with Rodney for more than its $3.9 million asking price. She also sold their former Little Holmby house (with an indoor pool) for more than $2.7 million and bought a new, 5,400-square-foot Art Deco–style home in the Hollywood Hills that boasted four bedrooms, five bathrooms, and city-to-ocean views.[3]

In August 2006, Joan filed a $2 million lawsuit in Manhattan Supreme Court against Tony Bevacqua, accusing him of locking her out of profits from Dangerfield's and falsely claiming full ownership of the comedy club, which was still going strong after over thirty-five years in business. "He is showing Rodney no respect—and it is just plain wrong," Joan said.

She claimed that, since Rodney's death two years earlier, Bevacqua refused to acknowledge what she contended was her 25 percent ownership stake in Dangerfield's. "Rodney would be proud of Mrs. Dangerfield's devotion and commitment to protecting his name and image," her attorney said. The suit was settled out of court in November 2007.[4]

In September 2006, shortly after filing suit against Tony Bevacqua, Joan filed a lawsuit in California claiming that Rodney's daughter, forty-two-year-old Melanie Roy-Friedman, peddled a video of Rodney to Comedy Central "for her own selfish purposes" for use in the network's on-air *Legends: Rodney Dangerfield* tribute to the late comedian, which aired September 10. "Melanie's actions hurt her father terribly," Joan said.

The copyright infringement lawsuit accused Melanie of not returning the original recording she made of Rodney's act in 1988—and that, while he protected his routine, he allowed his daughter to record it "so that her future children could see it." When Rodney asked Melanie to return the videotape, she kept the master tape for herself, the lawsuit alleged.[5]

The case dragged on for another two years and, in August 2008, as the case was headed for trial in federal court in Los Angeles, Joan and Melanie settled the lawsuit under terms that were confidential. "All copyrights to Rodney Dangerfield's act are held by Joan Dangerfield, who owns all of her late husband's intellectual property," Joan's attorney said. "Joan is very committed to my father's legacy," Melanie told the press. "He said that he loved her deeply and thought she was the nicest person in the world."[6]

Then, in September 2007, Joan filed a lawsuit in Los Angeles County Superior Court against David Permut, who had more than two hundred hours of videotaped footage of Rodney taken during the last years of his life. The material, she claimed, "is highly private, extremely sensitive and very personal," according to the lawsuit, and "was never intended to be made available for viewing by the public."

The suit claimed that Permut was editing the material into a documentary called *Respect* that he was hoping to air at the Sundance Film Festival in 2008—and that he violated an agreement he had with Joan giving her joint control over the material. The action sought a court order barring Permut from showing the footage until the dispute could be settled through arbitration.[7]

In October 2008, a judge ordered a permanent injunction against Permut not to distribute the video footage of Rodney. Attorneys for both parties declined to comment, noting the confidential terms of the settlement.

Six years later, in May 2014, Rodney was posthumously honored by Manhattanville College in Harrison, New York, which established the Rodney Dangerfield Institute for the Study of Comedy—and awarded Rodney an honorary posthumous doctorate deeming him "Dr. Dangerfield." That followed on the heels of the Dangerfield website, Rodney.com, still overseen by Joan, winning a Webby Award for its design and content. The Dangerfield Institute promised to offer a minor in the field of comedy to its students, to offer special scholarships, and to develop a "Dangerfield Archive" to "catalog and study Rodney's body of comedic work."[8]

Joan was proactive, too, three years later, after donating $1,000 toward a mural of Rodney in Kew Gardens, Queens. The mural was commissioned by 501 See Streets, a community group, and was painted in 2016, for free, by Italian artist Francesca Robicci on a brick wall near Lefferts Boulevard. Robicci worked from a photograph of Rodney taken by Joan. A letter from Joan's lawyer claimed the mural was "less-than-flattering."

"The situation here is that the artist left the country before making the revisions that were necessary," Joan told the *New York Post*, adding that she had approved a sample image that Robicci had submitted, but that the mural did not live up to it.

"As soon as I saw the image . . . I laid out the revisions that I thought would help improve it," she said. "I tried for three months. I thought the only solution at this point was to have it painted over. I don't want to embarrass the artist . . . hurt her, this is not a public stance against her."

Robicci told local television news station NY1 that she was willing to fly back from Italy to touch the mural up. "It was something that I wanted to do for that city, for the community, and also to have some kind of, as I said, exposure for my art," she said. "I was not expecting all this issue of this thing that came out as a gift."[9] Joan's lawyer eventually sent a cease-and-desist letter demanding that the artwork be removed.

That summer, Rodney was honored with a memorial plaque in Kew Gardens that was placed in front of a tree next to the Kew Gardens station for the Long Island Railroad, not far from where Rodney lived with his mother and sister in an apartment in the 1930s. The plaque was a gift from members of the Aquinas Honor Society at Immaculate Conception Catholic Academy in Jamaica Estates, who held a bake sale to raise money and enlisted Joan's support in the process. It features Rodney's image from his 1939 Richmond Hill High School graduation photo and lists *Caddyshack*, *Easy Money*, and *Back to School* among his achievements, along with his 1981 Grammy for *No Respect* and his 1983 "Rappin' Rodney" single.[10]

Joan was also front and center in founding the Rodney Dangerfield Institute at Los Angeles City College in honor of her late husband. It began in 2017 and offers classes, a stand-up workshop, joke writing, improvisational comedy, and an American film comedy genre class. It is the only comedy institute in the country housed within a community college. In September of that year, the college produced a stage reading of *Back to School* with *Everybody Loves Raymond* star Brad Garrett performing Rodney's role as Thornton Melon. Proceeds benefited the Rodney Dangerfield Institute.

Dangerfield's, the club into which Rodney poured so much of his heart, soul, and finances, continued to thrive in its location on 1st Avenue in Manhattan. But, in 2020, the club, like so many other businesses, was forced to shut down amidst the COVID-19 pandemic.

It remained shuttered until 2023, when it reopened as Rodney's, under the ownership of comic and attorney Mark Yosef. The newly rechristened club is brighter than the original Dangerfield's, with an Art Deco motif Yosef said is "modern and updated but keeps the foundations." There is a large portrait of Rodney placed directly across from the stage.[11]

Riffs on Rodney

RODNEY DANGERFIELD LEFT A LASTING IMPRESSION ON NEARLY everyone he encountered over his long and illustrious career.

The author interviewed many people for this book who shared their varied and in-depth memories of Rodney, only some of which could be included in the preceding pages.

Here, then, are more recollections and stories about Rodney Dangerfield culled from those interviews—and others conducted by the author—that shine a further light on his character and his personality.

THE PLAYERS (IN ALPHABETICAL ORDER):

Julie Ancis: Joe Ancis's daughter; family friend.

Dennis Arfa: Rodney's road manager.

Candice Azzara: Rodney's costar in *Easy Money*.

Harry Basil: Stand-up comedian; toured with Rodney and cowrote, directed, or produced *Back by Midnight, The 4th Tenor, My 5 Wives, Meet Wally Sparks, Ladybugs*.

Dennis Blair: Stand-up comedian; toured with Rodney.

Tom Dreesen: Stand-up comedian.

Dom Irrera: Stand-up comedian.

Carol Leifer: Stand-up comedian.

Maurice LaMarche: Stand-up comedian/voice-over artist. Toured with Rodney.

Jay Leno: Stand-up comedian and former host of *The Tonight Show with Jay Leno*.

Joseph Merhi: Producer and friend of Rodney's.

Bob Nelson: Stand-up comedian. Toured with Rodney.

David Permut: Friend of Rodney's.

Rita Rudner: Stand-up comedian.

Kevin Sasaki: Rodney's publicist.

Pauly Shore: Comedian and friend of Rodney's.

Robert Wuhl: Stand-up comedian.

Julie Ancis: I think Rodney relied on my father for his intellectual capacities, his ability to understand what's funny and what's not funny, for his ability to understand nuance. He relied on my dad for a lot of that. And, I think, for emotional support. My dad was there for him. And my dad was very loyal. He never said anything negative about Rodney, at any point in time.

Dennis Arfa: Rodney didn't want any angles. He didn't want the stress. He was very clear about that. He did what he had to do and paid what he had to pay. And that was it. He was an amazing character and an amazing artist to be close to and connected to.

Candice Azzara: We were up in his apartment rehearsing. I was more outgoing than he was. We talked about how he just wanted to be married and have a white picket fence and just have a natural life. He was kind of shy and a gentleman, and he had his robe on. I remember we were rehearsing, and his pants fell down. I don't know why he always had his pants open for some reason.

Harry Basil: As soon as he would come on the set he would go, "Harry, when am I going to move?" "You just got here!" He would get really impatient. He loved writing movies. He used to say this in interviews all the time: "You make a new movie, you think you're making *Gone with the Wind*." The anticipation doesn't live up to the realization. Movies take a long time to make. I always tried to shoot him first. Sometimes, I would save a scene where he didn't have much dialogue for the end of the day, so he didn't get high, because once he got high, he was like, "Hey, man, this is fucking great." He loved everybody. He didn't want to leave, but also he didn't have to have as many lines.

Tom Dreesen: We had a professional respect for one another, but you also liked him instantly. All the younger comedians, he liked them, and they liked him. He respected them. He respected the art of comedy, the art of stand-up comedy. When I first met him, I was doing *The Tonight Show*. I did sixty-one appearances on *The Tonight Show*, but my earlier times on the show I did a lot about going to Catholic school. I did four or five *Tonight Show*s like that. I used to get fan mail . . . that didn't say "to Tom Dreesen," it would say "to the Catholic comedian." When I met Rodney, he said, "Hey, Tommy, you're very funny, you've got the church going for ya." I never forgot that. That was Rodney's way of explaining things.

Dom Irrera: When I auditioned for Rodney's 1988 special, *Nothing Goes Right*, there were two guys ahead of me. One of them was Damon Wayans. Rodney wanted me to see his assistant, and then the guys ahead of me did twenty-five minutes each. I was so fucking pissed off. I didn't even do my act. I just laid into them. Rodney comes up to me and he goes, "You know, kid, you're funny, but you got no act. I'll come see you again." So, he comes to the Improv, and that's when I got the special. I had no clue how big it was. I go to Atlanta the next night. The tickets went in like an hour. Then it started. Then it was a big deal.

Carol Leifer: I do remember a funny story about Rodney, and I quote it a lot to people because I think it really encapsulates stand-up comedy. I remember being at the bar at Dangerfield's and a young comic walking over to Rodney and he was like, "Rodney, do you mind if I have a second of your time? I just want to ask you a question about comedy because I'm starting out." Rodney was very nice, and he was like, "Sure." And this kid launched into, "What do you think about this? What should I do about that? What about this situation?" It was like he was overloading Rodney with questions about stand-up. I remember Rodney just getting up and going, "You'll figure it out, kid, you'll figure it out," and he walked away. But to me it was not only so Rodney, but it was also like, that is the thing about stand-up comedy: you learn it by doing it. It's like no amount of advice or classes, or whatever is going to get around the fact that it's performing, and you have to get up onstage to learn the answers to all of these things.

Maurice LaMarche: Being on the road with Rodney was an experience. He was not into being on tour so we would only go out on weekends. Sometimes I would even stay at his house; I would fly into New York and stay at his house and we'd get on a tour bus and schlep out to Schenectady or Poughkeepsie or Scranton, P.A., and we would play the venue, then come back and I'd stay overnight at his place and then we would go out again. He only wanted to work weekends; he wanted his weeks to be free unless we worked Vegas and were there for a week or two weeks.

Jay Leno: When a joke bombed, Rodney would own up to it and he would feel terrible and look at the ground, like a bloodhound that can't find the snack. And he was a guy whose face grew into his act. Because when you're twenty-five years old, your life's pretty good and you're young, you're good-looking. When you get a little haggard, that's the real key. That's how you could tell real comedians. They don't really care what they look like.

Joseph Merhi: He offered me $100,000 to get high with him one time. He would call me at midnight or one in the morning and we would go to Jerry's Deli. "You awake?" "I'm awake now, Rodney." "Wanna go to Jerry's Deli? Let's get a sandwich." The place was open twenty-four hours a day at the time. He'd get out of the car slowly and pull up his pants, tuck in his shirt a little bit, look at the sign, and say, "You know, delis killed more Jews than Hitler." He would say that every time. Of course he was a sloppy eater; he would get shit all over the place. My wife refused to go to dinner with us and, if she did, she refused to eat. He would drip stuff on his shirt.

Bob Nelson: He would want you to work hard, too. He would tell me, "I'm only paying you $500 per show in Vegas, but they'll give you more money if you talk to them. If you get on the phone with them and try to negotiate, tell them, 'This is what Rodney is giving me, but could you guys help me out a little bit?'" He would do things like that.

David Permut: With me and Rodney, it was black and white and no gray. What you see is what you get. He always said what he felt to me—if he loved somebody, he would express it [and] if he didn't he would express that, too. There was that honesty. When you have someone close to you and you feel you have an honest relationship, you don't want to color anything—you call it like it is. Rodney did that. I loved his perception of things and people.

Rita Rudner: Dangerfield's was very dark, and it always felt like if the lights went out there would be something on the floor. There were little round tables, and they were somewhat spread out. Most of the [comedy] clubs at that point were people sitting close together . . . so you didn't get the boom of laughter you got in other clubs. You would go to the Comic Strip, and then I would go to Catch a Rising Star and then I'd go to Dangerfield's and then I would take a taxi downtown and do the Comedy Cellar. It was a little bit like a New York City tour of comedy.

Kevin Sasaki: Rodney wasn't that warm-and-fuzzy kind of guy that you could talk to about your mom. But you could tell his levels of affection, and he felt very comfortable with me, with regard to how he behaved. He was a very salt-of-the-earth kind of guy in so many ways. He would come to the door in his underwear or the bathrobe, hanging out. It didn't bother him.

Pauly Shore: I knew I was lucky to be in his presence, and I knew I was lucky to work with him, and I knew it was a snapshot in time that I would never get again. I knew I was blessed to be with him because of his ability to do comedy. There is no one who had his cadence and his style and his delivery. He was like a rapid-fire comic. It wasn't just long, drawn-out stories. It was all jokes. All killer, no filler, you know?

Robert Wuhl: Rodney doesn't get the credit for being one of the great comedy writers of his time. He wrote most of those jokes. At times I have to also say that Rodney would get upset about someone stealing his jokes, like any comic; however, he sometimes wrote a lot of jokes and other people came up with the same idea. I'd say, "Rodney, two people can do a joke about an airplane," but he was convinced that there were comics that stole his jokes, and they probably did. But there were other guys that didn't. In stand-up comedy, you're dealing with an honor code and not all people are honorable.

Dennis Arfa: He would tell me for years all the good things he did for me: "I gave you $43,000 to go start your company. I gave you good advice when your son was born. Don't argue with your wife in front of your kid or they will grow up fucked up." He would tell me over and over again how much good he did for me, which I have always acknowledged, but you know, he wanted to be confirmed. He was stupidly stubborn that way. It made surviving Rodney a bit of a task.

Candice Azzara: He was a very gentle soul, that's what I loved about him. I saw the sadness in him—such a deep sadness that, if you looked at his eyes, they were always sad even though he made a lot of jokes. He seemed like the saddest man I've ever known.

Harry Basil: I really loved Rodney's kids, Brian and Melanie. Anytime that I saw them, we had really nice times together and stuff. Brian was a funny guy. We had spent some time with him in Vegas, like going out, partying and stuff like that when we were all younger. And he was very charming, but I think he and his dad just had this weird relationship. There were so many times where Rodney could have said on these movies, "Hey, man, I want Brian to be a producer on this, I want him to learn the business. Make him a producer, teach him about the movie business," but he wouldn't do that. Rodney wouldn't give anyone a free ride, you know?

Tom Dreesen: When I worked Vegas a lot, Rodney would be in town, I would be in town, Joan Rivers, David Brenner. After our shows, we would all sometimes go over to the Riviera Coffee Shop and sit in the back, and we'd have like a big booth, and we would all talk about how the show went. I recall the night that Rodney and I were sitting in this oval booth, and he was sitting with a girl and there was a young waitress who was so nervous because she was waiting on all of us. I guess she was new. I don't know if she was intimidated or something, but she came around and she was pouring coffee, but as she was leaning, she went behind Rodney, and the girl with Rodney put her cup up behind Rodney's back and said, "Hey, honey, don't go away, pour some in here." Well, the girl was so nervous, she started to pour the coffee and she poured it down Rodney's back. She goes, "Oh, I'm so sorry." Rodney said, "Hey, it's not your fault. I was sitting here." It was such a Rodney line.

Dom Irrera: He said to me once, "What can I do for you, anything?" And it was just him and me. I said, "Rodney, you have already done enough. It's such a kick to have you as a friend now. Yeah, you can do something." He said, "What?" I said, "Close your robe. I can't eat anything if you don't close the robe, because it's making me sick to my stomach."

Maurice LaMarche: He loved my impressions. He knew that I did him, but he said, "Listen, man, I know you do me and you do me real good, but don't go out there and do me, okay? They're waiting for me; if you go out there and do me it takes something away, okay? There was one opening act that did that, and I didn't like it, okay?" He taught me quite a few things. I have a very warm spot in my heart for Rodney and I owe him a lot.

Jay Leno: I would hate a comedian who says, "How is everybody doing? Anybody from Boston?" Get to the fucking joke. Rodney was, "Here's the joke right now." Not a lot of phony filler and all this other nonsense. It was just pure comedy—a hundred percent real orange juice.

Joseph Merhi: Rodney was striving to find peace all his life. In the ten years that I knew him, he was looking and struggling to find peace. He would turn to marijuana to forget about life and stay up until four in the morning getting high, and then he would try to get excited about projects that he liked. He had very few friends. He was a wonderful man and I do miss him. I have a photo of him in my office and Rodney wrote on it, "Where have you been all my life?"

Bob Nelson: I liked Dangerfield's because it was very intimate. It was a little scary for me. I'm pretty physical when I do my stuff so when I moved around a lot, I was always afraid I was going to walk off the stage; sometimes I would bang into the piano. But it was a really good room. Sometimes it would be a little scary because if the audience wasn't with you right away you couldn't see anybody—and you couldn't tell if they were smiling.

David Permut: Rodney wore his emotions on his sleeve, and it wore heavy on him. He was consumed with being a good parent, consumed with having love in his life, consumed with finding happiness. "When I found pot, I found Shangri-La," he said. That was a great form of escape and relaxation for him. Rodney had many signatures—the red tie, the sweat, the way he moved, "no respect"—he checked every box.

Rita Rudner: I loved Rodney Dangerfield because of his character. He never broke character. Watching him on *The Tonight Show* with Johnny Carson was a real lesson to me in how to do panel. Because there's a difference when you do stand-up and when you do panel on a television show and how you approach it, so I kind of watched how Rodney separated those two activities.

Kevin Sasaki: To this day, his jokes are funny. There is not a time mark. It was just funny stuff. I will say that of all the people I represented, including Merv Griffin, Rodney was probably the most recognizable. Whenever I went anywhere with him people just lost it. "Hey, Rodney! No respect, Rodney!"

Robert Wuhl: He was from the East Coast, and I lived out here in L.A. and he came out here later. He lived right up the street from me. He was in Vegas a lot, and then he had some health problems. I remember the last time I spoke with him. He was in the hospital the day before he was going in for that double operation. He was smoking dope in the hospital. He said, "What are they gonna do to me now?" It wasn't like he was stoned all the time. There's a difference between being an alcoholic and having a drink at night.

Dennis Arfa: Melanie was the apple of his eye. Brian always seemed lost and down. I don't know how much contact they had. Not a lot. Melanie was the softer one about her dad. I remember when she had her Sweet Sixteen. Rodney missed it, so he had her Sweet Sixteen on her seventeenth birthday at Dangerfield's.

We would go out to play different venues on the weekends. He didn't really like theaters that were too big. I remember one night they put him on at Jones Beach, about ten thousand people, and he didn't like people yelling at him from the audience. Mostly we played three- to six-thousand-seat theaters. He played Radio City multiple times. He would do the Universal Amphitheatre in L.A. for our five nights in a row. He was kind of a rock star. His audience was young, a bunch of seventeen-year-olds; they were kids. The casino audience was older, but he had a young audience. One of the greatest things we did is that we would charge the last row at all of his performances $5—the "no respect" seats.

Another thing Rodney would do would be Opening Day for the baseball season. Rodney would throw out the ball on the second day. "No respect." I went with him a few times. The ballplayers and the cops were enamored with him. He knew basically shit about baseball, but he came in to throw the ball and we left. Anything to reinforce the "no respect" image. He did a lot of things like that.

Harry Basil: Rodney had the oldest clothes. He didn't like anything constricting. You know, the whole thing with tugging his shirt? He had a shirt collar that was made with one ply of material on the collar, and that's where the whole tugging thing came in. When he would wear socks, the elastic on the socks was too tight on his leg so he would take a scissors and cut them on either end, so they dropped down. He didn't like anything tight. As soon as he got home, he would take off his clothes and put on the robe. That's where that whole thing came from.

Dennis Blair: He referred to me and my wife as the "Happy Gentiles." He was not a happy man but, for some reason, he was protective of us happy Gentiles. He thought we were pure as the driven snow. So, he would never do anything in front of us. I mean, we knew. He had this little Seagram's pouch where he kept his various equipment or whatever he had in there. We knew it was drug related. He would take it out in front of us every once in a while but he never told us what it was. He protected us from that. I remember he would send the car around to get me and my wife and he would get in, and the first thing he would say was, "Man, it's all bullshit, man, what does it all mean?"

Tom Dreesen: I loved to watch Rodney kill it at the Laugh Factory. I would watch Rodney destroy those audiences. The young kids loved him, and his material always did well. One night we went in there and the room was packed with USC and UCLA students. For some reason, they did something joint together and they had the room for the night. I was following Rodney, and Rodney was doing all of his stuff. Everybody knew him on *The Tonight Show*, so he worked clean on *The Tonight Show*, as we all did, but this night he closed with . . . he said, "You got a lot of young kids out there, a lot of you young guys, and you're going to one day get married and I'm going to give you some advice. If you want to make your wife scream in the bedroom, when you're finished fucking her, get up and wipe your cock off on the drapes." There was a second and the audience erupted into laughter. That was his closer. Again, nobody ever saw him work blue because they always saw him on television, but he could be as blue as any comic out there.

Dom Irrera: I really felt like he was someone that would be in my heart forever. Not to be sappy. What a fucking character. On his eightieth birthday, he says, "Hey, kid, you want to get fucked up?" I said, "No, Rodney, I don't do drugs." He said, "That's all right. Wait here, don't go home."

Maurice LaMarche: I never saw cocaine [while on tour with Rodney] but he would smoke a little pot. He had a funny ritual before he would come on. I'd come off and immediately the "Rappin' Rodney" video would start to play, and he'd say, "How are they, kid?" And I'd say, "They're great, Rodney," or "They're a little dead tonight." He'd go, "It's all right, man, it's all right, we're gonna be good." He had a full-length mirror and a table in front of it. There would be two fingers of Scotch in a small glass, then a tumbler of water, no ice, then a second tumbler on the other side with two fingers of Scotch. Just as the video ended, he would throw back the Scotch, drink down all the water, then the second Scotch, then out onstage. It was all in time to the music. It was brilliant. I never saw him break that ritual in the year and a half I was on the road with him.

Bob Nelson: Rodney didn't want cursing in your act. He didn't want to censor you or anything, but that's why he would book people who could work clean. He would work with comedians who were a little blue, but we knew. It was an unwritten rule that you shouldn't say any four-letter words. It was okay to say the S-word or whatever, but he didn't want you to drop the F-bomb. He was like my crazy uncle.

David Permut: He was always very conscientious of the clock and of being punctual. "David, you gotta be here, I'll meet you at my place at eight." So, I ring the doorbell and it's like 8:05. "What happened? What happened?" He'd carry a watch with no band in his pajamas or his pants, but he took it out and was always looking at the time.

Kevin Sasaki: Rodney was interesting because he was a multigenerational comic. In other words, it wasn't just the wheelchair and walker audiences of his generation—there were young people, too . . . screaming. A lot of that probably had to do with the movies that continued to play, like *Caddyshack* and *Back to School*. A lot of movies that kids, to this day, probably still watch. And his *Tonight Show* appearances kept him relevant.

Robert Wuhl: Johnny Carson loved jokes and he loved Rodney. Rodney would say, "You gotta go out there and do damage"—he had, like, thirty-two jokes per second, around there, half of them in his stand-up and half in the panel segment with Johnny. It was set in stone. Rodney wasn't going to call an audible in telling his jokes. Johnny would just feed him; he was a great straight man. Anything that interrupted Rodney threw him. Carson wanted to see how he would react. He liked that.

Dennis Arfa: Working live was a big thing for him. He made a lot of money. It was a big part of his life. And he liked it. His DNA was comedy. It was just so who he was. He would sit around and all of a sudden he would see something or something would pop into his mind, a joke, and he would be writing it down. He was always on the edge of that.

Here I was observing this successful person and the price for what was going on in his head was part of where his brilliance came from, without a doubt, but he had to live with himself. He would say that. He went to Hawaii, out of the blue . . . and he comes back from this weeklong vacation. I said, "Rodney, how was your vacation?" He says, "How good could it be? I was with me." That is perfectly symbolic Rodney. Most people who associated with him didn't understand him. It was too overwhelming.

Harry Basil: Not a day goes by that I don't think about Rodney or tell a story about him. Even years later, the comedy club that I opened in Vegas . . . it was his club originally and we have a booth dedicated to him in the back and a statue of him. Sometimes when I'm alone in the club, I walk by it, and I'll kiss my hand and touch his cheek. I have a total of three clubs now. I got a writing career and a directing career and all of that just because of him.

Dennis Blair: I introduced Rodney to Sam Kinison. Rodney was raving about this comic that he saw a couple of nights before, he was in the club [Dangerfield's] and he was telling me about his act, and Sam came in one night and we were talking. He was talking about his act a little bit and I said, "I think Rodney saw you, do you want to meet him?" He said, "Yeah, sure," and we went downstairs to the dressing room and Rodney took a liking to him.

Tom Dreesen: I've been in this business a long time [and] 85 percent of all stand-up comedians that I've met in my life are insecure, neurotic, sometimes psychotic, love-starved wrecks. And the other 15 percent are gifted comics and people who say, "I know how to write a joke, and I know how to tell one." Rodney was in that first group. He was one of those insecure, neurotic . . . But, you know, that didn't make him any less funny, it made him a lot funnier. Every night it was like, "I've got to prove it again, prove it again." It wasn't like, "Look out for me, I'm going to wipe this audience out." He wasn't that way at all. There is an old cliché that most people live from day to day. A singer lives from song to song and a comedian lives from joke to joke. Except at the end of every joke, your option is up again. Rodney was that, personified.

Dom Irrera: I never heard anybody say anything bad about him, which is pretty amazing because people get jealous.

Maurice LaMarche: I remember one time we were in Latham, New York, at another theater-in-the-round, and the theater didn't put my name on the marquee. Rodney had a road manager at the time named Fitz, and he goes, "What the hell is this, Fitz? No fucking billing for Maurice? You tell them I'm not going on until they get his name up there." And, sure enough, I'm in my dressing room, showering and getting ready for the show, and Fitz comes to get me, and we open up the back door and he says, "Take a look at this." And there's a guy in a cherry picker, risking his life—the marquee looked like it was from *The Jetsons*, up in the clouds—and there he is with the suction cup, "L . . . A . . . M . . . A . . . ," so I got the billing. And Rodney would give me big letters, 50 percent billing in Las Vegas—people have to fight tooth and nail and give up money to get this type of billing, but Rodney would just hand me 50 percent billing on the marquee of Caesar's Palace. He was great to me.

Bob Nelson: My dad used to drink a little bit, and we're at the Westbury Music Fair and my dad's backstage and we're walking around. My dad walks up to Rodney, and he goes, "Hey, you know this whole crowd is here for my son." Now, Rodney had booked me on the show and all the shows were sold out. So, Rodney goes, "Is that so?" And my dad goes, "Yeah, you're not as funny as my boy. He blows you off the stage." And he's drunk. And Rodney goes, "Okay, whatever you say." And he says, "You know, it's very strange that your son drew all these people because it was sold out when I called him to open for me." And my dad just cursed him and goes back to my dressing room. I go, "Rodney, I'm so sorry," and he goes, "It's okay, kid, he tied one on. It's all right."

Robert Wuhl: Rodney transcended the generations because the jokes were so great. And people appreciate a good joke.

Dennis Arfa: Rodney was a good party boy. He would be on a plane and see a woman and he would start off with a question like, "Are you married? Are you available? Are you happily married?" He would cut to all the chases. He had big balls that way.

I'll tell you one thing with Rodney, and I saw this—he discarded people quickly. He got rid of a lot of people—cousins, comics, friends, nephews. If he thought you turned on him, you were dead. And I saw a lot of people vanish. And that includes family members.

There weren't that many professionals that stayed in his life. Estelle Endler would have been one. First of all, she was smart, and she knew her shit. And she could deal with him well. She was the only one. But when she passed, he was basically managing himself, which . . . didn't go quite as well. He did *Back to School* and that was his last really big movie. I think he cared, artistically, but he really wasn't the guy to do the business for himself. I think Rodney saw himself as a better businessman than he really was. He had a professional craft, but once he got into being his own guy, and didn't have a manager, and didn't really want one, or whoever stood in for five minutes . . . his career lost its direction.

Harry Basil: I think the first time I ever laid eyes on Rodney was when I was working as a doorman at the Comedy Store, probably 1983. And he climbed out of a limo with his pants unbuttoned. He was kind of pulling up the zipper and said, "Hey, how you doing? Everything all right?" I was like, "Wow!" Little did I know that I would be seeing a lot of that in the years to come.

I think the whole thing about Rodney and "no respect" is because everybody feels like they've been put down and whatnot, but if he ever felt like he was wronged by someone, even somebody he absolutely loved and was really close with, he could completely write them off. Or completely walk away from something. Rodney walked away from, like, $15 million worth of movies just because or on principle or what he thought was principle.

Dennis Blair: There was a part of him that was appreciative of his success. But even *Caddyshack* . . . he hated making it. He said, "You want to punish a kid, you make him write on the blackboard one hundred times. That's what making movies is like." It was hard to come by happiness with him.

Endnotes

Prologue

1 Elaine Dutka, "Dangerfield Rejected by Movie Group," *Boston Globe*, December 19, 1994, 61.
2 Dutka, "Dangerfield Rejected by Movie Group."
3 "Academy: Dangerfield Denied Membership to Group," *Los Angeles Times*, December 17, 1994, F12.
4 "Academy: Dangerfield Denied Membership to Group," *Los Angeles Times*.
5 Murry Frymer, "At 40, He Put on a Fresh Coat," *Newsday*, March 5, 1969, 64A.
6 Frymer, "At 40, He Put on a Fresh Coat," *Newsday*, 68A.
7 Donald Freedman, "Nobody Respects Poor Rodney, But They Sure Laugh at Him," *Miami Herald*, April 7, 1969, 45.
8 *The Howard Stern Show*, SiriusXM, July 14, 2020.
9 Author interview.

Chapter One

1 "Grand Theatre of Varieties," *Manchester Courier and Lancashire General Advertiser*, April 24, 1900, 8.
2 *Evening Star*, Washington, D.C., January 2, 1904, 22.
3 *Buffalo Courier*, August 21, 1910, 61.
4 *Bayonne Herald*, October 17, 1903, 3.
5 *Aberdeen Herald*, February 28, 1913, 8.
6 Eddie Cantor, *My Life Is in Your Hands* (New York: Cooper Square Press, 2000), 121.
7 *Edmonton Journal*, February 1, 1913, 26.
8 Cantor, *My Life Is in Your Hands*, 122.
9 *Virginian-Pilot and the Norfolk Landmark*, June 26, 1916, 4.
10 *Iowa City Press-Citizen*, February 16, 1916, 6.
11 *Calgary Herald*, June 16, 1923, 11.
12 "Good for the Disposition. New Palace Theatre Bill Is Rough on Grouches and Dyspeptics," *Fort Wayne Daily News*, January 18, 1916, 4.
13 Rodney Dangerfield, *It's Not Easy Bein' Me: A Lifetime of No Respect but Plenty of Sex and Drugs* (New York: HarperCollins, 2004), 4.

Chapter Two

1 Rodney Dangerfield, *It's Not Easy Bein' Me*, 6.
2 *It's Not Easy Bein' Me*, 13.
3 *It's Not Easy Bein' Me*, 8.
4 *It's Not Easy Bein' Me*, 16.

5   *It's Not Easy Bein' Me*, 10.

6   Lawrence Grobel, "One Banana Peel After Another," *Parade*, August 3, 1997, 9.

7   *Biography: Rodney Dangerfield*, A&E, 2012.

8   Ben Fong-Torres, "Rodney Dangerfield: America's Favorite Fall Guy Finally Gets Some Respect," *Rolling Stone*, September 18, 1980, 40.

9   *It's Not Easy Bein' Me*, 32.

Chapter Three

1   Jack Leahy, "What Makes Rodney Run . . . ," *New York Daily News*, June 1, 1969, 4.

2   *It's Not Easy Bein' Me*, 32.

3   *It's Not Easy Bein' Me*, 158.

4   Interview with Bobby Wygant, 1982 (YouTube.com).

5   Kliph Nesteroff, *The Comedians: Drunks, Thieves, Scoundrels and the History of American Comedy* (New York: Grove Press, 2015), 90–91.

6   *Biography: Rodney Dangerfield*, A&E, 2012.

7   *It's Not Easy Bein' Me*, 158.

8   *It's Not Easy Bein' Me*, 48.

9   *It's Not Easy Bein' Me*, 37.

10 *It's Not Easy Bein' Me*, 47.

11 *It's Not Easy Bein' Me*, 59.

12 *Biography: Rodney Dangerfield*, A&E, 2012.

13 Mary Mitchell, "For Rodney, Life Is Just a Bowl of Pits," *Journal-News*, October 21, 1973, 1E.

14 *Brooklyn Eagle*, April 23, 1948, 8.

15 Carol Kramer, "The Loser Image Pays for Rodney," *Chicago Tribune*, August 16, 1970, 2C.

16 Tom Shales, *Minneapolis Star*, September 11, 1977.

17 *New York Daily News*, April 4, 1946, 36.

18 Kliph Nesteroff, "An Interview with Van Harris," Classic Television Showbiz (blog), August 30, 2012.

19 Walter Winchell, "On Broadway," *Scrantonian*, July 2, 1950, 29.

20 Ed Sullivan, "Little Old New York," *New York Daily News*, January 13, 1951.

21 *The Boston Globe*, January 28, 1951, 70.

22 *Buffalo Evening News*, October 10, 1949, 9.

23 Earl Wilson, *Courier-Post*, August 2, 1951, 33.

24 *It's Not Easy Bein' Me*, 64.

25 *It's Not Easy Bein' Me*, 69.

Chapter Four

1   Martha Slud, "Aluminum Siding Celebrates Fiftieth Anniversary," *Washington Post*, September 9, 1995.

2   *It's Not Easy Bein' Me*, 65.

3   Jack Leahy, "What Makes Rodney Run . . . ," *New York Daily News*, June 1, 1969, 227.

4   "F.B.I. Arrests 15 in Home Loan Aid," *New York Times*, October 23, 1955.

5   Nathan Kanter and Loren Craft, "FBI Nabs 15 in Home Improvement Fraud,"
     New York Daily News, October 23, 1955, 37.

6   *It's Not Easy Bein' Me*, 74.

7   "Two Fined 6 Gs Each for Taking Part in 600-G Loan Racket," *Newsday*, Febru-
     ary 10, 1956, 17.

8   "Show Is Jammed with Ideas for Better Living," *Bergen Record*, March 8, 1957, S-2.

9   Nesteroff, *The Comedians*, 92.

10   Dan Lewis, "Don't Shed Tears for Rodney Dangerfield," *Bergen Record*, April 15,
     1969, 47.

11   Lewis Grossberger, "Respect at Last!," *Rolling Stone*, August 28, 1986, 41.

12   Grobel, "One Banana Peel After Another," *Parade*, August 3, 1997, 8.

13   Harvey Pack, "Now He's a Rich Loser," *Paterson News*, March 7, 1969, 17.

14   Jack Leahy, "What Makes Rodney Run."

Chapter Five

1   *New York Daily News*, June 1, 1969, 227.

2   Mike Kalina, "Rodney Dangerfield Don't Get No Respect, But at Six Figures a
     Year He Don't Care," *Pittsburgh Post-Gazette*, August 8, 1975, 23.

3   *It's Not Easy Bein' Me*, 79.

4   Fong-Torres, "America's Favorite Fall Guy," *Rolling Stone*, September 18, 1980, 41.

5   *Las Vegas Review-Journal*, December 8, 2005.

6   "Worry—and World Laughs," *Cincinnati Enquirer*, October 26, 1969, 4-I.

7   Frank Ross, "Sip and Sup," *New York Daily News*, October 11, 1963.

8   Joan Rivers, *Enter Talking* (New York: Delacorte Press, 1986), 346.

9   Bobby Wygant interview, 1982 (YouTube.com).

10   Albert Goldman, *Ladies and Gentlemen, Lenny Bruce!!* (New York: Random
     House, 1971), 105.

11   Goldman, *Lenny Bruce!!*, 105.

12   *It's Not Easy Bein' Me*, 242.

13   Author interview.

14   Al Cohn, "Tijuana Group Has Talent, All That Brass," *Newsday*, October 28, 1965, 102.

15   "At Mister Kelly's," *Chicago Tribune*, November 28, 1965.

16   Nesteroff, *The Comedians*, 94.

17   *Biography: Rodney Dangerfield*, A&E, 2012.

18   Earl Wilson, *Courier-Post*, January 20, 1966, 30.

19   *Bergen Record*, November 19, 1966, 39.

20   "Nightclub Review: 'Supremes,'" *Miami News*, April 9, 1966, 13.

21   Ken Barnard, *Detroit Free Press*, September 21, 1966, 34.

22   *Miami News*, January 21, 1967, 7.

23   Earl Wilson, *Morning Call*, January 7, 1967.

24   *Morning Sentinel*, January 11, 1967, 5.

25   Author interview.

26   *It's Not Easy Bein' Me*, 97.

27   Ruth Thompson, *Greenfield Recorder Gazette and Courier*, September 13, 1969, 15.

28   Larry Bonko, *Greensboro Daily News*, July 22, 1979, 69.

29   "Walter Winchell . . . of Broadway," *Lebanon Daily News*, April 20, 1967.

30   Walter Winchell, "The Broadway Lights," *Cincinnati Enquirer*, February 2, 1967, 16.

31   Ed Sullivan, "Little Old New York," *New York Daily News*, March 20, 1967, 135.

32   *Bristol Evening Post*, May 25, 1967, 12.

33   Earl Wilson, *Evansville Press*, January 24, 1968.

34   *It's Not Easy Bein' Me*, 99.

Chapter Six

1   *Biography: Rodney Dangerfield*, A&E, 2012.

2   *Greenfield Recorder Gazette and Courier*, September 13, 1969, 15.

3   Fong-Torres, "America's Favorite Fall Guy," *Rolling Stone*, September 18, 1980, 41.

4   Robert Klein, *The Amorous Busboy of Decatur Avenue* (New York: Touchstone, 2005), 306.

5   *New York Daily News*, November 25, 1973.

6   "Between The Acts," *The Record*, April 15, 1969, 47.

7   Ed Sullivan, "Little Old New York," *Morning Herald*, April 5, 1969, 4.

8   Frank Langley, *North Adams Transcript*, July 12, 1969, 19.

9   Norton Mockridge, "Dangerfield Lives Dangerously," *The News*, July 30, 1969, 30.

10   Jack Leahy, *New York Daily News*, June 1, 1969.

11   Jack O'Brian, "Voice of Broadway," *Asbury Park Press*, August 17, 1969, 63.

12   Vince Leonard, *Pittsburgh Press*, January 30, 1969, 48.

13   Dan Lewis, "Between the Acts," *Morning Call*, February 20, 1969, 44.

14   Bobby Wygant interview, 1982 (YouTube.com).

15   Donald Freeman, "Nobody Respects Poor Rodney But They Sure Laugh at Him," *Miami Herald*, April 7, 1969, 11-F

16   Fong-Torres, "America's Favorite Fall Guy."

17   Terry Kelleher, "Routine reality: It's not easy being Rodney," *Miami Herald*, April 23, 1982, 87.

18   *Bergen Record*, April 12, 1970.

19   Charles Champlin, "Dionne Warwick in Show at the Sands," *Los Angeles Times*, August 4, 1969, 70.

20   Jack Leahy, *New York Daily News*, June 1, 1969.

21   *North Adams Transcript*, July 12, 1969, 19.

22   Fong-Torres, "America's Favorite Fall Guy."

23   William Verigan, *Cincinnati Enquirer*, October 26, 1969, 132.

24   Author interview.

25   Author interview.

26   Author interview.

27   Author interview.

28   Biography.com/actors/rodney-dangerfield-i-dont-get-no-respect.

29   William Verigan, *Cincinnati Enquirer*, October 26, 1969.

30   Verigan, *Cincinnati Enquirer*, October 26, 1969.

31   Harvey Pack, "He Gets No Respect and No Award," *Morning Call*, January 12, 1972, 42.

32   Klein, *The Amorous Busboy of Decatur Avenue*, 342–344.

Chapter Seven

1   *It's Not Easy Bein' Me*, 140.
2   Jack O'Brian, *Paterson News*, January 23, 1970, 23.
3   John Huddy, "Poor Rodney Gets 'No Respect,'" *Miami Herald*, February 22, 1970.
4   *Bergen Record*, February 20, 1972.
5   McCandlish Phillips, "Singer Takes Charm to Rikers Island," *New York Times*, June 17, 1970.
6   Albert Goldman, "A 30-Year Loser Is a Winner," *Life* magazine, August 28, 1970, 8.
7   Ann Guarino, "Old Stars Add to Film," *New York Daily News*, January 18, 1971, 49.
8   Roger Greenspun, "Movie-House Fantasy Opens at Kips Bay," *New York Times*, January 18, 1971.
9   Museum of Modern Art, "The Projectionist. 1970. Written and directed by Harry Hurwitz."
10 Marvin Kitman, "Is Nothing Sacred?," *Newsday*, March 16, 1971, 97.
11 Klein, *The Amorous Busboy of Decatur Avenue*, 308.
12 Fong-Torres, "America's Favorite Fall Guy," *Rolling Stone*, September 18, 1980, 41.
13 Lewis Grossberger, "Respect at Last!," *Rolling Stone*, August 28, 1986, 85.
14 *It's Not Easy Bein' Me*, 73.
15 *Florida Today*, September 19, 1980, 9.
16 Author interview.
17 Author interview.
18 Author interview.
19 Author interview.
20 Author interview.
21 Dan Lewis, *Bergen Record*, August 6, 1972, 31.
22 *It's Not Easy Bein' Me*, 103.
23 Rodney Dangerfield, *I Couldn't Stand My Wife's Cooking, So I Opened a Restaurant* (New York: Jonathan David Publishers, 1972).
24 Rodney Dangerfield, *I Don't Get No Respect* (Los Angeles: Price/Stern/Sloan, 1973).
25 *It's Not Easy Bein' Me*, 153.
26 Author interview.
27 Mary Mitchell, *Journal News*, October 21, 1973, 53.
28 Author interview.

Chapter Eight

1   *San Francisco Examiner*, February 6, 1981, 5.
2   Author interview.
3   Author interview.
4   Larry Bonko, *Greensboro Daily News*, July 22, 1979.
5   "Caddyshack 'Cads' Wind Up Shooting," *Miami Herald*, November 15, 1979.
6   Author interview.

7   Earl Wilson, *Press-Telegram*, June 28, 1976, 17.

8   *Detroit Free Press*, June 1, 1979, 5-B.

9   *Minneapolis Star*, September 11, 1979, 1-C.

10   Author interview.

11   Author interview.

12   Larry Siddons, "Less filling or tastes great, Lite beer revives careers," *Marshall News Messenger*, December 10, 1981, 11.

13   Author interview.

14   David Hirshey, "Flacking for beer with the over-the-hill gang," *New York Daily News*, July 8, 1979.

15   Frank Deford, *Lite Reading* (New York: Penguin Books, 1984), 67.

16   *Sioux City Journal*, February 16, 1984.

17   "Phantom of a commercial," *Newsday*, June 6, 1986.

18   Author interview.

19   Author interview.

Chapter Nine

1   "Newhart's father leads campaign for Chicago reruns," *Clarion-Ledger*, December 13, 1981, 28.

2   Chris Nashawaty, *Caddyshack: The Making of a Hollywood Cinderella Story* (New York: Flatiron Books, 2018), 130.

3   *Biography: Rodney Dangerfield*, A&E, 2012.

4   Nashawaty, *Caddyshack*, 132.

5   Author interview.

6   Nashawaty, *Caddyshack*, 166.

7   Nashawaty, *Caddyshack*, 157.

8   Author interview.

9   Nashawaty, *Caddyshack*, 159.

10   Nashawaty, *Caddyshack*, 158.

11   *It's Not Easy Bein' Me*, 123.

12   Nashawaty, *Caddyshack*, 163.

13   Author interview.

14   Nashawaty, *Caddyshack*, 163.

15   Author interview.

16   Author interview.

17   *It's Not Easy Bein' Me*, 193.

18   Associated Press, "Comedian hurt during spoof," *Indiana Gazette*, December 22, 1979.

19   Rodneydangerfield.com (YouTube).

20   Karin Winegar, "Rodney (no-respect) Dangerfield hides, but . . . nobody seeks," *Minneapolis Star*, March 21, 1980.

21   Ernie Santosuosso, "Rodney Dangerfield, 'No Respect,' Casablanca," *Boston Globe*, July 17, 1980, 7.

22   Hugh Wyatt, *New York Daily News*, July 18, 1980, 25.

23   *Fort Lauderdale News*, September 5, 1980, 93.

24   Mike Kalina, "'Caddyshack' stars lug egos, hostility into match with media," *Pittsburgh Post-Gazette*, July 28, 1980.

25   *St. Louis Post-Dispatch*, July 24, 1980, 28.

26   John Stark, "The film is a turkey, not a birdie," *San Francisco Examiner*, July 25, 1980, E-3.

27   Joseph Gelmis, "A rowdy gagfest," *Newsday*, July 25, 1980.

28   Vincent Canby, "'Caddyshack,' 'Animal House' spinoff," *New York Times*, July 25, 1980, Section 3, 8.

29   Rex Reed, 'Dressed to Kill' tops in bad taste," *New York Daily News*, July 25, 1980, 3.

30   Anthony Bersani, "'Caddyshack: Bad Putt," *Atlantic City Press*, August 1, 1980, V3.

31   Author interview.

32   Author interview.

33   Tony Schwartz, "Dangerfield: 'It's Not Easy Bein' Me,'" *New York Times*, May 12, 1982, 85.

34   Dick Maurice, "Comedy star talks about marijuana," *Desert Sun*, December 9, 1980, B14.

35   Author interview.

36   Author interview.

37   Lawrence Christon, "Ungentled at the Genteel Pavilion," *Los Angeles Times*, February 28, 1982, 66.

38   "Lite Beer commercials our newest art form?," *Miami News*, March 2, 1982, 1.

39   Walter Kaner, "A China trip on agenda for judges," *New York Daily News*, August 4, 1983.

40   Author interview.

41   Tom Shales, "Rodney Dangerfield 'a ray of refracted sunshine,'" *Journal Herald*, April 29, 1982, 39.

42   *Santa Maria Times*, April 29, 1982, 2.

43   "Dangerfield special hilarious," *New York Daily News*, May 12, 1982, 64.

44   *It's Not Easy Bein' Me*, 227.

45   Author interview.

46   Nick Thomas, "Living With Rodney Dangerfield: Widow talks about love, laughs and legacy," thespectrum.com, September 25, 2018.

47   Author interview.

48   Author interview.

49   Author interview.

50   *Point of View: A Retrospective of Joe Sedelmaier*, sedelmaier.com.

51   *Chicago Tribune*, August 14, 1983, 14.

52   Author interview.

53   Roger Ebert, "Filmmaking is killin' Dangerfield," *Los Angeles Times*, March 27, 1983, 6.

54   Author interview.

55   Author interview.

56   Author interview.

57 Hal Lipper, "Dangerfield finds it hard to carry film," *Dayton Daily News*, August 18, 1983, 23.

58 Gary Graff, "Dangerfield should have stuck with stand-up comedy," *Detroit Free Press*, August 19, 1983, 31.

59 Janet Maslin, "Screen: 'Easy Money,' *New York Times*, August 19, 1983, 47.

60 *Hartford Courant*, September 2, 1983, 46.

61 Gene Siskel, "Funny how Rodney Dangerfield strikes it rich in 'Easy Money,'" *Chicago Tribune*, August 19, 1983, 55.

62 Richard Freedman, "'Easy Money' grossly unfunny," *Capital Times*, August 20, 1983, 10.

63 Author interview.

64 Author interview.

Chapter Ten

1 Lisa Faye Kaplan, "Hot Stuff!" *Journal News*, February 1, 1985, 23.

2 "No Respect? Loses Nugget in Atlantic City," *New York Daily News*, December 10, 1986.

3 Author interview.

4 *New York Daily News*, July 27, 1980, 172.

5 *Courier-News*, February 20, 1997, 37.

6 Author interview.

7 Author interview.

8 Author interview.

9 Author interview.

10 Author interview.

11 Bill Kinison and Steve Delshon, *Brother Sam: The Short, Spectacular Life of Sam Kinison* (New York: William Morrow & Co., 1994), 75–76.

12 *It's Not Easy Bein' Me*, 173.

13 *It's Not Easy Bein' Me*, 169.

14 Author interview.

15 Author interview.

16 Author interview.

17 Author interview.

18 David Bianculli, "Rodney Dangerfield is about to win some respect," *Akron Beacon Journal*, May 12, 1982, B8.

19 Author interview.

20 *Santa Cruz Sentinel*, June 6, 1986.

21 *Santa Cruz Sentinel*, June 6, 1986.

22 Author interview.

23 Lawrence Christon, "The Education of Rodney Dangerfield," *Los Angeles Times*, July 1, 1986.

24 Steven Rea, "Sally's match-up with Rodney was 'love at second sight,'" *Des Moines Register*, July 3, 1986, 44.

25 *It's Not Easy Bein' Me*, 202.

26 Author interview.

27   *Los Angeles Times*, June 12, 1986, 107.

28   Nina Darnton, *New York Times*, June 13, 1986, 72.

29   Hal Lipper, *Tampa Bay Times*, June 13, 1986, 69.

30   Rogerebert.com/reviews/back-to-school-1986.

31   Author interview.

32   "Rudeness keeps her employed," *North Jersey Herald-News*, August 30, 1986, A-14.

33   Author interview.

34   Author interview.

35   *Kansas City Star*, November 5, 1987, 41.

36   Author interview.

37   Author interview.

38   Richard Johnson, "He's not looking for respect," *Palm Beach Post*, January 30, 1988, 42.

39   Stephen Holden, "Stage: At the Hellinger, Rodney Dangerfield," *New York Times*, February 4, 1988, 79.

40   Laurie Stone, *Laughing in the Dark: A Decade of Subversive Comedy* (New York: The Ecco Press, 1997), 14–15.

41   Marilyn Beck, *Reporter Dispatch*, December 15, 1989, 37.

42   Associated Press, *Delaware Gazette*, August 25, 1990, 23.

43   "Rodney can't get any respect—won't settle lawsuit out of court," *Spokesman-Review and Spokane Chronicle*, September 10, 1990, B2.

44   "Rodney finally gets respect in Las Vegas courtroom," *St. Joseph News-Press Gazette*, September 15, 1990, 10A.

Chapter Eleven

1   Author interview.

2   Marilyn Beck, "Rodney Dangerfield plans to sing in 'Serenade Café,'" *News Tribune*, October 5, 1990, 52.

3   Charles Solomon, "Dangerfield's animated film gets no respect?," *Charlotte Observer*, September 25, 1991, 25.

4   Author interview.

5   Author interview.

6   Author interview.

7   Joe Baltake, "'Rover': family fare with bark, bite," *Sacramento Bee*, August 5, 1991, 18.

8   Jay Boyar, "'Rover'—a good howl," *Orlando Sentinel*, August 5, 1991, 25.

9   *It's Not Easy Bein' Me*, 210.

10   *It's Not Easy Bein' Me*, 121.

11   *Los Angeles Daily News*, October 12, 1991, C-5.

12   Chris Willman, "His New Club Gets Some Respect," *Los Angeles Times*, October 11, 1991, F-19.

13   Author interview.

14   Author interview.

15   Author interview.

16   Author interview.

17   Author interview.

18   Vincent Canby, "Coach Rodney Dangerfield and the Girls' Soccer Team," *New York Times*, March 28, 1992, L17.

19   Harry Haun, *New York Daily News*, March 28, 1992, 59.

20   "'Ladybugs' a dull comedy with bad acting," *Palm Beach Post*, March 30, 1992, 5D.

21   Author interview.

22   "Kinison: Colleagues Saddened," *Los Angeles Times*, April 12, 1992, A37.

23   *It's Not Easy Bein' Me*, 226.

24   *It's Not Easy Bein' Me*, 206.

25   Author interview.

26   *It's Not Easy Bein' Me*, 206.

27   *Biography: Rodney Dangerfield*, A&E, 2012.

28   Marilyn Beck and Stacy Jenel Smith, "Edict on 'Bishop' pic: Script must be divine," *New York Daily News*, August 15, 1994, 18.

29   Author interview.

30   Susan Spillman, "Dangerfield, Stone differ on comic's 'Killer' input," *San Bernadino County Sun*, September 5, 1994, D5.

31   Author interview.

32   Jeff Pearlman, *Newsday*, July 5, 2004, 55.

33   Author interview.

34   Bob Thomas, "'Natural Born Killers': Is this mindless mass murder a movie satire on violent society?," *The Reporter*, August 30, 1994, C3.

35   Mary Ann Lindley, "Reeling from 'Killers,'" *Des Moines Register*, September 10, 1994, 7A.

36   Robert Ebert, *Chicago Sun-Times*, August 26, 1994.

37   Author interview.

38   "No respect for Rodney—even in cyberspace," *Wichita Eagle*, October 30, 1995, 5A.

39   "Rose fever," *Detroit Free Press*, February 10, 1996, 3D.

40   Author interview.

41   Author interview.

42   Author interview.

43   Author interview.

44   Author interview.

45   Author interview.

46   Author interview.

47   Author interview.

48   Author interview.

49   Stephen Holden, "Take This TV Talk Show Host. Please.," *New York Times*, February 1, 1997.

50   Betsy Sherman, "'Wally': a lowbrow highlight reel for Rodney," *Boston Globe*, February 1, 1997, C3.

51   Rick Holter, "Host from hell fights for the airwaves," *The Record*, February 5, 1997, 48.

52   Author interview.
53   Author interview.
54   Author interview.
55   Author interview.
56   Lawrence Grobel, "One Banana Peel After Another," *Parade*, August 3, 1997, 9.
57   Author interview.
58   Author interview.

Chapter Twelve

1   Author interview.
2   Author interview.
3   Robin Rauzi, "More Does Not Mean Merrier in 'My Five Wives,'" *Los Angeles Times*, September 8, 2000.
4   *It's Not Easy Bein' Me*, 234.
5   Author interview.
6   Author interview.
7   Paul Brownfield, *Post-Star*, December 19, 2002.
8   Author interview.
9   Author interview.
10   Author interview.
11   Jason Hahn, "Jay Leno Speaks Out About His Battle with High Cholesterol: It's a 'Time Bomb,'" *People*, March 12, 2019.
12   Associated Press, "Comic Rodney Dangerfield back home from hospital," *Florida Today*, November 30, 2001.
13   Author interview.
14   "Comic undergoes brain surgery," *The State*, April 9, 2003.
15   Associated Press, "Rodney Dangerfield breathing on his own after brain surgery," *Sun-Journal*, April 15, 2003.
16   Associated Press, "After surgery, Rodney has jokes on the brain," *Newsday*, May 9, 2003.
17   Author interview.
18   *Biography: Rodney Dangerfield*, A&E, 2012.
19   Andy Seiler, "With respect to Rodney, comedy icon is still going strong," *Tulsa World*, July 22, 2003.
20   Associated Press, "No show for Rodney Dangerfield," *Daily Press*, June 19, 2003.
21   Author interview.
22   "Next generation also might get no respect," *The News & Observer*, October 13, 2003.
23   Associated Press, "Fox buys rights to comedian's book," *Indiana Gazette*, March 12, 2004.
24   *It's Not Easy Bein' Me*, ix.
25   Jeff Pearlman, "Rodney, laid bare," *Newsday*, July 5, 2004.
26   Erik Hedegaard, "Gone to Pot," *Rolling Stone*, June 10, 2004, 39–40.
27   Author interview.
28   Author interview.

29   Author interview.

30   "Rodney Dangerfield recuperating," *Lancaster New Era*, September 16, 2004.

31   "Rodney Dangerfield in coma after heart surgery," *Florida Today*, September 21, 2004.

32   "Dangerfield in coma after heart surgery," *Charlotte Observer*, September 22, 2004.

33   Howardstern.com/news/2020/07/14.

34   "Comedy Legend Rodney Dangerfield Passes Away," press release.

35   "Deep Respect marks Dangerfield's death," *Democrat and Chronicle*, October 6, 2004.

36   Mel Watkins, "Rodney Dangerfield, Comic Seeking Respect, Dies at 82," *New York Times*, October 6, 2004.

37   Dennis McLellan, "Rodney Dangerfield, 82; Comedic Icon Built a Career on Getting 'No Respect,'" *Los Angeles Times*, October 6, 2004, B8.

38   Tom Shales, "Comedian Rodney Dangerfield deserved and got our respect," *Kenosha News*, October 9, 2004.

39   Author interview.

40   Author interview.

41   Celebrityaccess.com and "A Heaven on Earth Sendoff for Rodney Dangerfield," http://scottweb2.frontrunnerpro.com/mysendoff/story/a-heaven-on-earth-send-off-for-rodney-dangerfield.

Coda

1   "SNL Transcripts: Queen Latifah: 10/09/04: Dangerfield Tribute," SNL Transcripts Tonight, snltranscripts.jt.org/04/04bdangerfield.phtml.

2   "Neurosurgery Division to Present Jay Leno With Rodney Dangerfield Legacy Award," University of California press release, September 14, 2005.

3   "Comedian's widow resettles in Hills," *Los Angeles Times*, May 15, 2005, K10.

4   Jose Martinez, "Dangerfield's wife hits biz pal," *New York Daily News*, August 4, 2006, 2

5   Jose Martinez, "No respect from Dangerfield's kid, either," *New York Daily News*, September 10, 2006, A28.

6   "Dangerfield widow, daughter settle lawsuit," *Abbotsford News Daily*, August 12, 2008, A7.

7   Associated Press, "Dangerfield's widow sues over film footage," *The Courier*, September 23, 2007, 2.

8   MWPR press release, "Doctor Dangerfield Goes Back to School," May 15, 2014.

9   Stephania Pagones and Danika Fears, "Rodney Dangerfield's widow doesn't respect his tribute mural," *New York Post*, March 1, 2017.

10   Corey Kilgannon, "The King of No Respect Finally Gets Some, in His Queens Hometown," *New York Times*, August 1, 2017.

11   Danielle Storm, "Look Inside: The Upper East Side's 'Newest' Comedy Club," East Side Feed, December 30, 2023.